THE ULT[IMATE]
ENTERTAINMENT
C O L L E C T I O N

Walter Foster
Jr.

ALL THE
MOVIES
TV SHOWS
BOOKS
TO EXPERIENCE
BEFORE
YOU GROW UP!

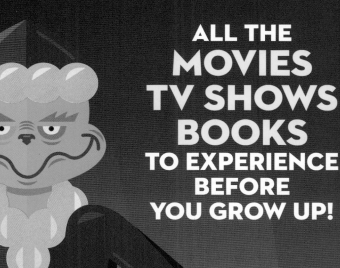

Brimming with creative inspiration, how-to projects, and useful
information to enrich your everyday life, Quarto Knows is a favorite
destination for those pursuing their interests and passions. Visit our
site and dig deeper with our books into your area of interest:
Quarto Creates, Quarto Cooks, Quarto Homes, Quarto Lives,
Quarto Drives, Quarto Explores, Quarto Gifts, or Quarto Kids.

101 Movies to See Before You Grow Up
Cover design by Steve Scott
Written by Suzette Valle
Illustrated by Natasha Hellegouarch

101 TV Shows to See Before You Grow Up
Written by Samantha Chagollan and Erika Milvy
Illustrated by Natasha Hellegouarch

101 Books to Read Before You Grow Up
Written by Bianca Schulze
Illustrated by Shaw Nielsen

6 Orchard Road, Suite 100
Lake Forest, CA 92630
quartoknows.com
Visit our blogs at quartoknows.com

Printed in China
1 3 5 7 9 10 8 6 4 2

MIX
Paper from
responsible sources
FSC® C016973

THE ULTIMATE
ENTERTAINMENT
COLLECTION

INTRODUCTION

Movies, television shows, and books are made to entertain! They can make you think, teach you lessons about life, introduce you to fascinating make-believe friends, or let you explore exciting fantasy worlds. This book is filled with hundreds of the most popular movies, TV shows, and books for families, children, and story-lovers of all ages. There is also a section at the bottom of each page where you can write in your own review!

IF YOU LOVE MOVIES...

Try tackling the movies section! Each film profile features basic information, such as the director, the stars, rating, release date, awards, and other quick facts. From classic films to modern flicks, including animated, adventure, action, sports, and musical genres, you'll find plenty of films to create your own bucket list. Grab some popcorn—the movie is about to start!

IF TV SHOWS ARE MORE YOUR THING...

Head over to the TV shows section! Use it as your own personal guide for what to watch next. Learn cool trivia and behind-the-scenes details to look out for as you watch each show. Each profile calls out essential details like who created the show, how many seasons were produced, when it aired, and other fun facts to impress your friends and family. Claim your spot on the couch, and let the fun begin!

IF BOOKS ARE MORE YOUR SPEED...

Check out the books section. Featuring a wide variety of books, from fairy tales and fantasy to sports and nonfiction, this personal bucket list is sure to have something you'll love! Each book profile features interesting facts and basic details, such as the year it was published, fun facts about the author, and why it is important. Find a comfy place to curl up, and let the story begin!

101 MOVIES

TO SEE BEFORE YOU GROW UP

Be sure to check the rating of each film, and ask your parents about movies rated "PG" or "PG-13," mate.

Look for the 🏆 symbol at the top of each page to see how many Academy Awards the movie has won.

Use the bottom of the page to mark off each movie after you watch it!

WRITTEN BY SUZETTE VALLE

ILLUSTRATED BY NATASHA HELLEGOUARCH

TABLE OF CONTENTS

The movies in this book are divided by film genre and listed in random order, so you can start watching wherever you like. We think it's practically perfect in every way!

1

IT'S A WONDERFUL LIFE

DIRECTOR:
Frank Capra

RELEASE DATE:
January 7, 1947

RATED:
NR
Not Rated

RUNTIME:
2 hours,
10 minutes

THE STORY

George Bailey (James Stewart) would rather die than live another miserable day. Clarence (Henry Travers), a guardian angel, is sent to Earth to save Bailey, but before he swoops in, he is shown flashbacks of George's life. At age 12, George lost hearing in one ear after rescuing his younger brother from a frozen pond. At 21, George's father unexpectedly died, and George unselfishly took over the family business, Bailey Building and Loan Association. Things go terribly wrong with the business after a large deposit is lost. George and his wife, Mary (Donna Reed), sacrifice their honeymoon money to help the business, but the bank still fails to thrive. Facing fraud and jail, George decides he's worth more dead than alive. He's about to jump off a bridge when Clarence is dispatched from heaven to save him. The angel shows George what his family and town would have been like without him, and he's shocked by what he sees. Seeing his life from a whole new perspective, George begs his guardian angel to let him live: "I want to live, Clarence!"

What does this famous Christmas film teach us? George Bailey already had a wonderful life, and he didn't even know it!

STARRING:
James Stewart, Donna Reed, and Lionel Barrymore

MUSIC:
Songs by Dimitri Tiomkin

SCREEN-PLAY WRITTEN BY:
Philip Van Doren Stern

DID YOU KNOW?

In 1939, Philip Van Doren Stern wrote "The Greatest Gift," which became *It's a Wonderful Life*. After he failed to find a publisher, he made 200 copies of the tale and sent them as Christmas cards in 1943.

Saw it! ☐ Rating: ☆☆☆☆☆

Date: ___ / ___ / _____ With: _____

Notes: _____

_____

2

HOME ALONE

DIRECTOR:
Chris Columbus

RELEASE DATE:
November 16, 1990

RATED:
PG
for comic action and mild language

RUNTIME:
1 hour, 43 minutes

THE STORY

Kevin McCallister (Macaulay Caulkin) is a cheeky and resourceful 8-year-old boy. As the youngest and smallest member of his family, he's tired of being picked on and ignored. Kevin secretly wishes that his family would disappear. The night before the big family Christmas trip to Europe, a power outage resets the alarm clocks. Everyone wakes up late the next morning and scrambles to get to the airport on time. In the chaos, Kevin is left behind! He wakes up to an empty house, and at first, he's thrilled! However, his joy is short-lived when he finds out two thieves, Harry (Joe Pesci) and Marv (Daniel Stern), are roaming the neighborhood planning to break in. Meanwhile, Kate McCallister (Catherine O'Hara), Kevin's mom, is frantically trying to get back to Chicago from Paris, but all of the flights are full. To protect his home from the bandits, Kevin rigs the house with booby traps. Will Mrs. McCallister and the rest of the family get home in time to save Kevin? Or is it really the bandits who need the saving from Kevin's elaborate contraptions?

WATCH OUT FOR

The success of *Home Alone* led to multiple films, *Home Alone 2: Lost in New York* (1992) and *Home Alone 3* (1997), and TV movies, *Home Alone 4* (2002) and *Home Alone: The Holiday Heist* (2012).

DID YOU KNOW?

Home Alone had a $15 million budget and grossed $477 million worldwide. *Home Alone* was entered into the Guinness Book of World Records as the "Highest Grossing Live Action Comedy" of 1990.

Saw it! ☐ Rating: ☆☆☆☆☆

Date: ___/___/_____ With: _____

Notes: _____

_____

👤👤👤 **3 ACADEMY AWARDS**

MIRACLE ON 34TH STREET

THE STORY

Kris Kringle (Edmund Gwenn) is inspecting the Macy's Thanksgiving Day parade lineup when he notices that the man hired by parade organizer Doris Walker (Maureen O'Hara) to play Santa Claus shows up drunk. Kringle turns up just in time, and Doris hires him on the spot. Kringle is a natural as Santa—beard, belly, and all—so Doris hires him to work as the store's Santa Claus as well. But when the jolly man recommends that customers buy from rival stores when they have better prices, Doris gets mad at first. But the customers love him, and they love Macy's for its kind heart!

However, Kris is so realistic as Santa that many of the children start believing he's the real thing! The store executives begin to get annoyed with Kris's persistence that he is the real Santa Claus, and they want to have his mental health evaluated by a judge. Fred Gailey (John Payne) is a lawyer and also a friend of Doris and her young daughter, Susan (Natalie Wood). At Kris's court hearing, Fred proves Kris Kringle is the real Santa Claus! On Christmas morning, Kris sends Fred, Doris, and Susan home through a shortcut. On the way, they see Doris's dream house with a "For Sale" sign, and they stop to see it. What they find inside makes them all firm believers.

DID YOU KNOW?

Before the first helium balloon (Felix the Cat) debuted at the Macy's Thanksgiving Day Parade in 1927, 200 live animals used to march along the six-mile route!

DIRECTOR:
George Seaton

RELEASE DATE:
May 2, 1947

RATED:
NR
Not Rated

RUNTIME:
1 hour, 36 minutes

Saw it! ☐ Rating: ☆☆☆☆☆

Date: ___/___/_____ With: _____

Notes: _____

_____

4

THE PARENT TRAP

DIRECTOR:
David Swift

RELEASE DATE:
June 21, 1961

RATED:
G
General
Audiences

RUNTIME:
2 hours,
9 minutes

Can you imagine having to act the part of two different people with different accents? In the 1961 Disney film, *The Parent Trap,* Hayley Mills plays the role of identical twin girls, one from Boston and the other from California.

THE STORY

Separated at birth when their parents divorced, Susan and Sharon each grew up living with one parent, unaware of the other twin's existence. Sharon

lives in Boston with her mother, while Susan lives with her father in California. They bump into each other for the first time at summer camp, and their first encounter is awkward! After some initial rivalry leads to campground mischief, the two become friends and realize they are sisters. Together they scheme to switch places to get to know the opposite parent—and get rid of their father's fiancée to reunite their parents.

In Disney's 1998 remake, Lindsay Lohan marvelously plays the role of the twins. One girl lives in London with her mother, a famous wedding gown designer, and the other lives in California with her dad. Hallie and Annie fabricate elaborate shenanigans to get their parents to reconcile and arrive at the expected happy ending.

WATCH OUT FOR

What makes *The Parent Trap* so interesting is that one actress plays two parts, which was an amazing feat for the filmmakers to achieve. Have a movie marathon with both films, and see how many differences you notice as you watch the same plot unfold twice, three decades apart!

STARRING:
Hayley Mills, Maureen O'Hara, and Brian Keith

MUSIC:
Songs by Richard M. Sherman and Robert B. Sherman

DID YOU KNOW?

Hayley Mills had to learn American slang since she's British. Lindsay Lohan was only 11 years old when she starred in *The Parent Trap* remake, and she learned to speak with a British accent!

SPECIAL FX:
Double exposure scenes using one actress to play twins

Saw it! ☐ Rating: ☆☆☆☆☆

Date: ___ / ___ / _____ With: _____

Notes: _____

_____

5

TO KILL A MOCKINGBIRD

DIRECTOR:
Robert
Mulligan

**RELEASE
DATE:**
March 16, 1963

RATED:

NR

Not Rated

RUNTIME:
2 hours,
9 minutes

WHY IT'S FAMOUS

This film's screenplay, based on the 1960 Pulitzer Prize-winning novel of the same name by Harper Lee, illustrates the profound racial problems and injustices of the 1930s in the Deep South.

THE STORY

Atticus Finch (Gregory Peck) is an honest, well-respected attorney and a widower. He is raising his two children, 6-year-old Scout (Mary Badham), and 10-year-old Jeremy "Jem" (Phillip Alford), on his own. Scout narrates the story about her family living in the fictional town of Maycomb, Alabama. The kids preoccupy themselves by spying on their strange neighbor, Arthur "Boo" Radley (Robert Duvall), who seems to never leave his house. Meanwhile, Mr. Finch is appointed to defend a black man, Tom Robinson (Brock Peters), who is accused of raping a white woman. The Finch family faces scorn from the townspeople, who believe the man is guilty of the crime even before he's tried. Atticus uses the situation to teach his children about prejudice and intolerance. Unexpectedly, the children are attacked by a bigoted, resentful citizen, but they're saved by an unlikely friend.

DID YOU KNOW?

Mary Badham was 10 years old when she played the role of Scout. She had never acted before, and was nominated for an Oscar for Best Supporting Actress.

Saw it! ☐ Rating: ☆☆☆☆☆

Date: ___/___/_____ With: _____

Notes: _____

_____

HOLES

THE STORY

At Camp Green Lake, a juvenile correction center located in the middle of the desert, there's no lake—only dirt and holes as far as the eye can see. The Warden, Louise Walker (Sigourney Weaver), and Mr. Sir (Jon Voight), the head counselor, are mean-spirited and make sure the boys at the camp stick to their punishment; each boy has to dig one hole a day, and every hole must be 5 feet deep and 5 feet wide. Stanley Yelnats IV (Shia LaBeouf) is from a nice family and was sent to Camp Green for stealing a pair of sneakers worn and donated by a famous ball player. If the boys dig up something interesting, such as a fossil, they earn a day off from digging under the hot sun. Stanley uncovers a lipstick tube with the initials K.B. engraved on it, but gives it to another boy who hasn't had a day off in six months! One day, Stanley ends up at the Warden's home. He notices old newspapers and wanted posters for Kissing Kate Barlow (Patricia Arquette), and they remind him of

DID YOU KNOW?

Stanley Yelnats' last name is a palindrome—written backwards, it spells his first name.

the initials on the lipstick tube. Zero (Khleo Thomas) and Stanley become friends, and they try to run away from camp together but face dangerous obstacles. Stories within stories start to unfold, which help us understand the lipstick and our young heroes' fate.

DIRECTOR:
Andrew Davis

RELEASE DATE:
April 18, 2003

RATED:
PG
for violence, mild language, and some thematic elements

RUNTIME:
1 hour, 57 minutes

Saw it! ☐ Rating: ☆☆☆☆☆
Date: ___/___/_____ With: _____
Notes: _____
_____

7

HOMEWARD BOUND: THE INCREDIBLE JOURNEY

DIRECTOR:
Duwayne
Dunham

RELEASE DATE:
February 12, 1993

RATED:

G

General
Audiences

RUNTIME:
1 hour,
24 minutes

THE STORY

Three pets are left with a friend at a ranch while their owners go on a trip. But Chance (Michael J. Fox), an American Bulldog puppy; Shadow (Don Ameche), an older Golden Retriever; and Sassy (Sally Field), a mischievous Himalayan cat, think they've been abandoned. They bravely escape from the ranch in search of their home and family. Their journey takes them over the breathtaking California Sierra Mountains, rivers, and forests. These wisecracking pals will crack you up throughout their rough adventure. Bears, mountain lions, and even the ferocity of Mother Nature won't keep these animals from their family!

WATCH OUT FOR

The animal stunts the trainers pulled off in this film are amazing. In one scene, a dog lures a mountain lion onto the end of a log, while another dog jumps on the other end to hurl the wildcat into the river!

DID YOU KNOW?

4 Golden Retrievers, 4 American Bulldogs, and 8 Himalayan cats were trained over 7 months to play the parts of Shadow, Chance, and Sassy.

UP NEXT

The adventures continue in *Homeward Bound II: Lost in San Francisco* (1996). The trio of pets once again find themselves trying to find their way home—this time in a big city!

Saw it! ☐ Rating: ☆☆☆☆☆

Date: ___/___/_____ With: _____

Notes: _____

_____

THE BRAVE LITTLE TOASTER

The Brave Little Toaster, common household appliances with simple names such as Toaster, Radio, Lampy, Blanky, and Kirby come to life. They go through harrowing adventures—but they prevail in the end. Hooray! Who doesn't like a happy ending, right? Well, it's not quite that simple. As in real life, a little struggle makes the happy ending that much sweeter.

THE STORY

These ordinary household appliances sit in Rob's summer cabin waiting for him to visit. As time goes by and their owner doesn't come back, they start to feel abandoned. But they refuse to accept the idea that their owner doesn't want them anymore. Toaster, the leader of the pack, tells the domestic devices that they must find Rob to once again feel loved. Convinced by Toaster, they set out to find their master. Along the way, the appliances learn the values of teamwork, bravery, friendship, and perseverance.

WHY IT'S FAMOUS

When John Lasseter was a junior animator at Disney, *The Brave Little Toaster* was his first attempt to make a computer-generated imagery (CGI) film. Though Disney rejected the idea, Lasseter went on to change the future of animation with the CGI concept and later became the chief creative officer for Walt Disney Animation and Pixar!

DIRECTOR:
Jerry Rees

RELEASE DATE:
July 10, 1987
(USA)

RATED:
NR
with mild scary scenes

RUNTIME:
1 hour,
30 minutes

Saw it! ☐ Rating: ☆☆☆☆☆

Date: ___ / ___ / _____ With: _____

Notes: _____

_____

9

BABE

DIRECTOR:
Chris Noonan

RELEASE DATE:
August 4, 1995

RATED:
G
General
Audiences

RUNTIME:
1 hour,
29 minutes

THE STORY

A little pig wants to be a sheepherder to save himself from certain death. Babe, an orphaned piglet whose mother was slaughtered, knows it's the only way he will survive living on Mr. Hoggett's farm. Babe went home with Mr. Hoggett as a prize from a county fair; however, Babe can't escape being eyed as the next centerpiece for Christmas dinner. Babe learns that humans eat pigs, so he decides to run away. When Hoggett finally finds him, he feeds him and sings to comfort him. Attempting to make himself useful around the farm, Babe tries to herd the farmer's sheep by speaking to them. When Mr. Hoggett sees Babe's talent, he enters him into a sheepherding competition that ends with the farmer acknowledging Babe's efforts by saying, "That'll do pig. That'll do."

WHY IT'S FAMOUS

Babe was nominated for several Academy Awards, winning for Best Visual Effects. It was also commended for raising awareness about animal abuse. During its time, *Babe* influenced many young people to rethink the food they were eating; and based on interactions between the animals in the film, many concluded that animals are capable of feeling sadness, happiness, and pain.

DID YOU KNOW?

The American Film Institute named *Babe* one of the most inspiring films of all time. According to *AFI's 100 Years of Cheers*, *Babe* "sends us from the theater with a greater sense of possibility and hope for the future."

Saw it! ☐ Rating: ☆☆☆☆☆

Date: ___/___/_____ With: _____

Notes: _____

_____

4 ACADEMY AWARDS

E.T. THE EXTRA-TERRESTRIAL

THE STORY

Elliot (Henry Thomas) is 10 years old when he finds a little goblin-like alien stranded in his backyard. Elliot, his older brother Michael (Robert McNaughton), and his little sister Gertie (Drew Barrymore), hide E.T. in their house. Elliot notices that E.T. copies his gestures, and he eventually begins to feel a strange connection with the alien. One day, the kids leave E.T. at home while they go to school, and the curious alien explores around the house. After looking through a comic book, E.T. gets the idea to build a device to call home. Elliot helps him make a contraption out of an electronic toy, a tin can, and miscellaneous metal parts. Soon the extraterrestrial's health starts to weaken, and Elliot also begins to get sick. Government agents show up at Elliot's house and isolate both him and E.T. Suddenly, Elliot and E.T. regain their strength, and with his brother's help, they escape authorities by flying into the night sky on a bicycle. Does E.T. make it home? Watch *E.T.* and find out!

DID YOU KNOW?

Elliot's parents are divorced in the film. When Steven Spielberg's parents were going through a divorce, the director made up imaginary friends who would help him temporarily escape his sadness.

DIRECTOR:
Steven Spielberg

RELEASE DATE:
June 11, 1982

RATED:
PG
for language and mild thematic elements

WHY IT'S FAMOUS

E.T. presents a remarkable portrait of childhood innocence, along with the heartwarming friendship between a boy and an alien. This classic piece of movie magic lives on as an ideal film for the whole family.

RUNTIME:
1 hour, 55 minutes

Saw it! ☐ Rating: ☆☆☆☆☆

Date: ___ / ___ / _____ With: _____

Notes: _____

_____

11

TOY STORY

DIRECTOR:
John Lasseter

RELEASE DATE:
November 22, 1995

RATED:

G

General Audiences

RUNTIME:
1 hour, 21 minutes

THE STORY

Classic toys (a cowboy named Woody and a space ranger named Buzz) come to life when their owner, a boy named Andy, is not around. Andy's family is moving, so he has an early birthday party. The adventure begins when Andy's mom tells him he can take only one toy to Pizza Planet for dinner. A jealous Woody (Tom Hanks) tries to hide Buzz (Tim Allen), who is convinced he's a real space ranger, so Andy will take him instead. In the heat of the moment, Woody accidentally pushes Buzz out of the bedroom window. Because he can't find Buzz, Andy reluctantly takes Woody—but Buzz manages to climb into the

car as it pulls out of the driveway. At the restaurant, Buzz jumps inside an arcade game that looks like a spaceship, and Woody follows, trying to convince Buzz to find Andy so the two can go home. Sid, Andy's toy-destroying next door neighbor, pulls Woody and Buzz from the machine and takes them home. Woody and Buzz learn they must work together to escape Sid and get back to Andy's house before he moves away!

UP NEXT

Toy Story was followed by *Toy Story 2* (1999) and *Toy Story 3* (2010). *Toy Story 4* is set to release in 2017.

WHY IT'S FAMOUS

Toy Story is the first full-length film to use computer-generated imagery (CGI). Its development and pioneering of CGI techniques made this first full-length computer-animated film a standout achievement in the film industry.

DID YOU KNOW?

Woody and Buzz Lightyear were brought to life by John Lasseter at Pixar Animation Studios. Lasseter worked at George Lucas's Industrial Light & Magic until Apple cofounder Steve Jobs bought the graphics group in 1986 and named the studio Pixar. *Toy Story* was a joint project between Pixar and Disney. After the success of *Finding Nemo*, *The Incredibles*, and other films, Disney purchased Pixar in 2006 for a whopping $7.4 billion.

STARRING:
Tom Hanks and Tim Allen

MUSIC:
Songs by Randy Newman

SPECIAL FX:
First feature film to use computer-generated imagery (CG1) animation

Saw it! ☐ Rating: ☆☆☆☆☆

Date: ___/___/_____ With: _____

Notes: _____

_____

12

FANTASTIC MR. FOX

DIRECTOR:
Wes Anderson

RELEASE DATE:
November 25, 2009

RATED:
PG
for adult content, mild violence

RUNTIME:
1 hour, 27 minutes

THE STORY

The Fox family is entirely proper. Mr. Fox (George Clooney) wears pants, a button-down shirt, and a tie. Felicity Fox (Meryl Streep) wears an apron in the kitchen to make sure her dress doesn't get dirty. Ash (Jason Schwartzman), their broody son, prefers to wear a cape and his pants tucked into his socks. Odd? No. He's just…different! The Fox family has decided to live a less risky life: Instead of stealing chickens and being chased by farmers, Mr. Fox does the next logical thing—he becomes a journalist!

But deep down, a fox will always be a fox. Mr. Fox goes behind Mrs. Fox's back and sneakily gets back into the chicken-nabbing business. Because he has to dig tunnels to capture his prey, he secretly gets help from his friends. But the angry farmers are on to them! The three neighboring farmers, Walter Boggis, Nathan Bunce, and Franklin Bean, stake out the fox's home, waiting for him to come up for food. Can the clever Mr. Fox outfox the farmers?

UP NEXT

Fantastic Mr. Fox is based on the children's book by Roald Dahl. Where have you heard this name before? He also wrote *Charlie and the Chocolate Factory*, *James and the Giant Peach*, and *Matilda*.

Saw it! ☐ Rating: ☆☆☆☆☆

Date: ___ / ___ / _____ With: _____

Notes: _____

_____

CHICKEN RUN

"Claymation," or clay animation, is the art of making clay figures come to life on screen with movement and voice. *Chicken Run* uses this technique to create the barracks-style coop life inhabited by two feisty fowl and their fellow chickens.

THE STORY

Mr. and Mrs. Tweedy run a chicken coop in England. They sell the chickens' eggs to make a living; however, the chickens are not happy with their living arrangement and want to escape! Ginger (Julia Sawalha), the leader of the group, can't stop thinking of ways to escape, but she fails each time they try to fly the coop. Why? Because chickens can't fly! But Ginger doesn't believe it. When a self-absorbed American rooster, Rocky (Mel Gibson), accidentally flies into the coop, Ginger thinks he can teach the hens to fly too. The urge to escape reaches a frantic peak when the hens find out the egg business isn't doing well, and that Mr. Tweedy (Tony Haygarth) is going to start selling chicken pot pies instead.

WATCH OUT FOR

The combination of the hens' proper British accents and the voice of Mel Gibson as Rocky, the big-headed American rooster, makes for a funny clash of cultures and an engaging film. *Chicken Run* is from the creators of the Wallace and Gromit short films and is their first feature-length, stop motion, claymation movie.

DIRECTORS:
Peter Lord and
Nick Park

RELEASE DATE:
June 23, 2000

RATED:
G
General
Audiences

RUNTIME:
1 hour,
24 minutes

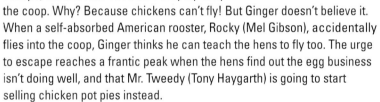

Saw it! ☐ Rating: ☆☆☆☆☆

Date: ___/ ___/ _____ With: _____

Notes: _____

_____

14

MONSTERS, INC.

DIRECTOR:
Pete Docter

RELEASE DATE:
November 2, 2001

RATED:

G

General Audiences

RUNTIME:
1 hour, 32 minutes

THE STORY

Children's screams power the city of Monstropolis, a parallel world where friendly monsters roam the streets. Sulley Sullivan (John Goodman) and Mike Wazowski (Billy Crystal) are "scarers" who work for Monsters, Inc., the power company responsible for collecting electricity-producing screams. However, the monsters of Monstropolis are terrified of children because they think human children are contaminated and dangerous to touch!

After work one night, a little girl walks through her closet door onto the scarefloor—and bumps right into Sulley! Chaos erupts when Boo, as Sulley nicknames her, escapes into Monstropolis. Boo thinks Sulley and Mike are really funny, and when she giggles, she creates a power surge! The villain, Randall (Steve Buscemi), wants to trap Boo and use her screams to power the city. Can Sulley and Mike save Boo and send her home?

UP NEXT

The CGI (computer-generated imagery) animated *Monsters, Inc.* has a prequel, *Monsters University* (2013). In this film, we find out how Mike and Sully met and became friends in college.

DID YOU KNOW?
After 16 nominations, Randy Newman finally won an Academy Award for Best Original Song in 2002 for "If I Didn't Have You," featured in *Monsters, Inc.*

Saw it! ☐ Rating: ☆☆☆☆☆

Date: ___ / ___ / _____ With: _____

Notes: _____

_____

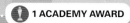

FINDING NEMO

Hop aboard the East Australian Current (EAC), dude! Join Dory, Marlin, and their sea turtle friends in an exciting quest to find Marlin's son, Nemo.

DIRECTORS:
Andrew Stanton and Lee Unkrich

THE STORY

Nemo and Marlin (Albert Brooks) live near the Great Barrier Reef. Nemo (Alexander Gould) has an unusually small fin, and after losing his mother when he was just an egg, his dad constantly worries about him. On his first day of school, Nemo gets kidnapped by a scuba diver! The scuba diver, a dentist from Sydney, puts Nemo in a fish tank in his office, and he plans to give Nemo to his mischievous niece, Darla (LuLu Ebeling), as a birthday gift. Marlin searches for his son across the ocean as he travels toward Sydney. Along the way, Marlin meets Dory (Ellen DeGeneres), a royal blue tang fish with short-term memory loss. Together they "just keep swimming," and with the help of a few unexpected friends, Marlin and Dory work together to rescue Nemo and bring him home!

> **DID YOU KNOW?**
> John Lasseter, the head of Pixar, assigned crew members who worked on *Finding Nemo* to get scuba-diving certifications.

RELEASE DATE:
May 30, 2003

RATED:
G
General Audiences

WHY IT'S FAMOUS

Finding Nemo showcases Pixar's vivid, flawless CGI (computer-generated imagery) animation. To create this undersea world, crew members traveled to the Great Barrier Reef in Australia to see the natural wonder firsthand. *Finding Dory*, the sequel, followed in June 2016.

RUNTIME:
1 hour, 40 minutes

Saw it! ☐ Rating: ☆☆☆☆☆

Date: ___/___/_____ With: _____

Notes: _____

_____

16

RATATOUILLE

DIRECTOR:
Brad Bird and
Jan Pinkava

**RELEASE
DATE:**
June 29, 2007

RATED:
G
General
Audiences

RUNTIME:
1 hour,
51 minutes

THE STORY

Remy (Patton Oswalt) is a rat with a gift for smell and an exquisite taste in food. After his family is forced to leave their home, he finds himself lost in Paris. Resting on a skylight above Gusteau's, a famous French restaurant started by chef Auguste Gusteau (Brad Garrett), he watches as Linguini, the clumsy garbage boy, accidentally spills a pot of soup. Linguini (Lou Romano) tries to make another pot, but it tastes awful! Remy can't resist, and he secretly fixes the soup. Linguini sees Remy adding spices to the soup, but before he can say anything, the restaurant's new owner chases the rat out of the kitchen. In the scuffle, the soup is mistakenly served and the customers love it! Colette (Janeane Garofalo), the female chef, thinks it was Linguini who made the soup and hires him as a cook. With Remy's clever (and secret) help, Linguini learns to cook and the restaurant gains popularity. Anton Ego (Peter O'Toole), a famous food critic, decides to visit the restaurant. The night of the review, Remy is hurt because Linguini takes Colette's cooking advice over his own. After they argue, Remy brings his rat family to infest the pantry and steal food. Linguini catches Remy red-handed, but he realizes he owes his success to Remy and has treated him badly. He apologizes and tells the staff about his rat sidekick—and they all leave! But the restaurant still has to impress Ego and get a good review. What will they do?

DID YOU KNOW?

The ratatouille recipe used in this movie was created by Chef Thomas Keller for his famous restaurant, French Laundry, in Napa Valley, California.

Saw it! ☐ Rating: ☆☆☆☆☆

Date: ___ / ___ / _____ With: _____

Notes: _____

_____

WALL-E

THE STORY

As one of the last robots left on earth, WALL-E's job is to collect the garbage, compress it into perfect cubes, and stack them on top of each other, building enormous skyscrapers. WALL-E (Ben Burtt) carries a small cooler with him to collect any special objects he finds. Each night, WALL-E empties the cooler and reviews the day's treasures; a spork, an iPod, a Rubik's Cube, and a green plant he keeps in an old shoe. He then takes off his tread wheels and powers down for the night. One day, his routine is forever changed by the arrival of a mysterious spaceship. EVE (Elissa Knight), a modern and powerful scouting robot, flies out of the ship and captures WALL-E's attention. They communicate in a stream of distinct whirls and purring sounds. WALL-E falls in love with EVE and doesn't feel lonely anymore. But when EVE finds WALL-E's plant, she grabs it, stores it inside her compartment, and deactivates. WALL-E doesn't understand that EVE was sent to find any signs of life left on Earth. The spaceship arrives to pick up EVE, and WALL-E hitches a ride to *Axiom*, the mother ship, to try to protect his friend. When they arrive, WALL-E and EVE discover that the fate of mankind rests in their hands.

DID YOU KNOW?

EVE stands for "Extraterrestrial Vegetation Evaluator." WALL-E means "Waste Allocation Load Lifter, Earth Class."

DIRECTOR:
Andrew Stanton

RELEASE DATE:
June 27, 2008

RATED:
G
General Audiences

RUNTIME:
1 hour, 37 minutes

Saw it! ☐ Rating: ☆☆☆☆☆
Date: ___ / ___ / _____ With: _____
Notes: _____

18

THE IRON GIANT

DIRECTOR:
Brad Bird

RELEASE DATE:
August 6, 1999

RATED:

PG

for fantasy action
and mild language

RUNTIME:
1 hour,
26 minutes

This animated movie takes place in 1957 during the Cold War when the Soviet Union was America's worst enemy. During the same year, the Russians launched Sputnik, the first satellite to orbit the earth.

THE STORY

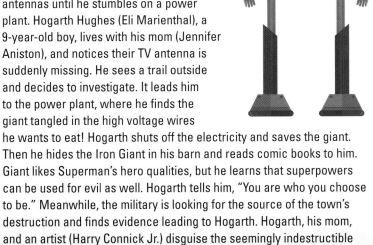

Near Maine, people gazing at Sputnik as it moves across the sky don't notice the Iron Giant (Vin Diesel) crash into the ocean. He stomps his way through the forest eating small metal sources like TV antennas until he stumbles on a power plant. Hogarth Hughes (Eli Marienthal), a 9-year-old boy, lives with his mom (Jennifer Aniston), and notices their TV antenna is suddenly missing. He sees a trail outside and decides to investigate. It leads him to the power plant, where he finds the giant tangled in the high voltage wires he wants to eat! Hogarth shuts off the electricity and saves the giant. Then he hides the Iron Giant in his barn and reads comic books to him. Giant likes Superman's hero qualities, but he learns that superpowers can be used for evil as well. Hogarth tells him, "You are who you choose to be." Meanwhile, the military is looking for the source of the town's destruction and finds evidence leading to Hogarth. Hogarth, his mom, and an artist (Harry Connick Jr.) disguise the seemingly indestructible giant—but can they save him?

Saw it! ☐ Rating: ☆☆☆☆☆

Date: ___/___/_____ With: _____

Notes: _____

_____

26

JAMES AND THE GIANT PEACH

This film includes a mix of live action and stop motion animation. The director chose this combination to reinforce the transition from reality to fantasy.

DIRECTOR:
Henry Selick

THE STORY

James (Paul Terry) lives happily with his mom and dad in England. The family dreams of visiting New York City. When James's parents are killed, things abruptly change—he's sent to live with his horrible aunts, Spiker and Sponge, who mistreat him. Sad and lonely, James meets an old man with a bag full of crocodile tongues. The stranger gives James the bag and tells him the tongues are magical and that they'll make his life better. But he can't let them get loose! James turns around and promptly trips, spilling the tongues on the ground. That night, right in that very spot, a giant peach starts to grow, and it becomes as big as his house! One day, James takes a bite out of the peach and discovers a tunnel into the fruit. He climbs through and finds amazingly oversized bugs: Old Green Grasshopper (Simon Callow), Centipede (Richard Dreyfuss), Spider (Susan Sarandon), Earthworm (David Thewlis), and Ladybug (Jane Leeves). Together they take a trip to New York aboard the giant peach!

RELEASE DATE:
April 12, 1996

DID YOU KNOW?

Roald Dahl refused to let anyone make a movie about his book *James and the Giant Peach* while he was alive. However, after his death in 1990, his wife Felicity Dahl sold the film rights to Walt Disney.

RATED:
PG
for some frightening images

RUNTIME:
1 hour, 19 minutes

Saw it! ☐ Rating: ☆☆☆☆☆

Date: ___ / ___ / _____ With: _____

Notes: _____

_____

20

BRAVE

DIRECTORS:
Mark Andrews
and Brenda
Chapman

**RELEASE
DATE:**
June 22, 2012

RATED:
PG
for some scary
action and rude
humor

RUNTIME:
1 hour,
39 minutes

THE STORY

Brave is a computer-animated fantasy film about a feisty Scottish princess battling traditions to make her own path. Merida (Kelly Macdonald) doesn't want to marry one of the three suitors chosen from the neighboring clans. Queen Elinor (Emma Thompson) pleads with her stubborn daughter to allow one of the young men to marry her—if she refuses, the Dunbroch clan could face war with the other clans. Like many young girls, Merida takes her anger out on her mother. The fiery redhead follows the will-o'-the-wisps, tiny spirit-like fairies, into the forest. There, Merida meets a sorceress who gives her a bewitched cake that turns her mom into a bear! The witch tells Merida that unless the bond between her and her mother is restored by the second sunrise, Queen Elinor will remain a black bear forever. Merida regrets her behavior and is desperate to find a way to reverse the curse. In the meantime, the clans are already waging war against each other. Can the actions of a single girl change the kingdom's long-standing traditions and allow a princess to marry who and when she wants?

DID YOU KNOW?
Terms like "bunch of galoots" (many fools) and "jiggery pokery" (nonsense) used in the film are real Scottish words and phrases.

Saw it! ☐ Rating: ☆☆☆☆☆

Date: ___/___/_____ With: _____

Notes: _____

_____

A BUG'S LIFE

Have you ever wondered what happens when ants disappear through the tiny pinhole on top of an anthill? We get an up-close, bug's eye view of life underground in this computer-animated movie!

THE STORY

In a moment of panic, an ant screams, "I'm lost! Where's the line?" A leaf has fallen on the trail and blocked the path. The rescue ants come over and say, "Now, stay calm. We are going around the leaf!" The ants are in a hurry to gather enough food for the winter, not only for the colony, but also for a troop of demanding grasshoppers that have made the ants their slaves. Flik (Dave Foley) is a clever ant in the colony who always thinking outside the box. He is tired of Hopper (Kevin Spacey), the leader of the grasshoppers, threatening the colony and stealing their food. However, the Queen (Phyllis Diller), Princess Atta (Julia Louis-Dreyfus), and Mr. Soil (Roddy McDowall) want Flik to stop causing trouble. They encourage Flik to leave the colony to find a band of soldiers that can help protect the colony from the grasshoppers. Flik brings back a silly-looking group of performers from P.T. Flea's Circus. Can they save the colony from the terrifying Hopper?

DID YOU KNOW?

The film crew put Lego wheels on a tiny camera and mounted it on a stick. They rolled it through the garden at Pixar Animation's studio to see what the bugs actually saw!

DIRECTORS:
John Lasseter
and
Andrew Stanton

RELEASE DATE:
November 25, 1998

RATED:

G

General Audiences

RUNTIME:
1 hour, 35 minutes

Saw it! ☐ Rating: ☆☆☆☆☆

Date: ___ / ___ / _____ With: _____

Notes: _____

_____

THE INCREDIBLES

🏆🏆 **2 ACADEMY AWARDS**

DIRECTOR:
Brad Bird

RELEASE DATE:
November 5, 2004

RATED:
PG
for action violence

RUNTIME:
1 hour, 55 minutes

THE STORY

Posing as a regular family under the Superhero Relocation Program, the Incredibles are famous superheroes trying to fit in with normal folks. Bob (Craig T. Nelson) and Helen (Holly Hunter), formerly Mr. Incredible and Elastigirl, and their kids, Violet (Sarah Vowell), Dashiell (Spencer Fox), and Jack-Jack (Eli Fucile, Maeve Andrews) are now known as the Parr family. The government forced all supers into leading normal lives due to the collateral damage and lawsuits caused by their heroics. Helen becomes a mom raising her kids, Violet uses her force field bubbles to hide from bullying kids at school, and Dash has to slow down at school track meets so his break-neck speed won't raise suspicions. Bob has a desk job—and he hates it. His old pal, Frozone (Samuel L. Jackson) is also a relocated superhero. They secretly sneak out at night to fight crime, telling their wives they're just bowling. But evil is everywhere! A robot named Omnidroid 7, created by one of Mr. Incredible's former fans, Syndrome (Jason Lee), wants to kill all of the superheroes. Once again, it's up to the Incredibles to save the world!

DID YOU KNOW?
After a search for someone to voice Edna Mode failed, Brad Bird decided to voice her himself.

WATCH OUT FOR

The Incredibles is the first full-length CGI (computer-generated animation) movie to feature all human characters. Take special notice of Violet's long flowing hair. This was a huge technical achievement!

Saw it! ☐ Rating: ☆☆☆☆☆
Date: ___/___/_____ With: _____
Notes: _____
_____

UP

THE STORY

After Carl Fredricksen's wife dies, he becomes a recluse who doesn't want to leave his house. Now a retired balloon maker, Carl (Ed Asner) dreams of taking a trip to Paradise Falls in South America, a journey he and his wife had planned to take together. They wanted to visit the place where the famous explorer Charles F. Muntz (Christopher Plummer) claims he discovered a large, strange bird. When crabby old Mr. Fredricksen is about to be forced into a retirement home, he escapes using thousands of colorful balloons to lift his house into the sky! Young Wilderness Explorer Russell (Jordan Nagai) is standing on Carl's porch about to knock on the door when the entire house takes flight. A 78-year-old and an 8-year-old aren't the best traveling buddies, but they manage to survive a storm and make it to Paradise Falls. They meet a talking dog named Dug (Squirrel!), and a rare 13-foot-tall bird that Russell affectionately names Kevin. After an angry pack of dogs leads them to their master, they discover the mysterious owner is Muntz himself! But Muntz isn't who Carl thought he was, and when Muntz turns on the travelers, the only way to escape the villain is to get the house airborne again. Can they do this without balloons?

DID YOU KNOW?

Up was the first Disney movie (and the first 3-D animated film) to open the Cannes Film Festival in France.

DIRECTORS:
Pete Docter and Bob Peterson

RELEASE DATE:
May 29, 2009

RATED:

PG
for mild peril and action

RUNTIME:
1 hour, 36 minutes

Saw it! ☐ Rating: ☆☆☆☆☆

Date: ___ / ___ / _____ With: _____

Notes: _____

_____

24

A CHRISTMAS STORY

DIRECTOR:
Bob Clark

RELEASE DATE:
November 18, 1983

RATED:
PG
for strong language

RUNTIME:
1 hour, 34 minutes

THE STORY

A Christmas Story is a classic comedy about an all-American family living in the Midwest. Mrs. Parker (Melinda Dillon) is the pillar of the family in the face of calamity; the Old Man, whom they call Mr. Parker (Darren McGavin), is obsessed with the failing furnace; and 9-year-old Ralphie (Peter Billingsley) and his brother face bullies at school and deal with double- and triple-dog dares. The family's quirky nature brings the holiday season into perspective for Ralphie, as he pines for a Red Ryder Carbine Action 200-Shot Range Model Air Rifle for Christmas.

WHY IT'S FAMOUS

This seemingly typical family is affectionately known for its pretty unusual behavior. When all Ralphie wants for Christmas is a Red Ryder BB gun, the adults all tell him the same thing, "You'll shoot your eye out!" But he can't imagine anything better than that BB gun! Things take a bizarre turn when Mr. Parker wins a major prize—a lamp shaped like a woman's leg. Mrs. Parker doesn't like it one bit! She also doesn't like Ralphie to swear. *A Christmas Story* is a go-to family film for the season that brings some sense to the craziness of the holidays.

DID YOU KNOW?
Ralphie Parker repeats the name of his most-wanted Christmas present, a Red Ryder Carbine Action 200-Shot Range Model Air Rifle, 28 times during the movie. Count them yourself!

Saw it! ☐ Rating: ☆☆☆☆☆
Date: ___/___/_____ With: _____
Notes: _____
_____

THE NIGHTMARE BEFORE CHRISTMAS

What do you get when you combine Halloween, Christmas, and Tim Burton? *The Nightmare Before Christmas!* Although Tim Burton did not direct this film, he wrote the story, produced the film, and created its unique-looking characters.

THE STORY

This stop motion animated musical is about a well-intentioned skeleton from Halloween Town who takes over Christmas and poses as Santa Claus, aka "Sandy Claws." He delivers gruesome toys on Christmas Eve, scaring the kids of Christmas Town in the process.

Jack Skellington is the Pumpkin King of Halloween Town. He's in charge of organizing the annual Halloween celebration for the citizens, a creepy collection of ghouls, goblins, vampires, and other monsters. Tired of doing the same thing year after year, Jack wants to do something more meaningful. Strolling through the forest one night, he enters Christmas Town through a portal. He sees how the people there are happily preparing for their annual holiday. Santa even has cheerful helpers—unlike the gloomy folks of Halloween Town! Jack wants to take part in the Christmas celebrations as well, so he decides to kidnap Santa and take his place! Although Jack's intentions are good, the Pumpkin King's experience lies more with spooky Halloween traditions than with the quaint, friendly customs of the winter holiday.

DIRECTOR:
Henry Selick

RELEASE DATE:
October 29, 1993

DID YOU KNOW?

The Nightmare Before Christmas took three years to complete. It took a week to shoot only one minute of the stop motion movie.

RATED:
PG
for some scary images

RUNTIME:
1 hour, 16 minutes

Saw it! ☐ Rating: ☆☆☆☆☆
Date: ___/___/_____ With: _____
Notes: _____
_____

26

THE GOONIES

DIRECTOR:
Richard
Donner

**RELEASE
DATE:**
June 7, 1985

RATED:

PG

for adult situations
and language,
violence

RUNTIME:
1 hour,
54 minutes

THE STORY

A band of preteen boys call themselves "Goonies" because they live in an Oregon neighborhood called the Goon Docks. Their families are being forced to move out of their homes to make way for a country club to be built on the land, and they're desperate to save their homes. While

"Goonies never say die!" —Mikey Walsh

hanging out in their friend Mike Walsh's (Sean Astin) house one last time, the boys decide to snoop around the attic, where they discover an old treasure map belonging to a pirate named One-Eyed Willy. The nonstop adventure begins when they follow the clues, leading them to a secret cave and bringing them face-to-face with criminals!

The map leads them to a cavern under a restaurant used by the delinquent Fratelli family to make counterfeit money. The Fratellis manage to capture Chunk (Jeff Cohen), the chubby clown of the gang, and squeeze him for information about the other kids' whereabouts. He spills the beans, telling the thieves about his pals' treasure hunt. After overcoming a series of traps left by pirates to protect the booty, the kids find One-Eyed Willy's long-lost pirate ship, but unknowingly lead the Fratelli family to the treasure too. Time is running out, and the country club builders are demanding to begin construction. Can this group of clever kids escape the clutches of the wicked Fratelli family and find the treasure while saving their homes?

DID YOU KNOW?
Chris Columbus, the writer of *The Goonies* screenplay, later directed two of the *Harry Potter* movies: *Sorcerer's Stone* and *Chamber of Secrets*.

STARRING:
Sean Astin,
Josh Brolin,
Jeff Cohen,
and Corey
Feldman

**SCREEN-
PLAY
WRITTEN
BY:**
Chris
Columbus

**FILM
LOCATION:**
Astoria,
Oregon

Saw it! ☐ Rating: ☆☆☆☆☆

Date: ___/___/_____ With: _____

Notes: _____

_____

27

HOW THE GRINCH STOLE CHRISTMAS

DIRECTOR:
Ron Howard

RELEASE DATE:
November 17, 2000

RATED:
PG
for some crude humor

RUNTIME:
1 hour,
44 minutes

Theodor Geisel, also known as Dr. Seuss, is the author and illustrator of the book *How the Grinch Stole Christmas* (1957). His unique characters from the book are recreated in human form in the movie of the same title, *How the Grinch Stole Christmas*, which was released in 2000. The original animated short film was made for television in 1966.

THE STORY
The Grinch (Jim Carrey) and his faithful dog Max live in a dark cave on a snow-covered mountaintop high above Whoville. The cheerful town below is preparing for Christmas, and the Whos laugh and sing as they put up

elaborate decorations and gather food for the huge celebration. The Grinch, who has a heart "two sizes too small," doesn't like all the hustle and bustle of the season. The racket and over-the-top decorations are too much for him, and he decides this year to stop Christmas from coming.

Speeding down the steep mountain on a sleigh with Max dressed as a reindeer, the Grinch hatches the perfect plan to disguise himself as Santa Claus—but instead of delivering presents, the green Santa will take everything away, including their favorite dinner, the great roast beast! On Christmas Eve, the Grinch slides down each chimney stealing everything, but one tiny Who, Cindy Lou Who (Taylor Momsen), catches him in the evil act. After fooling Cindy Lou, he escapes with all the trimmings of Whoville's Christmas piled on his sleigh and rides back to his cave. Convinced he'll hear the sound of disappointment coming from Whoville on Christmas morning, the Grinch is shocked to hear just the opposite.

WHY IT'S FAMOUS

How The Grinch Stole Christmas continues to teach a universal message: the true meaning of the season lives in our hearts.

DID YOU KNOW?

How the Grinch Stole Christmas was the first Dr. Seuss book to be made into a full-length motion picture.

STARRING:
Jim Carey, Jeffrey Tambor, and Christine Baranski

BOX OFFICE:
$345.1 million

MUSIC:
James Horner

Saw it! ☐ Rating: ☆☆☆☆☆

Date: ___/___/_____ With: _____

Notes: _____

_____

28

EDWARD SCISSORHANDS

DIRECTOR:
Tim Burton

RELEASE DATE:
December 14, 1990

RATED:
PG-13
for suggestive humor, some teen drinking, and language

RUNTIME:
1 hour,
45 minutes

THE STORY

This film begins with a grandmother telling her granddaughter a story about where snow comes from. She tells her about a young man named Edward (Johnny Depp). As a result of his inventor's (Vincent Price) sudden death, Edward, a gothic Frankenstein-like human, is left with large scissors for hands. He grows up isolated, hiding in a dark castle perched on a hill overlooking a cheerful suburban residential area. One day, the local Avon Lady, Peg Boggs, comes calling at the castle. She sees that the speechless young man dressed all in black is alone and decides he's harmless. She takes Edward into her home where her daughter Kim (Winona Ryder), eventually falls in love with him. He becomes popular with some people because he trims hedges and hair with flair! To show his love, Edward uses his hands to create an ice sculpture of Kim. As he's working, the shaved ice flies into the sky and falls like snow. But this love story is not meant to be. Edward's hands cause havoc with the neighbors and the town wants him gone. Edward retreats to his dark castle and is never seen again. Kim, now an old woman, tells her granddaughter that the only sign he's still alive is the yearly snow that still falls over the town.

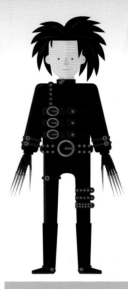

DID YOU KNOW?

This film was the first-ever collaboration between Johnny Depp and Tim Burton. They have since made 8 films together over a span of 25 years.

Saw it! ☐ Rating: ☆☆☆☆☆

Date: ___/___/_____ With: _____

Notes: _____

_____

FLY AWAY HOME

THE STORY

Amy Alden (Anna Paquin) and her mother are in a car accident in New Zealand. Amy survives, but her mother doesn't. Her parents are divorced. Her father, Thomas Alden (Jeff Daniels), is a sculptor and inventor who lives in Ontario, Canada. After the accident, Amy leaves New Zealand to live with her dad. Things are awkward at first, especially when her dad's girlfriend, Susan (Dana Delany), is around. One day, Amy finds some goose eggs and takes them home. She hides them in a drawer in the barn. When the eggs hatch, the

first thing the chicks see is Amy, and now they think she's their mother! Amy's dad lets her keep the chicks as pets; however, the birds need to migrate for the winter. Without a mother to teach them how to fly, they may not survive. The game warden tells the Aldens they can't keep the geese unless their wings are clipped so they can't fly. Thomas figures out that the birds can be taught to fly, and since the chicks already follow Amy around everywhere, they'll likely follow her up into the sky too. He makes a special homemade light aircraft and teaches Amy how to fly the machine, turning Amy into a human Mother Goose!

WHY IT'S FAMOUS

Fly Away Home is loosely based on the real-life events of William Lishman and his daughter Carmen. In 1993, Lishman led 16 birds from Ontario to Virginia. The following year, 13 geese returned.

DIRECTOR:
Carroll Ballard

RELEASE DATE:
September 13, 1996

RATED:

PG

for an opening accident scene and some mild language

RUNTIME:
1 hour, 47 minutes

Saw it! ☐ Rating: ☆☆☆☆☆
Date: ___ / ___ / _____ With: _____
Notes: _____
_____

30

THE PRINCESS BRIDE

DIRECTOR:
Rob Reiner

RELEASE DATE:
October 9, 1987

RATED:

PG

for adult situations/ language

RUNTIME:
1 hour, 38 minutes

THE STORY

An old man reads a story to his grandson, who is home sick from school. Buttercup (Robin Wright) lives on a farm in the fictional country of Florin. Her loyal farm boy, Westley (Cary Elwes), loves her and always answers her commands with, "As you wish." Buttercup realizes that she also loves Westley, but before they can get married, Westley sails away to seek his fortune. His ship is attacked by the Dread Pirate Roberts, and no one survives. Five years later, Buttercup is engaged to marry Prince Humperdinck (Chris Sarandon). Before the wedding, Buttercup is kidnapped by an odd trio: Vizzini (Wallace Shawn), Fezzik (André the Giant), and a Spanish fencer Inigo Montoya (Mandy Patinkin) who wants to avenge his father, who was killed by a six-fingered man. Montoya practices for revenge by repeating, "Hello, my name is Inigo Montoya. You killed my father. Prepare to die."

DID YOU KNOW?
This film made the American Film Institute's 100 Greatest Love Stories.

Meanwhile, along with a mysterious masked man, the prince goes after the outlaws who took Buttercup. Atop the Cliffs of Insanity, the masked man defeats Montoya in a swordfight and crushes the band of outlaws. He grabs Buttercup and tells her that he is the Dread Pirate Roberts. Thinking he killed her beloved Westley, Buttercup pushes him down a hill. As he falls he yells, "As you wish!" The grandson asks his grandfather to read the story again. The ending will answer all your questions too!

Saw it! ☐ Rating: ☆☆☆☆☆

Date: ___/___/_____ With: _____

Notes: _____

_____

THE SECRET GARDEN

THE STORY

Mary Lennox (Kate Maberly) lives in India with her parents, where she is cared for by a nanny and servants. One day, tragedy strikes and her parents are killed in an earthquake. Now an orphan, Mary is shipped off to England to live with her uncle, Lord Archibald (John Lynch), at Misselthwaite Manor in Yorkshire. Lord Archibald's wife died many years before, and heartbroken, he has since spent his days traveling, away from the manor. Mrs. Medlock (Maggie Smith) manages the estate and looks after Lord Archibald's son and Mary's cousin, Colin, a 9-year-old sickly, bedridden boy. A boy named Dickon Sowerby, a relative of one of the manor servants, befriends Mary. With Dickon's help, Mary discovers a hidden garden on the castle grounds and the key that unlocks the garden's door. Mary and Dickon inspire Colin to walk and show him that happiness can be found.

WHY IT'S FAMOUS

This British film is based on the 1911 book by Frances Hodgson Burnett, which was inspired by her own life experiences.

DID YOU KNOW?

A fountain dedicated to Burnett at the Conservatory Garden in New York City's Central Park is said to be of the two main characters in *The Secret Garden*, Mary and Dickon.

DIRECTOR:
Agnieszka Holland

RELEASE DATE:
August 13, 1993

RATED:

G

General Audiences

RUNTIME:
1 hour, 41 minutes

Saw it! ☐ Rating: ☆☆☆☆☆

Date: ___/___/_____ With: _____

Notes: _____

_____

32

PRIDE & PREJUDICE

DIRECTOR:
Joe Wright

RELEASE DATE:
November 23, 2005

RATED:
PG
for some mild thematic elements

RUNTIME:
2 hours, 9 minutes

THE STORY

Five sisters live in the British countryside with their parents,
Mr. Bennet (Donald Sutherland) and Mrs. Bennet (Brenda Blethyn):
Jane (Rosamund Pike), Elizabeth (Keira Knightley), Mary (Talula Riley),
Kitty (Carey Mulligan), and Lydia (Jena Malone). It's their mother's
business to marry off her daughters, and she must find a suitable suitor
for each one, starting with the oldest. Back then, marriage was only a
matter of money—love was expected to gradually form over time.
Mr. Bingley (Simon Woods), an eligible bachelor with a substantial
income, moves near the Bennet's country home, and Mrs. Bennet begins
to scheme about how to introduce him to her daughters. Mr. Bingley
brings his friend Mr. Darcy (Matthew Macfadyen) to a local dance, and
the two meet Jane and her sister Elizabeth. Jane and Mr. Bingley like
each other right away, but Mr. Darcy does not like Lizzy because she is
from a lower class. He carelessly voices his opinion of Elizabeth within
earshot and tells Mr. Bingley that she is "tolerable, but not handsome
enough to tempt me." Lizzy, a stubborn woman who knows what she
wants, swears she will hate Mr. Darcy forever. This film marvelously
wraps you up in the complicated courtships indicative of this time. Will
Mr. Darcy and Elizabeth learn to let go of their pride and the inherent
prejudices of their society?

STARRING:
Keira
Knightley,
Matthew
Macfadyen,
Brenda
Blethyn,
and Donald
Sutherland

**ORIGINAL
STORY BY:**
Jane
Austen

DID YOU KNOW?

Pride & Prejudice is based on a Jane Austen novel
published in 1813. Although Austen wrote about love
and marriage, she never married herself.

**FILM
LOCATION:**
England

Saw it! ☐ Rating: ☆☆☆☆☆
Date: ___/___/_____ With: _____
Notes: _____
_____

33

DESPICABLE ME

DIRECTORS:
Pierre Coffin
and
Chris Renaud

**RELEASE
DATE**:
July 9, 2010

RATED:
PG
for rude humor
and mild action

RUNTIME:
1 hour,
35 minutes

THE STORY

Gru (Steve Carell) is a grumpy supervillain anxious to recapture his glory as the world's best villain. His fellow villain, Vector (Jason Segel), has stolen the Great Pyramid of Giza and become top dog in the world of evil. Gru cooks up a plan to steal the moon, but he first needs an influx of cash to invent a powerful shrink ray. Gru borrows money from the Bank of Evil, and together with his army of irresistibly cute minions, they create the shrink ray—only to have Vector take it from them. Enraged, Gru adopts three orphan girls, Margo (Miranda Cosgrove), Edith (Dana Gaier), and Agnes (Elsie Fisher) to use them for a wicked plan. Posing as Girl Scouts selling cookies, Gru plans to use the girls to fool Vector into letting them into his house to steal back the shrink ray—and it works! Gru successfully shrinks and steals the moon. While in his care, the adorable girls run amuck at Gru's house, and amid the chaos,

Gru and the girls start to feel like a family. However, Vector kidnaps the girls and offers to trade them for the moon. Will Gru save the girls from Vector's diabolical hands?

This 3-D film also includes the comedy voice talents of Will Arnett, Ken Jeong, Kristin Wiig, Russell Brand, and Danny McBride.

UP NEXT

The success of this film led to the sequel *Despicable Me 2* (2013), as well as the spin-off movie *Minions* (2015). *Despicable Me 3* is set to hit theaters in 2017.

STARRING:
Steve Carell,
Jason Segel,
Miranda
Cosgrove,
and Russell
Brand

BOX OFFICE:
$543.1
million

DID YOU KNOW?

Pharrell Williams produced *Despicable Me*'s soundtrack. Williams also wrote, produced, and performed "Happy" for the *Despicable Me 2* film soundtrack.

MUSIC:
Songs by
Hans Zimmer
and Pharrell
Williams

Saw it! ☐ Rating: ☆☆☆☆☆
Date: ___/___/_____ With: _____
Notes: _____
_____

34

ICE AGE

DIRECTORS:
Chris Wedge
and Carlos
Saldanha

**RELEASE
DATE:**
March 15, 2002

RATED:

PG

for mild peril

RUNTIME:
1 hour,
21 minutes

THE STORY

This digitally animated movie follows three prehistoric animals that find a human baby and make a pact to return him to his family. Manny (Ray Romano), a warm hearted woolly mammoth; Sid (John Leguizamo), a fast-talking sloth; and Diego (Denis Leary), a menacing saber-toothed tiger, bond as they cross the frozen tundra, going in the opposite direction of the seasonal animal migration. Along their cold and comedic journey, you'll see amazing scenes of snow-covered mountains, glistening glaciers, and expansive land during the Ice Age. The movie also follows an out-of-control, long-toothed squirrel named Scrat. Scrat is desperately trying to gather food for the winter, but faces many hilarious, terrifying obstacles in an effort to save his prized acorn—which is about as big as he is!

UP NEXT

Get ready for an *Ice Age* marathon, because this film became a franchise with three more films: *Ice Age: The Meltdown* (2006), *Ice Age: Dawn of the Dinosaurs* (2009), and *Ice Age: Continental Drift* (2012). *Ice Age 5* is set to hit theaters in 2016.

DID YOU KNOW?

After 40 different attempts, John Leguizamo came up with Sid's voice watching documentaries about sloths. He learned that these slow animals store food in their cheek pouches. To mimic the sound, the actor put a sandwich in his mouth and tried to talk!

Saw it! ☐ Rating: ☆☆☆☆☆

Date: ___/___/_____ With: _____

Notes: _____

_____

1 ACADEMY AWARD

SHREK

THE STORY

Shrek (Mike Myers) is an ogre living alone in his swamp, and he likes it that way. But one day, his peace and quiet is interrupted by a group of fairy tale characters—the Three Little Pigs, the Three Blind Mice, the Gingerbread Man, and Pinocchio, among others—who show up and ask Shrek for help. The mean, power-hungry Lord Farquaad (John Lithgow) kicked them out of the kingdom, and they don't have anywhere to live. Farquaad asks the Magic Mirror for a bride to choose from: Cinderella, Snow White, or Princess Fiona (Cameron Diaz)—who's cursed, lives in a tower, and turns into an ogre at night. The Magic Mirror tries to tell Farquaad this small detail, but he doesn't listen! The fast-talking Donkey (Eddie Murphy) joins Shrek on the way to Duloc to talk to Farquaad. When they arrive, Shrek and Farquaad make a deal: The ogre slays the dragon, rescues Fiona from the tower, and brings her to him. In exchange, Farquaad will ban the fairy tale creatures from Shrek's swamp.

WATCH OUT FOR

Two sequels followed, *Shrek 2* (2004) and *Shrek the Third* (2007).

DIRECTORS:
Andrew Adamson and Vicky Jenson

RELEASE DATE:
May 18, 2001

DID YOU KNOW?

Mike Myers asked to re-record all of his lines in the Scottish accent he learned from his mom when she read him bedtime stories when he was young!

RATED:

PG

mild language and some crude humor

RUNTIME:
1 hour, 30 minutes

Saw it! ☐ Rating: ☆☆☆☆☆

Date: ___ / ___ / _____ With: _____

Notes: _____

_____

DRUMLINE

DIRECTOR:
Charles Stone III

RELEASE DATE:
December 13, 2002

RATED:
PG-13
for innuendo and language

RUNTIME:
1 hour, 58 minutes

THE STORY

Devon (Nick Cannon) is an African-American teenager from Harlem with a big attitude and an even bigger desire for success. He scores a full scholarship to the fictitious A&T University in Atlanta, Georgia, to play drums in the marching band. Devon likes to show off, but band director Dr. Lee Jones (Orlando Jones) is more traditional; his players need to know how to read music, play a variety of classics, and work as a team: "One band, one sound." Devon is more interested in Laila (Zoe Saldana), the dance team captain, than in teamwork. Problems begin when he antagonizes the section leader and news gets out that he can't read music. Devon gets demoted within the drumline and is eventually kicked out of the band. However, the school's president tells Dr. Lee that they need to win the BET television-sponsored Big Southern Classic competition. He needs to modernize the band's sound or he's out! Devon's slick drum moves earn him a spot back in the band to help beat their rivals (and real band champions) Morris Brown College.

DID YOU KNOW?

The Georgia Superdome was filled with 50,000 extras to film the final drumoff. The marching bands from Morris Brown College, Clark Atlanta University, Bethune-Cookman University, and Grambling State University are featured in the scene.

Saw it! ☐ Rating: ☆☆☆☆☆

Date: ___/___/_____ With: _____

Notes: _____

_____

WHALE RIDER

THE STORY

A 12-year-old Maori girl named Pai (Keisha Castle-Hughes) lives in present-day New Zealand and wants to become the leader of her people, which is traditionally a man's role. After her twin brother and mother die during childbirth, the little girl is named Paikea, after a mythic ancestor of the Maoris. According to legend, Paikea led the tribe to settle in Whangara by riding a whale. Since then, descendants of the great leader have become tribe chiefs, and the name Paikea is reserved for the first-born male of a family. Pai's dad, Porourangi (Cliff Curtis), is an artist and leaves New Zealand, leaving Pai to be raised by her grandparents: Koro (Rawiri Paratene), the leader of the tribe, and Nanny Flowers (Vicky Haughton). One day, Koro gathers all of the teenage boys to teach them how to be a Maori. Pai is not invited. As you can imagine, she is disappointed. However, this movie is anything but disappointing—the ending is so surprising that whatever you might guess, you'll likely be surprised.

    Whale Rider shows us the struggle native cultures face to maintain traditions, and that girls have the ability to be strong leaders!

DID YOU KNOW?

Keisha Castle-Hughes had never acted before *Whale Rider*. She was 13 years old when she was nominated for the Academy Award for Best Actress in a Leading Role, the youngest actress ever nominated for an Oscar in this category.

DIRECTOR:
Niki Caro

RELEASE DATE:
August 29, 2003 (USA)

RATED:
PG-13
for brief language and a momentary drug reference

RUNTIME:
1 hour, 41 minutes

Saw it! ☐ Rating: ☆☆☆☆☆

Date: ___ / ___ / _____ With: _____

Notes: _____

_____

THE CHRONICLES OF NARNIA: THE LION, THE WITCH AND THE WARDROBE

1 ACADEMY AWARD

DIRECTOR:
Andrew Adamson

RELEASE DATE:
December 9, 2005

RATED:

PG

for battle sequences and frightening moments

RUNTIME:
2 hours, 23 minutes

THE STORY

In this first film, Peter (William Moseley), Susan (Anna Popplewell), Edmund (Skandar Keynes), and Lucy Pevensie (Georgie Henley) are evacuated from London to save them from Nazi raids during World War II. They move in with Professor Kirke (Jim Broadbent) at his vast home in the English countryside. Playing hide-and-seek, Lucy stumbles upon a wardrobe that leads to the magical land of Narnia, a parallel fantasy world. She shows her siblings the portal, and they all travel through the closet into a snow-covered land inhabited by strange creatures. Narnia has been cast in a perpetual winter for a century by a spell from the evil White Witch (Tilda Swinton). The children meet Aslan (Liam Neeson), a talking lion, and together they set out to hunt down the White Witch. Can the Pevensies defeat the White Witch and return to reality?

UP NEXT

Two more books in the series were turned into movies, *Prince Caspian* (2008) and *The Voyage of the Dawn Treader* (2010).

DID YOU KNOW?

Clive Staples Lewis, better known as C.S. Lewis, wrote the seven-book series *The Chronicles of Narnia*. He taught at Oxford University in England along with his colleague and good friend, J.R.R. Tolkien, who wrote *The Lord of the Rings* trilogy.

Saw it! ☐ Rating: ☆☆☆☆☆

Date: ___/___/_____ With: _____

Notes: _____

_____

WHERE THE WILD THINGS ARE

This movie is adapted from Maurice Sendak's beloved 1963 children's tale *Where the Wild Things Are*. The entire book consists of 10 sentences — that's 37 pages or 388 words. The reader's imagination is left to interpret the author's muted drawings to get the whole story. Now this abbreviated classic is a feature-length motion picture.

THE STORY

Max (Max Records) is a mischievous 9-year-old boy who escapes his complicated home life by hiding in his imagination. After an argument with his sister and throwing a tantrum in front of his mom, Max goes to his room, throws on a wolf costume, and travels on a boat to an island inhabited by The Wild Things: Carol (James Gandolfini), Ira (Forest Whitaker), Judith (Catherine O'Hara), Alexander (Paul Dano), Douglas (Chris Cooper), and K.W (Lauren Ambrose). The horned, 10-foot-tall monster-like creatures accept Max as their king because he promises to use his magic to help them solve their problems—something Max wishes he were able to do in his real life.

DID YOU KNOW?
Max Records was 8 years old when he was chosen for the role of Max.

WATCH OUT FOR

To convincingly re-create the story's furry creatures for the film, the director used a combination of live people inside costumes and computer animation.

DIRECTOR:
Spike Jonze

RELEASE DATE:
October 16, 2009

RATED:
PG
for mild thematic elements, some adventure action, and brief language

RUNTIME:
1 hour, 41 minutes

Saw it! ☐ Rating: ☆☆☆☆☆
Date: ___/___/_____ With: _____
Notes: _____
_____

40

HAPPY FEET

DIRECTOR:
George Miller,
Warren Coleman,
and Judy Morris

**RELEASE
DATE:**
November 17, 2006

RATED:
PG
for some mild peril
and rude humor

RUNTIME:
1 hour,
48 minutes

THE STORY

Mumble (Elijah Wood) is born without a proper "heartsong," the sounds penguins make to attract a mate. Mumble's parents, Norma Jean (Nicole Kidman) and Memphis (Hugh Jackman) worry that without it he may never find true love. However, Mumble has a special talent: He can tap dance like no other Emperor Penguin in the colony! But since Mumble is simply too strange to be part of Emperor Land, Noah the elder penguin banishes him and his "hippity-hoppity" feet. Drifting alone across the white landscape, Mumble meets the Adelies, a joyful trio of penguins. They're impressed with his moves and Ramon (Robin Williams), leader of these misfit penguins, invites Mumble to party with them. However, when Mumble ends up confined at Marine World in Australia, all hope for his return home seems lost. Can Mumble go back to his arctic habitat and find a mate in spite of the odds set against him?

DID YOU KNOW?
Tony Award-winning dancer Savion Glover, was responsible for the dance sequences in *Happy Feet*.

Happy Feet sends a valuable message. One penguin shows up with a set of plastic six-pack rings around his neck and a seagull wearing a yellow band on his leg claims he was "tagged by aliens." These references to humans' intrusion on the environment are wrapped up in this movie's broader message about acceptance and being unique.

UP NEXT
Happy Feet 2 followed in 2011.

Saw it! ☐ Rating: ☆☆☆☆☆
Date: ___/___/_____ With: _____
Notes: _____
_____

THE LEGO® MOVIE

THE STORY

In this original computer-animated movie, construction worker Legos band together to battle against the evil Lord Business (Will Ferrell). Vitruvius (Morgan Freeman), a wise Lego wizard, prophesies that whoever finds the Piece of Resistance is "The Special"—the chosen one destined to save the Lego universe from a superweapon called the Kragle. Emmet (Chris Pratt) is a construction worker who encounters Wyldstyle (Elizabeth Banks) scavenging on the construction site. He tries to help her and falls into a hole where the Piece of Resistance attaches to his back. Wyldstyle takes Emmet to Vitruvius, where he learns they are both Master Builders, meaning they don't need instructions to build. They must battle Lord Business because he wants to destroy their creativity. Emmet recalls a vision he had of "The Man Upstairs," a human who glues his Lego creations after building them by following the instructions. Emmet encourages the Legos to work as a team to defeat him. Can the Lego people use their creativity to defeat Lord Business? Will Emmet reach the real world in time?

DID YOU KNOW?

Inspired by these classic building blocks, Legoland® operates seven theme parks around the world. Two are located in the United States, in California and Florida.

DIRECTORS:
Phil Lord and Christopher Miller

RELEASE DATE:
February 7, 2014

RATED:
PG
for mild action and rude humor

RUNTIME:
1 hour, 40 minutes

Saw it! ☐ Rating: ☆☆☆☆☆
Date: ___/___/_____ With: _____
Notes: _____
_____

42

WRECK-IT RALPH

DIRECTOR:
Rich Moore

RELEASE DATE:
November 2, 2012

RATED:

PG

for some rude humor and mild action/violence

RUNTIME:
1 hour, 41 minutes

THE STORY

Nicelanders don't like Wreck-It Ralph (John C. Reilly). He destroys everything in the Fix-It Felix Jr. game because that's what he's coded to do! Felix (Jack McBrayer) fixes what Ralph destroys. After being the bad guy for 30 years, Ralph decides to get advice from a video game villains' support group. They tell him he can't change the game's program. Disappointed, he leaves the game world of Niceland through the electric cables in search of a medal from the new Hero's Duty video game—everyone loves heroes! Sgt. Calhoun (Jane Lynch) is getting ready to attack a player when Ralph arrives, accidentally shoots the player, and ends the game. He sees a medal hanging in midair and grabs it, but then accidentally steps on a Cy-Bug egg that tries to attack him. He escapes to the Sugar Rush game next and then jumps from game to game trying to escape attacks and gain a medal. In the meantime, a girl tries to play Fix-It Felix Jr., but the game doesn't work because Ralph is missing. She reports the game is out of order, and the arcade owner plans to pull the plug on it the next day. Fearing this, Felix leaves his game to find Ralph. Can Felix find Ralph in time, and will Ralph finally earn the respect he desires?

DID YOU KNOW?

The British Royal Wedding influenced the Nicelanders' outfits since it was big news in 2011 when the characters were being designed.

Saw it! ☐ Rating: ☆☆☆☆☆

Date: ___/___/_____ With: _____

Notes: _____

_____

MRS. DOUBTFIRE

THE STORY

Mrs. Doubtfire is secretly a mister! Daniel Hillard (Robin Williams) is a divorced father of three. He's an unemployed voice actor who loves his children very much. However, he's also a rather irresponsible adult. He prefers to play with his kids rather than discipline them. Miranda Hillard (Sally Field), the children's mother, needs a nanny to care for the kids while she's at work. Daniel can't stand the thought of seeing his kids only one day a week, so without telling his ex-wife, he comes up with the perfect solution—he decides to become their nanny. With help from his brother, a professional makeup artist, Daniel transforms himself from a fun-loving dad into a stern British nanny—and the whole family adores him…umm, her! Mrs. Doubtfire cooks, cleans, and helps with homework. Only Miranda's boyfriend Stu (Pierce Brosnan) thinks the nanny is a bit strange, but otherwise no one has a clue about the disguise. However, after several close calls, Mrs. Doubtfire forgets to shut the door to the bathroom and one of the kids sees "her" do something weird—and Daniel's cover is blown! What happens next? You'll have to watch *Mrs. Doubtfire* to find out.

DID YOU KNOW?

It took four hours to put the heavy makeup on Robin Williams that transformed him into Mrs. Doubtfire.

DIRECTOR:
Chris Columbus

RELEASE DATE:
November 24, 1993

RATED:
PG-13
for some sexual references

RUNTIME:
2 hours, 5 minutes

Saw it! ☐ Rating: ☆☆☆☆☆
Date: ___/___/_____ With: _____
Notes: _____
_____

44

FORREST GUMP

DIRECTOR:
Robert Zemeckis

RELEASE DATE:
July 6, 1994

RATED:
PG-13
for drug content, some sensuality, and war violence

RUNTIME:
2 hours, 22 minutes

"Momma always said life was like a box of chocolates. You never know what you're gonna get." —Forrest Gump

THE STORY

Forrest Gump (Tom Hanks) is a slow, naïve but honest man who lives in Alabama. While waiting at the bus stop, Forrest starts telling his life story to the riders waiting next to him. His mother (Sally Field) told him simple truths as a child, such as "Stupid is as stupid does," and encouraged him to be proud of himself no matter how the world treated him. He recounts how he wore leg braces as a kid and was bullied for being a cripple. One day, bullies surrounded and threatened him. His best friend Jenny (Robin Wright) screamed, "Run, Forrest! Run!" He ran so fast that his leg braces flew right off his legs.

This is how Forrest ends up with a college football scholarship. From this point on, specifically between 1950 and 1980, Forrest is somehow involved in every major American historical event. He's awarded the Medal of Honor for his service in Vietnam, becomes a ping-pong champion, and later a millionaire after he and his friend, Lieutenant Dan (Gary Sinise), invest in "some kind of fruit company" called Apple. But does he find true love?

WHY IT'S FAMOUS

This charming film takes a look at our own culture and history. While Forrest's life takes him to key moments in American history as a war veteran, we also glimpse what prominent 1960s subcultures were like through the eyes of Jenny, Forrest's love interest. She becomes a hippie and an anti-Vietnam war protester. We find ourselves desperately wanting Forrest to find love and happiness, and the bittersweet conclusion to this movie is very satisfying.

STARRING:
Tom Hanks,
Robin Wright,
Gary Sinise,
and Sally Field

BOX OFFICE:
$677.9 million

DID YOU KNOW?

Robert Zemeckis used real TV footage and inserted Forrest into the clips: Lyndon B. Johnson awarding Forrest the Medal of Honor; Forrest at college during George Wallace's Stand in the Schoolhouse Door; Forrest visiting Nixon at the White House; and Forrest at the Watergate Hotel. An interview with Dick Cavett even results in Forrest inspiring John Lennon to write the song "Imagine."

MUSIC:
Alan Silvestri

Saw it! ☐ Rating: ☆☆☆☆☆
Date: ___/___/_____ With: _____
Notes: _____
_____

45

THE RED BALLOON

DIRECTOR:
Albert Lamorisse

RELEASE DATE:
1956 (France);
March 11, 1957
(USA)

RATED:

G

General
Audiences

RUNTIME:
34 minutes

This short film has resonated with children for over half a century. *The Red Balloon*'s heartwarming, almost-silent script won the Oscar for Best Original Screenplay in 1957, making it the only short film to win an Academy Award outside of the short film categories.

THE STORY

A simple story about a boy who encounters a red balloon that starts following him around his Parisian neighborhood seems like a child's dream come true. A balloon that thinks and moves on its own? It's pure childhood imagination at its best! The fun soon turns

"LE BALLON ROUGE" (ORIGINAL TITLE) FRANCE

into a nuisance for Pascal, the young boy, when the red balloon starts causing commotion. In one instance, the pesky balloon even sneaks into his school and disrupts class! Pascal then meets a little girl with the same problem, except her balloon is blue. Pascal, Sabine, and their colorful balloons manage to have fun adventures in the dull and neglected streets of Paris. However, reality sets in for Pascal and his helium-filled friend when a bunch of bullies pop the red balloon, destroying Pascal's seemingly perfect dream. But don't worry, the young hero's sadness is lifted by a surprising twist, and his heart takes flight!

WHY IT'S FAMOUS

The Red Balloon is full of life lessons and visual splendor. Having a friend to count on and share what can sometimes be an overwhelming world with is special, like the friendship between Pascal and his balloon. This movie also serves as a reminder that some moments in life can seem magical! Taking place on the streets in Paris, the City of Lights, only adds to the visual experience of this enchanting movie.

STARRING:
Pascal Lamorisse, Sabine Lamorisse, and Georges Sellier

SCORE BY:
Maurice Leroux

SCREEN-PLAY WRITTEN BY:
Albert Lamorisse

DID YOU KNOW?
The two children featured in this movie are film director Albert Lamorisse's own son and daughter, Pascal and Sabine Lamorisse.

Saw it! ☐ Rating: ☆☆☆☆☆
Date: ___/___/_____ With: _____
Notes: _____
_____

46

MY NEIGHBOR TOTORO
"TONARI NO TOTORO" (ORIGINAL TITLE) JAPAN

DIRECTOR:
Hayao Miyazaki

RELEASE DATE:
April 16, 1988 (Japan);
May 7, 1993 (USA)

RATED:
G
General Audiences

RUNTIME:
1 hour,
26 minutes

THE STORY

Totoro is a friendly spirit that lives in an old camphor tree in the forest and can only be seen by children. Although Totoro is huge compared to the children that he encounters, this cute character is gentle and playful. When sisters Mei (Chika Sakamoto) and Satsuki (Noriko Hidaka) move to the Japanese countryside, they do what any curious child would do in a new neighborhood; they set out to explore their new surroundings. They discover magical creatures that take them on wild adventures.

WATCH OUT FOR

The animated characters in this beloved tale are a concept of the imaginative Japanese storyteller, Hayao Miyazaki. This film will introduce you to the world of Japanese animation, which is noticeably different from the American cartoon style. Though this movie does not rely on common American themes, it does have a little bit of everything: sadness, surprise, joy, and a lesson.

UP NEXT

Also from Miyazaki: *Kiki's Delivery Service* (1989), *Princes Mononoke* (1997), *Spirited Away* (2001), and *Ponyo* (2008). Disney's English-language adaptation of *My Neighbor Totoro* (2005) includes the voices of sisters Dakota and Elle Fanning as Satsuki and Mei. The Disney adaptation of *Ponyo* (2009) features the voices of Tina Fey, Cate Blanchett, Liam Neeson, Betty White, Lily Tomlin, Noah Cyrus (Miley Cyrus's brother), and Frankie Jonas (the youngest of the Jonas Brothers).

Saw it! ☐ Rating: ☆☆☆☆☆
Date: ___/___/_____ With: _____
Notes: _____
_____

CHILDREN OF HEAVEN
"BACHEHA-YE ASEMAN" (ORIGINAL TITLE) IRAN

THE STORY

In a very poor area in the south of Tehran, Iran, 9-year-old Ali (Amir Farrokh Hashemian) picks up his sister's only pair of shoes from the cobbler and stops at the market on his way home. He puts the bag down to buy potatoes, but when he looks back down it's gone! A blind garbage collector mistook the bag for trash. In a panic, Ali goes home and tells 7-year-old Zahra (Bahare Seddiqi), what happened and begs her not to tell their parents. He's afraid to make their father angry. They agree to find a solution on their own and spare their parents more grief. However, the problem is a big one: Zahra doesn't have another pair of shoes to wear to school. Ali and Zahra agree to share Ali's sneakers; Zahra wears them to school in the morning, and at midday they switch, so Ali can wear them in the afternoon. A few days later, a solution materializes. There's a running competition with other schools coming up, and the third place prize is a new pair of sneakers. Ali just has to place third, and the problem will be solved!

Ali runs in the race, and the outcome surprises everyone!

DID YOU KNOW?

The director chose Amir Farrokh, who had never acted before, after seeing him crying in his classroom because he forgot his notebook. Majidi asked the boy why he was crying, and Amir lied and said he had amnesia, making him the perfect Ali!

DIRECTOR:
Majid Majidi

RELEASE DATE:
February 1997 (Iran); January 22, 1999 (USA)

RATED:

PG

for some mild language

RUNTIME:
1 hour, 29 minutes

Saw it! ☐ Rating: ☆☆☆☆☆

Date: ___/___/_____ With: _____

Notes: _____

_____

48

CROUCHING TIGER, HIDDEN DRAGON

DIRECTOR:
Ang Lee

RELEASE DATE:
July 8, 2000 (China); January 12, 2001 (USA)

RATED:

PG-13

for martial arts violence and some sexuality

RUNTIME:
2 hours

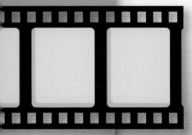

"WO HU CANG LONG" (ORIGINAL TITLE)
AMERICAN-CHINESE CO-PRODUCTION

THE STORY

Emotions run very high in this powerful martial arts action drama about love, loyalty, and the conflicts that arise when these two feelings collide. *Crouching Tiger, Hidden Dragon* follows the pursuit of Green Destiny, a legendary holy sword stolen by an unlikely thief. This event unleashes a series of ambitious martial arts battles to recover the sword. Both male and female warriors engage in fights that look more like aerial acrobatics; the characters gracefully float high above bamboo trees and perform spectacular gravity-defying stunts.

WHY IT'S FAMOUS

Much of the captivating beauty of this motion picture is due to the breathtaking locations. From the remote corners of the Gobi Desert to the Anji bamboo forest in Jiangsu, China, the cinematography alone is worth watching. Most of the fight scenes were filmed with the actors, not stunt artists. Taiwanese director Ang Lee (*Life of Pi*, 2012) was proud of this accomplishment, since it's very uncommon to have actors suspended across 60-foot-high bamboo branches!

This film features daring stunts and fight sequences by the famous Chinese martial arts choreographer Youen Woo-ping. He is also responsible for the extraordinary action scenes in *The Matrix* (1999).

UP NEXT

This film is based on the fourth book of the Crane Iron Pentalogy, a series of five books written by the Chinese author Wang Dulu and published between 1938 and 1942. A sequel debuted simultaneously on Netflix and IMAX in early 2016.

DID YOU KNOW?
The world-famous cellist Yo-Yo Ma performs in the soundtrack.

STARRING:
Chow Yun-Fat
and
Michelle Yeoh

BOX OFFICE:
$213.5 million

SCORE BY:
Tan Dun

Saw it! ☐ Rating: ☆☆☆☆☆
Date: ___/___/_____ With: _____
Notes: _____
_____

3 ACADEMY AWARDS

49

LIFE IS BEAUTIFUL "LA VITA È BELLA" (ORIGINAL TITLE) ITALY

DIRECTOR:
Roberto Benigni

RELEASE DATE:
December 20, 1997 (Italy); February 12, 1999 (USA)

RATED:
PG-13
for Holocaust-related thematic elements

RUNTIME:
1 hour, 56 minutes

In *Life Is Beautiful*, Roberto Benigni manages to disguise the tragedies of the Holocaust with a little humor and a lot of imagination.

THE STORY

Guido Orefice (Roberto Benigni) is a happy-go-lucky Jewish storeowner with a wife and young son. Their enchanted life is uprooted when the Nazis occupy their small Italian town during World War II. The family is captured and taken to a concentration camp. Guido, a joker at heart, uses this quality to help his son, Joshua (Giorgio Cantarini), persevere through the most unbearable stages of their captivity. Guido shelters Joshua from the frightening events at the concentration camp by turning them into a big game. He promises his son that if he wins, the prize is a real tank!

Guido sets the stage for the elaborate game as soon as they arrive at the concentration camp. Instead of telling Joshua what the Nazi guard is really shouting in German, the ingenious father translates it in a much gentler way:

"The game starts now. You have to score one thousand points. If you do that, you take home a tank with a big gun. Each day we will announce the scores from that loudspeaker. The one who has the fewest points will have to wear a sign that says 'Jackass' on his back. There are three ways to lose points: One, if you cry; two, if you ask to see your mother; and three, if you're hungry and ask for a snack."

Saw it! ☐ Rating: ☆☆☆☆☆

Date: ___/___/_____ With: _____

Notes: _____

_____

1 ACADEMY AWARD

CLOSE ENCOUNTERS OF THE THIRD KIND

THE STORY

Roy Neary (Richard Dreyfuss) has visions he can't explain—one is of a mountain in Wyoming he's sure he's never visited before, and he's drawn to go see it. Others experience strange things too; for example, a young boy's battery-powered toys suddenly turn on in his room. Meanwhile, scientists are mystified when they discover intact planes from a flight mission that had gone missing 30 years before. One night, Roy sees an unidentified flying object (UFO) and the bright, violent, flashing lights leave a burn mark on his face. People around the world also begin to have encounters with UFOs and report that they hear strange musical sounds—as if the UFOs are trying to communicate. Roy heads to the mountain along with the others, but the military wants to keep people away while they prepare a secret landing zone for the UFOs. Will they see aliens?

DID YOU KNOW?
Making *Close Encounters* was top secret. Costing $18 million, it was Spielberg's most expensive film at the time.

WATCH OUT FOR

Director Steven Spielberg went to great lengths to protect the film from being spoiled by early leaks of the spectacular ending. Spielberg consulted experts about the reported UFO sightings that have taken place around the world, and used that information to create a believable outcome for *Close Encounters*.

DIRECTOR:
Steven Spielberg

RELEASE DATE:
December 25, 1977

RATED:
PG
for some intense sci-fi action, mild language, and thematic elements

RUNTIME:
2 hour, 17 minutes

Saw it! ☐ Rating: ☆☆☆☆☆

Date: ___/___/_____ With: _____

Notes: _____

_____

51

STAR WARS

DIRECTOR:
George Lucas

RELEASE DATE:
May 25, 1977

RATED:

PG

for sci-fi violence
and brief mild
language

RUNTIME:
2 hours,
1 minute

THE STORY

Star Wars tells the story of Luke Skywalker, Han Solo, Obi-Wan Kenobi, and Princess Leia, who together lead the Rebel Alliance against Darth Vader and the evil Empire. After Obi-Wan teaches Luke about the "Force," an invisible power that only true Jedi knights can control, the space cowboys, along with the princess and two amusing droids, R2-D2 and C-3PO, plot to destroy the Death Star space station.

WHY IT'S FAMOUS

This film was considered ahead of its time, and it has survived the test of time. *Star Wars* was later re-titled *Star Wars Episode IV A New Hope*, but any self-respecting fan refers to it simply by its birth name. Besides introducing us to some out-of-this-world characters,

"A long time ago, in a galaxy far, far away..."

galaxies, spaceships, and lightsabers, *Star Wars* pioneered a new special-effects industry. George Lucas wrote and directed the film. He also established a new company called Industrial Light & Magic (ILM) to accommodate the groundbreaking computer-generated visual effects he created for the movie. In 2012, The Walt Disney Company bought ILM as part of the $4 billion Lucasfilm deal.

Luke Skywalker and the rest of the rebels made two more films, *The Empire Strikes Back* (1980) and *Return of the Jedi* (1983). Together these three films (which you can binge-watch in one session if you are a true fan!) are known as the Star Wars Trilogy.

UP NEXT

Decades later, the obsession with *Star Wars* continues. A prequel trilogy was released between 1999–2005, including the films *The Phantom Menace, Attack of the Clones,* and *Revenge of the Sith. Star Wars: Episode VII,* the next installment, hit theaters in December 2015, and featured original *Star Wars* cast members Mark Hamill as Luke Skywalker, Harrison Ford as Han Solo, and Carrie Fisher as Princess Leia.

Disney plans to complete the third trilogy as well as release a string of spin-off films spotlighting various characters, meaning there will be new Star Wars movies for years to come!

DID YOU KNOW?
This film influenced our popular culture in so many ways that *Star Wars* is now part of the National Film Registry at the Library of Congress for being "culturally, historically, and aesthetically significant."

BOX OFFICE:
$775.3 million

MUSIC:
John Williams

SCREEN-PLAY WRITTEN BY:
George Lucas

Saw it! ☐ Rating: ☆☆☆☆☆
Date: ___/___/_____ With: _____
Notes: _____
_____

52

RAIDERS OF THE LOST ARK

DIRECTOR:
Steven
Spielberg

**RELEASE
DATE:**
June 12, 1981

RATED:

PG

for intense
sequences of
violence, graphic
images, brief
language and
sensuality

RUNTIME:
1 hour,
55 minutes

Indyyy! Iiinnndddyyy! That's short for Indiana Jones. The demanding tone heard in this hero's nickname means someone is in trouble and needs his help. Though Dr. Jones doesn't always have a rescue plan in mind, you can count on this whip-smart professor to make one up on the fly, nearly every time.

THE STORY

Harrison Ford plays the role of Dr. Indiana Jones in *Raiders of the Lost Ark*. Set in the 1930s, the U.S. government hires Jones to spoil a Nazi plan to dig up the famous biblical artifact, the Ark of the Covenant.

MUSIC:
John Williams

According to legend, whoever finds the Ark will possess infinite power, and Adolf Hitler wants to use it to create the most powerful army in the world. Professor Jones's knowledge of archeology and antiquities helps him determine the essential missing clue that points to the location of the Ark. From the jungles of Peru to the snowy mountains of Nepal to the hot sands of Egypt, we follow Indy on his quest to find the Ark before the enemy.

In a way, Indiana Jones was the 1980s version of a superhero. However, his outfit of choice was a pair of pants, shirt, leather jacket, hat (which he never lost!), and bullwhip. Jones was able to dash into a dangerous situation and save the day without having to change into tights or wear a cape!

BOX OFFICE:
$389.9 million

UP NEXT

Raiders of the Lost Ark was so popular it led to three more films: *Indiana Jones and the Temple of Doom* (1984), *Indiana Jones and the Last Crusade* (1989), and *Indiana Jones and the Kingdom of the Crystal Skull* (2008). *Raiders of the Lost Ark* also inspired the television series, *The Young Indiana Jones Chronicles* (1992–1993), which were followed by a series of made-for-TV films that were produced from 1994–1996.

DID YOU KNOW?

Indiana Jones has inspired over a dozen video games! The popularity of this film also inspired rides and live shows at Disney theme parks in the United States, France, and Japan.

SCREEN-PLAY WRITTEN BY:
Lawrence Kasdan

Saw it! ☐ Rating: ☆☆☆☆☆

Date: ___ / ___ / _____ With: _____

Notes: _____

_____

53

GHOSTBUSTERS

DIRECTOR:
Ivan Reitman

RELEASE DATE:
June 8, 1984

RATED:

PG

for some
language,
suggestive
humor,
frightening
images

RUNTIME:
1 hour,
45 minutes

THE STORY

A trio of unemployed university parapsychologists (investigators of paranormal and psychic phenomena) establish a business to investigate and exterminate ghosts. They invent sophisticated equipment to trap spirits and work out of a neglected fire station in New York City. The highly intelligent scientists are hired to catch a ghost, and after trapping their first goblin, the Ghostbusters find themselves in high demand all over the city. Drs. Venkman (Bill Murray), Stantz (Dan Aykroyd), and Spengler (Harold Ramis) get into some funny, yet frightening, situations with phantoms and monsters when the Big Apple is caught in the middle of a poltergeist outbreak!

The government discovers that the popular ghost wranglers are not disposing of their wispy catches properly—the ghosts are being held in a containment unit in the firehouse basement. Ordered by the Environmental Protection Agency to release the ghouls, they set them free, causing mayhem in Manhattan. The mayor finds that he needs to bring order to a chaotic city. So, who's he gonna call? That's right: Ghostbusters!

WHY IT'S FAMOUS

Ghostbusters gave us a few of the most memorable lines in movie history. "I ain't afraid of no ghost," is just one of the famous sayings from *Ghostbusters*. The catchy phrase is from the film's extremely successful theme song by Ray Parker Jr. The movie became a pop culture phenomenon and led to a second film, *Ghostbusters II*, released in 1989.

It's worth mentioning that even though this film is rated PG, in 1984 the PG-13 rating wasn't around. There are some very scary super-natural beings in this movie and also some inappropriate language and behaviors that may not be suitable for the PG audience of today.

DID YOU KNOW?
Ghostbusters is on the American Film Institute's "AFI's 100 Years...100 Laughs" list.

STARRING:
Bill Murray, Dan Aykroyd, Harold Ramis, and Sigourney Weaver

BOX OFFICE:
$295.2 million

SCREEN-PLAY WRITTEN BY:
Dan Aykroyd, Harold Ramis, and Rick Moranis

Saw it! ☐ Rating: ☆☆☆☆☆

Date: ___/___/_____ With: _____

Notes: _____

_____

54

BACK TO THE FUTURE

DIRECTOR:
Robert Zemeckis

RELEASE DATE:
July 3, 1985

RATED:
PG
for adult situations/
language and
violence

RUNTIME:
1 hour,
56 minutes

One of Michael J. Fox's most memorable roles is Marty McFly in *Back to the Future*. In the movie, Marty travels back to 1955 in a modified DeLorean that a local inventor, the bizarre Dr. Emmett "Doc" Brown (Christopher Lloyd), has turned into a time machine. Powered by a flux capacitor, the car propels Marty into a series of events that threaten to change the course of history.

THE STORY

Marty finds himself 30 years in the past, in his hometown of Hill Valley, looking at the teenage versions of his mother and father. He sees his nerdy dad, George McFly (Crispin Glover), bullied by a meathead named Biff (Thomas F. Wilson).

"Great Scott!"

Marty tries to toughen up George so he can charm Lorraine, Marty's mother. Marty's life depends on them falling in love, after all! But instead of becoming smitten with George, Lorraine (Lea Thompson) starts liking Marty. Marty has to make sure his parents fall in love before he permanently alters time, meaning he would cease to exist in 1985—the year he came from. Harnessing 1.21 gigawatts of energy to fuel the car and return Marty to 1985 turns into the most electrifying scene of this back-in-time movie.

WATCH OUT FOR

Back to the Future is an iconic 1980s movie. Its amazing success led to two more films: *Back to the Future, Part II* (1989) and *Back to the Future, Part III* (1990).

"The Power of Love" was written and performed by Huey Lewis and the News for this film. Huey Lewis has a small cameo in the movie. When Marty and his band are playing "The Power of Love" during an audition, Lewis is the judge that tells the band they are too loud!

STARRING:
Michael J. Fox, Christopher Lloyd, Crispin Glover, Thomas F. Wilson, and Lea Thompson

BOX OFFICE:
$381.1 million

DID YOU KNOW?

At the end of *Back to the Future*, Doc Brown returns to Hill Valley from a trip to the future. He tells Marty to get in the DeLorean so he can take him to see the future where "we don't need roads." The date he declares he's just come from is October 21, 2015. Roads? Yes, we still need them!

MUSIC:
Alan Silvestri

Saw it! ☐ Rating: ☆☆☆☆☆

Date: ___ / ___ / _____ With: _____

Notes: _____

_____

55

HARRY POTTER AND THE SORCERER'S STONE

DIRECTOR:
Chris Columbus

RELEASE DATE:
November 16, 2001

RATED:
PG
for some scary moments and mild language

RUNTIME:
2 hours, 32 minutes

This is the first film of eight in the Harry Potter film franchise and is based on the first of seven novels written by author and creator J.K. Rowling, who unleashed a powerful spell on the world with her magical pen.

THE STORY

Harry Potter (Daniel Radcliffe) arrived at the dreary Dursley home as a baby in a basket with a note attached. His parents, both wizards, were killed by the evil Lord Voldemort (or "He Who Must Not Be Named"), but Harry survived the attack, which left only a bolt-shaped scar on his forehead as evidence. When he is 11 years old, Harry starts getting letters of admission from Hogwarts School of Witchcraft and Wizardry, but Mr. and Mrs. Dursley, both Muggles (non-magical humans), throw them away, refusing to believe that Harry is a wizard. Rubeus Hagrid, a giant wizard, eventually delivers an acceptance letter to Harry in person. Hagrid takes Harry to Diagon Alley, a hidden wizard's market-place. Harry buys a cape and scarf, books, ingredients for potions, and visits a shop where magic wands choose their owners. Shockingly, the wand that chooses Harry is companion to Lord Voldemort's wand—both contain a feather from the same phoenix. Harry and Hagrid then travel to Platform 9¾ in London where he boards a train to Hogwarts. On board, he meets his future best friends, Hermione Granger (Emma Watson) and Ron Weasley (Rupert Grint), who are also headed to the school. Once at Hogwarts, Harry is assigned to Gryffindor, one of the four student houses,

and becomes a member of the flying Quidditch team. Headmaster Albus Dumbledore (Richard Harris), Professor McGonagall (Maggie Smith), and Hagrid (Robbie Coltrane) know Lord Voldemort is dying and that he seeks the magic of the Sorcerer's Stone to regain his strength. Harry eventually realizes that his unfriendly potions teacher Severus Snape (Alan Rickman) is after the stone as well. Can Harry find the powerful stone before it falls into the hands of evil Lord Voldemort?

UP NEXT

The spellbinding film franchise that captivated adults and children alike includes: *Harry Potter and the Chamber of Secrets* (2002), *Harry Potter and the Prisoner of Azkaban* (2004), plus five more movies detailing the adventures of the young wizard and his friends.

WHY IT'S FAMOUS

Upon the release of the last movie in the franchise in 2011, The American Film Institute recognized the entire series with a special award, saying "The Harry Potter series marks the final triumphant chapter of a landmark series; eight films that earned the trust of a generation who wished for the beloved books of J.K. Rowling to come to life on the silver screen. The collective wizardry of an epic ensemble gave us the gift of growing older with Harry, Ron, and Hermione as the magic of Hogwarts sprung from the films and into the hearts and minds of Muggles around the world."

STARRING:
Daniel Radcliffe,
Emma Watson,
Rupert Grint,
and
Alan Rickman

BOX OFFICE:
$974.7 million

DID YOU KNOW?

If you decide to binge-watch the entire Harry Potter series, it would take you 21 hours and 49 minutes!

MUSIC:
John Williams

Saw it! ☐ Rating: ☆☆☆☆☆
Date: ___/___/_____ With: _____
Notes: _____
_____

56

HARRY POTTER
AND THE GOBLET OF FIRE

DIRECTOR:
Mike Newell

RELEASE DATE:
November 18, 2005

RATED:

PG-13

for sequences of fantasy violence and frightening images

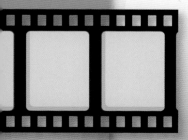

RUNTIME:
2 hours,
37 minutes

Beginning with the fourth film, the rest of the Harry Potter series takes on a darker tone. The young wizards Harry Potter, Ron Weasley, and Hermione Granger grow up before our eyes and begin to face much more difficult and serious adventures in the wizarding world.

THE STORY

Now 14 years old, Harry's name is the fourth spit out by the Goblet of Fire to compete in the Triwizard Tournament. Traditionally, the contest only has three representatives, each required to be 17 years old. Dumbledore can't protect Harry from the goblet's choice, which prompts the question: Who submitted Harry's name? As the tournament begins, a dark and fearsome tempest of Death Eaters ominously descends on the arena and attacks. This can only mean one thing: Voldemort (Ralph Fiennes) is back!

The attack is thwarted, and the students return to Hogwarts, where a convivial gathering of the finalists competing in the Triwizard Cup takes place. Joining Harry and Cedric Diggory (Robert Paattison) from Hogwarts are Viktor Krum (Stanislav Ianevski) from

Durmstrang and Fleur Delacour (Clémence Poésy) from Beauxbatons, two neighboring schools of witchcraft and wizardry. They face each other in terror-inducing challenges involving dragons, rescuing prisoners from a dark lagoon, and finding their way out of a seemingly endless maze that holds an extra-chilling encounter for Harry. However, the fury of these tasks doesn't compare to Harry's next challenge—asking a girl to the Yule Ball.

Will Harry come face to face with his nemesis, Voldemort, and will the evil man's identity finally be revealed? Who put Harry's name in the Goblet of Fire, and why? All is revealed in this action-packed, sinister installment in the Harry Potter film series.

UP NEXT

The final four films in the Harry Potter franchise are: *Harry Potter and the Order of the Phoenix* (2007), *Harry Potter and the Half-Blood Prince* (2009), *Harry Potter and the Deathly Hallows: Part 1* (2010), and *Harry Potter and the Deathly Hallows: Part 2* (2011).

DID YOU KNOW?

This is the first film of the series that doesn't start out at 4 Privet Drive, the Dursley residence where Harry Potter grew up. This address and home are real. A replica of the street and its homes was built on the Warner Bros. studio lot in Leavesden, England, for filming.

STARRING:
Daniel Radcliffe, Emma Watson, Rupert Grint, and Alan Rickman

BOX OFFICE:
$896.9 million

MUSIC:
Patrick Doyle with main theme by John Williams

Saw it! ☐ Rating: ☆☆☆☆☆

Date: ___/___/_____ With: _____

Notes: _____

_____

57

BATMAN

DIRECTOR:
Tim Burton

RELEASE DATE:
June 23, 1989

RATED:
PG-13
for violence and gore, intense scenes, mild profanity and some sensuality

RUNTIME:
2 hours,
6 minutes

This film is considered responsible for the live-action superhero film genre so popular today. It is based on the DC Comics character Bruce Wayne, a billionaire and secret vigilante crime fighter known as Batman. In this movie, an incredible art deco Gotham City, Batcave, Batmobile, and Bat Signal all leap off the comic book pages and onto the big screen.

THE STORY

As a child, Bruce Wayne witnessed his parents' murder at the hands of a mugger and is traumatized by this event. Now an adult, Bruce lives in a mansion with his loyal butler, Alfred Pennyworth (Michael Gough), the only person who knows his double identity.

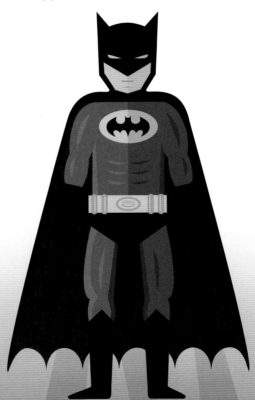

The story begins as mob boss Carl Grissom (Jack Palance) and Harvey Dent (Billy Dee Williams), the corrupt Gotham City District Attorney, plan to have their partner in crime, Jack Napier (Jack Nicholson), killed at the Axis Chemicals plant. Batman (Michael Keaton) and Commissioner James Gordon (Pat Hingle) thwart their plan, but Napier falls into a container of chemicals in the shootout and is left for dead. Years later, Bruce meets a reporter, Vicki Vale (Kim Basinger), who's looking into a vigilante helping the police and taking out criminals. At an art gallery fundraiser, a terribly disfigured man sets a trap for Vale while his cronies vandalize the artwork and scare guests. Batman arrives just in time to save the reporter, but the strange man whispers something to him that he recalls hearing from his parents' murderer. Batman realizes the man calling himself The Joker is his archenemy, and the pursuit is on.

UP NEXT

Many more Batman films and Batman series spin-off films have been made. Those that directly followed the 1989 movie include *Batman Returns* (1992), *Batman Forever* (1995), and *Batman & Robin* (1997). In 2005, Christopher Nolan directed a new Batman trilogy, including *Batman Begins* (2005), *The Dark Knight* (2008), and *The Dark Knight Rises* (2012).

DID YOU KNOW?

Prince wrote the soundtrack for *Batman* (1989).

STARRING:
Jack Nicholson, Michael Keaton, and Kim Basinger

BOX OFFICE:
$411.3 million

SCREEN-PLAY WRITTEN BY:
Sam Hamm and Warren Skaaren

Saw it! ☐ Rating: ☆☆☆☆☆

Date: ___/___/_____ With: _____

Notes: _____

_____

58

SPIDER-MAN

DIRECTOR:
Sam Raimi

RELEASE DATE:
May 3, 2002

RATED:

PG-13

for stylized
violence and
action

RUNTIME:
2 hours,
1 minute

THE STORY

This film introduces us to a web-entangled high school
student named Peter Parker (Tobey Maguire). While
on a field trip at Oscorp Industries with his friend Harry
Osborn (James Franco) and love interest Mary Jane
Watson (Kirsten Dunst), Peter is bitten by a genetically
engineered spider. Peter notices his vision and body
starting to change and that he can suddenly produce
webs from his hands! He realizes he has superhuman
speed with the ability to stick to walls and climb tall
buildings. Meanwhile, power-hungry Oscorp-owner
Norman Osborn (Willem Dafoe)—Harry's father—wants faster
progress on an experimental military drug to benefit his company,
so he tests a dose of a performance vapor on himself in his lab,
transforming him into the evil Green Goblin. Peter decides to use his
new powers for good, and wears a costume to keep his new identity
as a crime-fighting superhero a secret. Can Spider-Man save the city
from the Green Goblin, keep his identity a secret, and win Mary Jane's
heart in the process?

UP NEXT

Based on the Marvel Comics character by Stan Lee, *Spider-Man* has
two sequels: *Spider-Man 2* (2004) and *Spider-Man 3* (2007). The franchise was re-booted with *The Amazing Spider-Man* (2012) and
The Amazing Spider-Man 2 (2014) with Andrew Garfield as Spidey.
Spider-Man will also reappear in Marvel's Cinematic Universe in
Captain America: Civil War (2016) and is slated for another stand-alone
film in 2017.

Saw it! ☐ Rating: ☆☆☆☆☆
Date: ___/___/_____ With: _____
Notes: _____
_____

 **3 ACADEMY AWARDS**

JURASSIC PARK

THE STORY

John Hammond (Richard Attenborough) is the rich CEO of a bioengineering company who discovers how to clone dinosaurs from fossils. He builds Jurassic Park, a theme park located on an isolated island off the coast of Central America, where tourists can admire the prehistoric animals safely behind 10,000-volt-electrified fences. However, after an employee is killed by a Velociraptor, the park is deemed unsafe and must be certified by experts before it is allowed to open to the public. Hammond invites archeologists Dr. Alan Grant (Sam Neill) and Dr. Ellie Sattler (Laura Dern), along with mathematician Dr. Ian Malcolm (Jeff Goldblum), to tour the park and support his cause against the government safety officials. However, the scientists are not convinced that bringing dinosaurs back to life is such a good idea. One stormy night, an attempted employee theft shuts down the security systems throughout the park. Things begin to go terribly wrong, and the entire park begins to lose power, including the soaring electric enclosures keeping the dinosaurs contained. Can the scientists and park employees find a way to escape the island before the dinosaurs harm anyone else?

UP NEXT

Spectacular special effects made this Michael Crichton book series a successful film franchise. *The Lost World: Jurassic Park* (1997) and *Jurassic Park III* (2001) followed the original film. *Jurassic World* premiered in June 2015.

DIRECTOR:
Steven Spielberg

RELEASE DATE:
June 11, 1993

RATED:
PG-13
for intense science fiction terror

RUNTIME:
2 hours,
7 minutes

Saw it! ☐ Rating: ☆☆☆☆☆

Date: ___/___/_____ With: _____

Notes: _____

_____

60

TITANIC

DIRECTOR:
James Cameron

RELEASE DATE:
December 19, 1997

RATED:
PG-13
for disaster-related peril and violence, nudity, sensuality, and brief language

RUNTIME:
3 hours,
14 minutes

This epic story begins with actual footage shot by James Cameron of the *Titanic* sitting at the bottom of the North Atlantic Ocean. A team searches the wreckage for a rare diamond necklace that legend claims went down with the ship. They find a safe with a drawing of a woman wearing the necklace inside, and they discover that she is still alive. They invite the woman, Rose Dawson Calvert, to visit and she tells the crew what occurred on the RMS *Titanic* on April 15, 1912, the day the ship famously sank on its maiden voyage.

THE STORY

The RMS *Titanic* is the most luxurious ship ever built and leaves Southampton, England, with a score of wealthy passengers, such as Colonel John J. Astor, founder of the Astoria Hotel; Isidor Straus, founder and co-owner of Macy's; Benjamin Guggenheim, a successful businessman from Pennsylvania; and "the unsinkable" Molly Brown (Kathy Bates). Among them are first-class passengers Rose DeWitt Bukater (Kate Winslet); her fiancé, Cal Hockley (Billy Zane); and her mother, Ruth (Frances Fisher). Hockley gives Rose the Heart of the Ocean, a rare blue diamond necklace, as an engagement present.

Rose's mother is forcing her to marry Hockley for his money, and Rose feels trapped, so much so that she considers jumping off the bow of the ship! Jack Dawson (Leonardo DiCaprio), a flat-broke artist who managed to swindle his way onto third class, encounters Rose about to go overboard. He talks her out of it, and they become improbable friends from opposite social classes. Hockley sees the two and becomes suspicious of their friendship, but Rose tells him Jack saved her from falling overboard. As a reward, Rose invites Jack to dinner in first class. During the course of the voyage, Jack and Rose fall in love.

Hockley notices the pair becoming close and, out of jealousy, frames Jack for the theft of the necklace—which he plants in Jack's coat pocket—and has him handcuffed to a pipe belowdecks. Meanwhile, the ill-fated ship hits an iceberg and water pours into the hull. As women and children are evacuated, Rose jumps out of the lifeboat to find and save Jack. The re-imagined tragedy unfolds with striking detail as passengers plunge into the freezing waters, while others remain trapped in their third-class staterooms.

Can Rose and Jack hold on until help arrives? Does the team find the legendary Heart of the Ocean 85 years later?

STARRING:
Leonardo DiCaprio, Kate Winslet, Billy Zane, and Kathy Bates

BOX OFFICE:
$2.1 billion

DID YOU KNOW?

Titanic is tied with *Ben-Hur* (1959) and *The Lord of the Rings: The Return of the King* (2003) for Most Oscar Wins.

MUSIC:
James Horner

Saw it! ☐ Rating: ☆☆☆☆☆
Date: ___/___/_____ With: _____
Notes: _____
_____

HOW TO TRAIN YOUR DRAGON

DIRECTOR:
Dean DeBlois and
Chris Sanders

**RELEASE
DATE:**
March 26, 2010

RATED:

PG

for intense
action
sequences,
peril, and
some violence

RUNTIME:
1 hour,
38 minutes

Hiccup Horrendous Haddock III (Jay Baruchel), the son of Chief Stoick the Vast (Gerard Butler), guides us through a computer-animated Viking world where fire-breathing dragons are the perceived enemy.

THE STORY

Fire-breathing dragons have been stealing Berk's livestock and burning down its buildings for seven generations, and young Vikings are taught to slay dragons on sight. Hiccup, the Chief's scrawny and accident-prone son, is Gobber (Craig Ferguson) the blacksmith's apprentice, and he learns to use tools and make unusual inventions.

One night, Hiccup strikes down a Night Fury, the most dangerous and rare type of dragon. When he finds the small dragon and realizes he is hurt and can't fly, he doesn't have the heart to kill him. Hiccup brings the dragon food and names him Toothless because he has retractable teeth. In time, Toothless begins to trust Hiccup, and the two become friends. Hiccup learns that dragons aren't so bad after all—they only attack if they're attacked first. Hiccup makes Toothless a prosthetic fin for his tail and teaches him to fly with it. On a practice flight, Toothless takes Hiccup and his friend Astrid (America Ferrera) to the dragon's colony where a giant dragon, Red Death, feeds on smaller dragons and stolen livestock offered by the other dragons to keep it at bay. Hiccup wants to keep the location a secret, but word gets out, and the villagers mount an attack on the colony. Can Hiccup save the dragons and his village from the terrible dragon, Red Death?

UP NEXT

This clever and witty 3-D movie from DreamWorks Animation spurred two more films: *How To Train Your Dragon 2* (2014) and *How To Train Your Dragon 3,* scheduled for release in 2018.

STARRING:
Jay Baruchel,
Gerard Butler,
Craig Ferguson,
and America
Ferrera

BOX OFFICE:
$494.8
million

DID YOU KNOW?

This film is loosely based on British author Cressida Cowell's book *How to Train Your Dragon*, which is part of a 12-book children's series.

MUSIC:
John Powell

Saw it! ☐ Rating: ☆☆☆☆☆

Date: ___/___/_____ With: _____

Notes: _____

_____

62

DIRECTOR:
Peter Jackson

RELEASE DATE:
December 19, 2001

RATED:
PG-13
for epic battle
sequences
and some scary
images

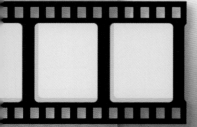

RUNTIME:
2 hours,
58 minutes

THE LORD OF THE RINGS: THE FELLOWSHIP OF THE RING

The Lord of the Rings trilogy is based on a series of books by J.R.R. Tolkien. The first of these epic fantasy films, *The Fellowship o f the Ring*, introduces us to the imaginary Middle-earth and its core characters.

THE STORY

Dark Lord Sauron (Sala Baker) wants to take over Middle-earth using the almighty power of the One Ring. But the ring is taken from Sauron during a battle with Isildur. Although Sauron's body is gone, the power of the ring holds his life force, and he survives as long as the ring remains. Orcs kill the corrupt Isildur, and the ring is lost in the river Anduin until Gollum (Andy Serkis) finds it thousands of years later. Hundreds of years pass until the hobbit Bilbo Baggins (Ian Holm) takes the ring for safekeeping. Sixty years later, Bilbo gives it to his nephew, Frodo Baggins (Elijah Wood), who learns from the wizard Gandalf the Grey (Ian McKellen) that Sauron's forces will hunt him down to recover

the ring. Frodo sets off to return the ring to its birthplace at Mount Doom, the only place it can be destroyed once and for all. On the way, Frodo and his companion Samwise Gamgee (Sean Astin) avoid the Nazgûl, Sauron's soldiers, with help from Aragorn (Viggo Mortensen), who hides the pair in Rivendell. There, a meeting is called to figure out what to do with the ring—and the Fellowship is born! Together with our hobbit hero, the Fellowship travels across a vast imaginary land, encountering many obstacles, wicked creatures, and magical forces that covet the ring's power to use it for evil.

Can the Fellowship resist the ring's powerful draw, which tempts the members to use it for their own benefit? Will Frodo and the Fellowship make it to Mordor and finish their quest?

WATCH OUT FOR

The incredible detail conceived by Tolkien in his books was brought to life by Peter Jackson's extraordinary imagination. The enormity of the sets, the technical achievements, and the superb special effects will make this film trilogy transcend many generations.

The two sequels that follow are *The Two Towers* (2002) and *The Return of the King* (2003).

STARRING:
Elijah Wood, Ian McKellen, Viggo Mortensen, Cate Blanchett, Liv Tyler, and Orlando Bloom

BOX OFFICE:
$871.5 million

DID YOU KNOW?

The Return of the King won 11 Oscars, making it the film with the most awards in the trilogy, and tied with *Titanic* and *Ben-Hur* for most Oscar wins.

MUSIC:
Howard Shore

Saw it! ☐ Rating: ☆☆☆☆☆
Date: ___/___/_____ With: _____
Notes: _____
_____

63

PIRATES OF THE CARIBBEAN: THE CURSE OF THE BLACK PEARL

DIRECTOR:
Gore Verbinski

RELEASE DATE:
July 9, 2003

RATED:
PG-13
for action/
adventure
violence

RUNTIME:
2 hours,
23 minutes

An unsteady Captain Jack Sparrow (Johnny Depp) takes us across the high seas and into the world of undead pirates, cursed Aztec gold, and fierce swordfights unlike any you've ever seen in a pirate film!

THE STORY

Will Turner (Orlando Bloom) and Elizabeth Swann (Keira Knightley) have been friends since childhood, but their opposing social status hinders their union. Elizabeth saved Will as a boy from a burning ship, keeping a gold medallion necklace she took from him to prevent him from being identified as a pirate. Now a woman, Elizabeth faces a marriage proposal from the straight-laced Commodore Norrington (Jack Davenport). Distraught about the unwanted offer, she faints and falls into the bay.

Her medallion touches the water and secretly signals the *Black Pearl* and its cursed crew to Port Royal, where they capture Elizabeth and the medallion. The coin is part of a cursed Aztec treasure, and the immortal pirates need to return all of the gold coins to the original chest to break the terrible curse. Meanwhile, Captain Jack is set on getting revenge on Captain Barbossa (Geoffrey Rush) for the mutiny and theft of his ship, the *Black Pearl*. Years ago, Barbossa betrayed Sparrow and left him stranded on an island so he could find and steal the Aztec treasure; but little did Barbossa know that the loot was cursed. Sparrow joins Will to save Elizabeth from the clutches of the rogue pirates. Can Captain Jack and Will save Elizabeth, the treasure, and return the *Black Pearl* to its rightful owner?

UP NEXT

Inspired by the Pirates of the Caribbean ride at Disneyland, this swashbuckling fantasy film starring Johnny Depp as Captain Jack Sparrow led to four sequels: *Pirates of the Caribbean: Dead Man's Chest* (2006), *Pirates of the Caribbean: At World's End* (2007), *Pirates of the Caribbean: On Stranger Tides* (2011), and *Pirates of the Caribbean: Dead Men Tell No Tales* (2017).

STARRING:
Johnny Depp,
Geoffrey Rush,
Orlando Bloom,
and Keira
Knightley

BOX OFFICE:
$654.2 million

DID YOU KNOW?

Pirates of the Caribbean is ranked among the highest-grossing film series, behind *Harry Potter, Star Wars, Batman, The Lord of the Rings, James Bond, Spider-Man, Shrek, Twilight, Transformers,* and *X-Men.*

MUSIC:
Klaus Badelt

Saw it! ☐ Rating: ☆☆☆☆☆
Date: ___/___/_____ With: _____
Notes: _____
_____

64

AVATAR

DIRECTOR:
James Cameron

RELEASE DATE:
December 18, 2009

RATED:
PG-13
for intense epic battle sequences and warfare, sensuality, language, and some smoking

RUNTIME:
2 hours,
42 minutes

Written, directed, co-produced, and co-edited by James Cameron, this epic science-fiction film will show you the powerful vision of one of this generation's most innovative directors.

THE STORY

In the year 2154, humans have depleted Earth of its energy resources and are looking for other sources. A ship transporting people to Pandora, a distant moon as lush as a rainforest, arrives carrying civilians, scientists, and military personnel. As the ship approaches the landing site, the passengers see huge machines mining the ground for unobtanium, a mineral needed on Earth to ensure its survival.

Jake Sully (Sam Worthington), a former Marine in a wheelchair, travels six years in cryosleep to take over his scientist brother's project—Jake is a match for his deceased twin brother's Avatar, a genetically attached Na'vi and native of Pandora, who can breathe in the non-human environment.

There's an added bonus for Jake—as an Avatar he can walk again. Avatars are genetic copies of the Na'vi, controlled by their human counterparts' consciousness while they are asleep and wired to a machine that controls the slim, blue-skinned, 12-foot-tall creatures. Colonel Miles Quaritch (Stephen Lang) immediately instructs Jake and the new base residents to follow Pandora rules if they want to stay alive. They are there on a mission: They must take possession of the land where the quarry for unobtanium is located. To do this, they must convince the Na'vi to leave, or they will kill them.

The Na'vi live in harmony with nature. They've learned to tame dragon-like birds and ride them. Jake finds out the hard way that the oversized creatures of Pandora have an indiscriminant appetite, but he's saved by the gentle blue Princess Neytiri (Zoe Saldana). After getting to know the natives and understanding their way of life, Jake starts to find it very difficult to remain focused on his mission. Forced to take a stand, the future of Pandora and the Na'vi is in his hands.

UP NEXT

James Cameron is working on several *Avatar* sequels, with the next installment to come in 2017.

DID YOU KNOW?

It took 15 years for James Cameron to develop the full concept for *Avatar*. Along with the technical achievements, Cameron created the otherworldly planets, the native beings, and a new language for the Na'vi humanoids.

STARRING:
Sam Worthington, Zoe Saldana, and Sigourney Weaver

BOX OFFICE:
$2.7 billion

MUSIC:
James Horner

Saw it! ☐ Rating: ☆☆☆☆☆

Date: ___ / ___ / _____ With: _____

Notes: _____

_____

65

THE HOBBIT: AN UNEXPECTED JOURNEY

DIRECTOR:
Peter Jackson

RELEASE DATE:
December 14, 2012

RATED:

PG-13

for extended sequences of intense fantasy, action, violence and frightening images

RUNTIME:
2 hours, 49 minutes

Prodigious director Peter Jackson takes us on another fantasy adventure with three films based on J.R.R. Tolkien's novel *The Hobbit*, published in 1937.

THE STORY

Bilbo Baggins (Ian Holm) tells his nephew, Frodo Baggins (Elijah Wood), the story of his adventure 60 years earlier. Young Bilbo (Martin Freeman) is a hobbit living in the Shire who likes his orderly comfort. But his life of leisure changes overnight after the wizard Gandalf the Grey (Ian McKellen) visits him out of the blue. Gandalf proposes that Bilbo join a group of 13 dwarves (an unlucky number), led by Thorin Oakenshield (Richard Armitage), the legendary fighter and

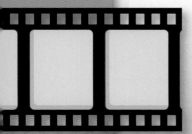

prince of Erebor, who wants to take back the long-lost dwarven kingdom that lies beneath the Lonely Mountain. The dwarves' land is rich in gold and jewels, but it was taken from them by the dragon Smaug. Gandolf wants the nimble and compact hobbit to be the group's burglar when the need arises, but Bilbo doesn't want any part of the chaos. However, the next morning he changes his mind and decides to go on this unexpected journey with the company. Bilbo is very grumpy during the trek eastward to the Lonely Mountain—his pony is giving him bum sores. But his worries only grow as the crew is suddenly attacked by trolls, goblins, orcs, and Gollum—the creature who will change his fate in ways the hobbit can't even imagine. During his skirmish with Gollum, Bilbo sees a small ring fly out of the creature's pocket. He soon discovers that the golden band has magical powers, which he uses to escape Gollum's clutches.

The harrowing trip to the Lonely Mountain tests the dwarves, Gandolf, and Bilbo to their limits. Will the dwarves be able to reclaim their homeland? And what will Bilbo do with the One Ring?

WHY IT'S FAMOUS

The Hobbit: An Unexpected Journey, *The Desolation of Smaug* (2013), and *The Battle of the Five Armies* (2014) are considered prequels, taking place 60 years before *The Lord of The Rings* trilogy.

STARRING:
Martin Freeman, Ian McKellen, Ian Holm, and Richard Armitage

BOX OFFICE:
$1 billion

DID YOU KNOW?

The Hobbit trilogy is based on a single 300-page book. Now that's stretching the imagination!

MUSIC:
Howard Shore

Saw it! ☐ Rating: ☆☆☆☆☆

Date: ___/___/_____ With: _____

Notes: _____

_____

66

IRON MAN

Tony Stark is Stan Lee's 1963 comic book creation and the first of the Marvel Cinematic Universe's live-action film superheroes.

DIRECTOR:
Jon Favreau

RELEASE DATE:
May 2, 2008

RATED:
PG-13
for intense sci-fi action, violence, and brief suggestive content

RUNTIME:
2 hours, 6 minutes

THE STORY

The eccentric engineer, Tony Stark (Robert Downey Jr.), is captured by terrorists in Afghanistan after demonstrating Stark Industries' newest missile, Jericho. Stark is injured in the skirmish. Yinsen (Shaun Toub), a fellow engineer and prisoner, saves Stark by implanting a permanent electromagnet in his chest to keep the shrapnel from reaching his heart and killing him. The terrorists want

Stark to build them Jericho, and they give him the tools to do it. Stark instead builds an armored, flame-throwing suit powered by a mini arc reactor that propels him through the air, and he escapes. Meanwhile, Obadiah Stane (Jeff Bridges), his father's old business partner, plots to take over Stark Industries. He steals Tony's chest arc reactor to duplicate the Iron Man suit. Tony sends his assistant, Pepper Potts (Gwyneth Paltrow), to investigate Stane's activities, and she discovers a dark truth. Potts meets with Agent Phil Coulson (Clark Gregg) of S.H.I.E.L.D. to alert him of Stane's sinister plans.

WATCH OUT FOR

Watch the post-credits scene to see Nick Fury (Samuel L. Jackson) visit Tony Stark to discuss the *Avengers*. The final moments of *Iron Man* set the stage for the series of films released as part of the Marvel Cinematic Universe: *Iron Man 2* (2010), *Captain America: The First Avenger* (2011), *The Avengers* (2012), *Iron Man 3* (2013), and *Captain America: The Winter Soldier* (2014).

STARRING:
Robert Downey Jr., Terrence Howard, Gwyneth Paltrow, and Jeff Bridges

BOX OFFICE:
$585.1 million

DID YOU KNOW?

Iron Man director Jon Favreau wears a hairpiece and plays the role of Happy Hogan, Tony Stark's driver and loyal friend.

MUSIC:
Ramin Djawadi

Saw it! ☐ Rating: ☆☆☆☆☆

Date: ___/___/_____ With: _____

Notes: _____

_____

67

THE SOUND OF MUSIC

DIRECTOR:
Robert Wise

RELEASE DATE:
March 2, 1965

RATED:

G

General Audiences

RUNTIME:
2 hours,
54 minutes

The Sound of Music was a 1959 Broadway musical before it became a movie in 1965. The musical was inspired by the book *The Story of the Trapp Family Singers* by Maria Augusta Trapp. This classic film turned 50 in 2015!

THE STORY

The seven von Trapp children live in Austria during World War II, amid the Nazi takeover. Their father, Austrian naval captain Georg von Trapp (Christopher Plummer), is a widower and requests a governess from Nonnberg Abbey to help with the children. The Mother Superior of the abbey asks Maria (Julie Andrews), a young and rebellious nun, to take the job. When she arrives at the stately von Trapp home, she discovers that Captain von Trapp has been disciplining the children in a militaristic style—he even uses a whistle to call them to attention! Maria steps in, and while the captain is away, she introduces the children to fun and music. As the Germans advance into Austria, the von Trapp family devises a clever plan to escape.

WHY IT'S FAMOUS

The Sound of Music won five Oscars, including one for Best Music. "Do-Re-Mi," "Sixteen Going on Seventeen," "My Favorite Things," and "So Long, Farewell" were written for the original musical, but were also included in the movie, helping make it a huge success.

STARRING:
Julie Andrews, Christopher Plummer, and Charmian Carr

BOX OFFICE:
$158.6 million (domestic)

DID YOU KNOW?
Julie Andrews was busy filming *Mary Poppins* when she was approached for the role of Maria in *The Sound of Music*.

MUSIC:
Richard Rogers and Oscar Hammerstein III

Saw it! ☐ Rating: ☆☆☆☆☆

Date: ___/___/_____ With: _____

Notes: _____

_____

68

MARY POPPINS

DIRECTOR:
Robert Stevenson

RELEASE DATE:
August 26, 1964

RATED:

G

General
Audiences

RUNTIME:
2 hours,
19 minutes

Mary Poppins is a musical film based on the 1934 fantasy book series written by P.L. Travers. It took Walt Disney 20 years to convince the author to allow Disney to turn her novel into a movie!

THE STORY

The film is set in 1910 in London, England. Mr. Banks works at a bank and is concerned with his work more than his home. Mrs. Banks is too busy trying to help women gain voting rights, and her two children, Jane (Karen Dotrice) and Michael (Matthew Garber), need someone to care for them. The family places an ad in the newspaper for a new nanny. After a strong wind blows away the line of nannies waiting for an interview, Mary Poppins (Julie Andrews) floats down from the sky and introduces herself to the Banks family. As the new nanny, she makes life

perfectly magical for the Banks children; toys and rooms are picked up at the snap of her fingers, and tea parties take place on the ceiling! With the help of her performer friend Bert (Dick Van Dyke), Mary Poppins shows the Banks children how to bring a sunny attitude and whimsical sense of adventure into everyday life.

WHY IT'S FAMOUS

The most magical part of this film is the hand-drawn animated cartoon characters that mingle and dance with real-life human actors—a cinematic feat that had not been done before! Computer animation was nowhere in sight in 1964, when Mary Poppins and her talking umbrella flew into theaters. Also, Disney animators didn't have green-screen technology to help them bring animated characters together with actors on film. Leave it to Disney to pioneer the combination of fantasy with reality in one endearing motion picture!

"Chim Chim Cher-ee" won the Oscar for Best Original Song in 1964. It is one of the many cheery songs in this five-time Academy Award-winning movie.

Mary Poppins turned 50 years old in 2014. Disney celebrated this milestone by restoring and releasing the 50th Anniversary Edition of the movie on DVD.

STARRING:
Julie Andrews, Dick Van Dyke, and David Tomlinson

BOX OFFICE:
$102.2 million (domestic)

DID YOU KNOW?

The story of how *Mary Poppins* became a movie was brought to the screen in the 2013 Disney film *Saving Mr. Banks*. And just FYI: Supercalifragilisticexpialadocious is not a real word!

MUSIC:
Richard M. Sherman and Robert B. Sherman

Saw it! ☐ Rating: ☆☆☆☆☆

Date: ___/___/_____ With: _____

Notes: _____

69

WILLY WONKA & THE CHOCOLATE FACTORY

DIRECTOR:
Mel Stuart

RELEASE DATE:
June 30, 1971

RATED:
G
General Audiences

RUNTIME:
1 hour,
40 minutes

THE STORY

This story centers around Charlie (Peter Ostrom), a poor boy who passes by the eccentric, wonderful, and very mysterious Willy Wonka Chocolate Factory every day on his way home from school. The candy factory is securely locked from the outside world to guard its famous recipes. Charlie sees the other children crowd into a nearby candy shop to get a treat on their way home from school, but he can't afford one—he has to use his money to buy a loaf of bread for his family. One day, news breaks out that five lucky winners will get a private tour of the Wonka factory if they find a golden ticket hidden inside a Wonka Bar.

WHY IT'S FAMOUS

The deep lessons of this movie lie with the five golden-ticket winners. Mr. Wonka (Gene Wilder) takes it upon himself to teach these ill-raised kids a thing or two about how to behave properly.

UP NEXT

In 2005, the film was remade as *Charlie and the Chocolate Factory*, starring Johnny Depp as Willy Wonka.

DID YOU KNOW?

This classic fantasy film is based on the 1964 book *Charlie and the Chocolate Factory* by the prolific author Roald Dahl, who also wrote the screenplay.

Saw it! ☐ Rating: ☆☆☆☆☆
Date: ___/___/_____ With: _____
Notes: _____
_____

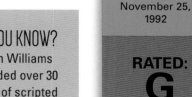

2 ACADEMY AWARDS

ALADDIN

THE STORY

In Agrabah, the evil Jafar, advisor to the Sultan, is searching for a thief—a "Diamond in the Rough"—to go into the Cave of Wonders and retrieve a magic lamp that holds a powerful genie. Meanwhile, Princess Jasmine (Linda Larkin) is sulking because according to tradition, she must marry before her next birthday—which is in three days! But Jasmine wants to choose her own suitor and marry for love. Unhappy with her palace life, she escapes. In the marketplace, she meets Aladdin (Scott Weinger), a street rat constantly running from palace guards because he must steal to eat. The two become friends, but Aladdin and his pet monkey, Abu (Frank Welker), are arrested and thrown into the palace dungeon. Jafar convinces Aladdin to go into the Cave of Wonders to get the lamp, but the two become trapped in the cave. Aladdin rubs the lamp, and a genie appears. Genie (Robin Williams) informs Aladdin he will grant him three wishes. Aladdin's first wish is to become a prince so Jasmine will marry him. But Jafar steals the lamp and forces Genie to help him take over the city. Aladdin decides that the only way to save the kingdom is to tell Jasmine the truth about who he really is and together defeat Jafar.

DID YOU KNOW?
Robin Williams recorded over 30 hours of scripted and improvised dialogue for *Aladdin*.

DIRECTORS:
Ron Clements and John Musker

RELEASE DATE:
November 25, 1992

RATED:

G

General Audiences

RUNTIME:
1 hour, 30 minutes

Saw it! ☐ Rating: ☆☆☆☆☆
Date: ___/___/_____ With: _____
Notes: _____
_____

71

THE MUPPET MOVIE

DIRECTOR:
James Frawley

RELEASE DATE:
June 22, 1979

RATED:

G

General Audiences

RUNTIME:
1 hour,
35 minutes

THE STORY

The Muppet Movie explains how Kermit the Frog, Miss Piggy, Gonzo, Fozzie, and the rest of the Muppets meet for the first time. When a Hollywood agent (Dom DeLuise) hears Kermit singing in the swamp, he convinces him to pursue a career in show business. Kermit sets off on a cross-country road trip from Florida to California and meets the other Muppets along the way. The trip hits some speed bumps when a fast-food chain owner sees Kermit and wants him to become the mascot for the fried-frog-legs restaurant.

WHY IT'S FAMOUS

The greatest challenge for the filmmakers was making the puppets seem lifelike and walk on their own two feet for their first full feature-length movie! When Kermit pedals his bike, you don't see strings, rods, or puppeteers. Where is Jim Henson, creator of The Muppets, while Kermit sits on a log in the pond singing? Apparently, Henson was below the surface in a water-resistant contraption, where he communicated with the crew on a walkie-talkie.

Steve Martin, Bob Hope, Mel Brooks, and Orson Welles all appear in this movie. However, the real stars are Jim Henson and the master puppeteers who magically work behind, over, and under the scenes to bring The Muppets to life!

UP NEXT

There are 12 more movies featuring The Muppets, from *The Great Muppet Caper* (1981) to *Muppets Most Wanted* (2014), which stars Tina Fey and Ricky Gervais.

Saw it! ☐ Rating: ☆☆☆☆☆

Date: ___/___/_____ With: _____

Notes: _____

_____

THE LITTLE MERMAID

THE STORY

Disney's musical animated film introduces us to Ariel, a mermaid princess, who has everything a 16-year-old girl could wish for but still dreams of life on land. When Ariel (Jodi Benson) yearns to go above water, Sebastian (Samuel E. Wright), her crab sidekick and King Triton's trusted adviser, reminds her that contact with humans is forbidden!

One night, Ariel swims to the surface and sees Prince Eric (Christopher Daniel Barnes) celebrating his birthday on a passing ship. A storm comes, and Prince Eric's ship catches fire and sinks. Ariel saves Prince Eric from drowning and falls in love with him. Desperate to be human, Ariel makes a deal with Ursula the sea witch (Pat Carroll)—she gives up her beautiful singing voice in exchange for legs. However, if the prince doesn't fall in love with her in three days, Ariel will lose her voice permanently and become Ursula's prisoner. Ariel is faced with a tough decision: is her true love worth the risk?

WHY IT'S FAMOUS

The Little Mermaid marked the beginning of the Disney Renaissance. Walt Disney Animation Studios changed the animation landscape by combining classic stories with stage musical-quality songs in a string of successful animated films.

DID YOU KNOW?

The Little Mermaid was first a fairy tale. In 1837 Danish author Hans Christian Andersen wrote a story about a mermaid who wanted to become a human.

DIRECTORS:
Ron Clements and John Musker

RELEASE DATE:
November 17, 1989

RATED:

G

General Audiences

RUNTIME:
1 hour, 23 minutes

Saw it! ☐ Rating: ☆☆☆☆☆

Date: ___/___/_____ With: _____

Notes: _____

_____

73

BEAUTY AND THE BEAST

DIRECTOR:
Gary Trousdale
and Kirk Wise

**RELEASE
DATE:**
November 22, 1991

RATED:

G

General
Audiences

RUNTIME:
1 hour,
24 minutes

"A tale as old as time..."

Beauty and the Beast is a fairy tale that has been around for centuries. As Disney did with other classic stories, the animation studio adapted the traditional story into a unique Disney musical.

THE STORY

Belle (Paige O'Hara) loves reading stories about faraway places, and she secretly wishes for more than just an ordinary life. This makes her different from the other girls in town who do chores at home and don't like to read. Belle's father, Maurice (Rex Everhart), is an inventor and doesn't fit in with the rest of the town either. One day, Maurice leaves the village to enter his newest invention at a fair, and he gets lost in the woods. He stumbles upon a dark and abandoned castle. He goes inside looking for directions, but meets the angry Beast (Robby Benson), who throws him in the dungeon! Beast was once a handsome prince, but a wandering witch disguised as an ugly, old beggar woman cast a spell over him after he arrogantly denied to help her when she knocked on the castle doors. Belle goes to the castle to save her father, but when she meets the horrible Beast, she offers to take her father's place so he can go free. Can Belle save herself, her father, and break the Beast's spell?

DID YOU KNOW?
Mrs. Potts (a teapot), Chip (a teacup),
Lumière (a candelabrum), and Cogsworth (a clock) are new characters Disney created to transform the classic
Beauty and the Beast tale into a timeless film.

MUSIC:
Alan Menken

BOX OFFICE:
$424.9 million

ORIGINAL STORY BY:
Jeanne-Marie Leprince de Beaumont

Saw it! ☐ Rating: ☆☆☆☆☆
Date: ___/___/_____ With: _____
Notes: _____
_____

74

THE LION KING

DIRECTORS:
Roger Allers and
Rob Minkoff

**RELEASE
DATE:**
June 24, 1994

RATED:

G

General
Audiences

RUNTIME:
1 hour,
29 minutes

THE STORY

The Lion King is a completely original story and centers on Simba, an overconfident lion cub next in line to become king of the Pride Lands in the African savanna. His jealous uncle, Scar (Jeremy Irons), tricks Simba into thinking he caused his father Mufasa's (James Earl Jones) death. Scar tells him that the other lions will blame Simba and leaving is the only way he can save himself. Overwhelmed with shame, little Simba (Jonathan Taylor Thomas) runs into the desert, and Scar takes over as king. Simba meets Timon (Nathan Lane), a meerkat, and Pumbaa (Ernie Sabella), a warthog, and they become an irresistible trio of friends. Timon and Pumbaa's motto for living in the jungle is "Hakuna Matata," a Swahili phrase that means "no worries." Is it because they only have to worry about what their next meal will be? Simba (Matthew Broderick) grows up, and returns with his childhood friend Nala to the Pride Lands to reclaim his proper place as king.

The Academy Award winning music, including Elton John's "The Circle of Life" and "Can You Feel the Love Tonight," is ingrained in the Millennial generation like a historical event.

DID YOU KNOW?

After 57 years and 54 films, Pumbaa is the first character to fart in a Disney movie.

UP NEXT

In addition to two home entertainment sequels, *The Lion King* also became a successful stage musical.

Saw it! ☐ Rating: ☆☆☆☆☆

Date: ___/___/_____ With: _____

Notes: _____

_____

THE PRINCESS AND THE FROG

THE STORY

Tiana dreams of opening an elegant restaurant in New Orleans where she can serve her father's special gumbo and sweet beignets. Her rich friend Charlotte dreams of marrying a handsome prince. Tiana's father tells her that wishing for something is just the start; she needs to work hard to make her dreams come true.

Prince Naveen, a broke, fun-loving royal from Maldonia, travels to New Orleans looking for a rich Southern belle to marry. Charlotte's father, Big Daddy La Bouff (John Goodman), hosts a masquerade ball in honor of the prince. Earlier that day, Naveen meets Dr. Facilier (Keith David), an evil witch doctor who promises to make all his dreams come true. Dr. Facilier's voodoo spell turns the prince into a frog and disguises his valet as the prince! At Charlotte's ball, Tiana is dressed as a princess, and Naveen convinces her to kiss him to break the spell. Instead of reversing the spell, Tiana turns into a frog too!

DIRECTORS:
Ron Clements
and
John Musker

RELEASE DATE:
December 11, 2009

WHY IT'S FAMOUS

After 72 years, *The Princess and the Frog* introduced Disney's first-ever African-American princess.

RATED:
G
General Audiences

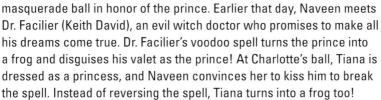

DID YOU KNOW?
Grammy winner Alicia Keys auditioned three times for the part of Tiana, but she ultimately lost to Tony Award-winner Anika Noni Rose.

RUNTIME:
1 hour,
37 minutes

Saw it! ☐ Rating: ☆☆☆☆☆

Date: ___/___/_____ With: _____

Notes: _____

_____

76

DIRECTORS:
Chris Buck and
Jennifer Lee

**RELEASE
DATE**:
November 27, 2013

RATED:

G

for some action
and mild rude
humor

RUNTIME:
1 hour,
42 minutes

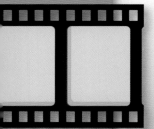

FROZEN

This musical fantasy was inspired by *The Snow Queen*, the 1844 fairy tale written by Hans Christian Andersen. *Frozen* beat records for Disney and the film industry as a whole, becoming the highest-grossing animated film of all time.

THE STORY

Princess Elsa (Idina Menzel) has a strange, magical gift that allows her to create ice and snow at will—and sometimes by accident too. As a little girl, Elsa was playing with her sister Anna (Kristen Bell), when she accidentally let a blast of cold knock Anna unconscious. Her parents, the King and Queen of Arendelle, sought help from a magical troll, who erased Anna's memories of Elsa's magical powers and restored her health. From that day onward, Elsa stayed hidden within the castle to keep from hurting Anna or revealing her powers to anyone else. Many years go by and Elsa and Anna's parents are killed in a shipwreck. The sisters, once close, are now distant.

Elsa turns 21 and is now of age to take the throne. Since she hasn't been seen in years, the city is bursting with excitement in preparation for her coronation. No one is more anxious to see Elsa than her younger sister Anna. At the coronation, Anna meets Prince Hans and they quickly bond. Meanwhile, Elsa is frightened she won't be able to control her emotions, which may unleash the blasts that freeze anything they touch. Nevertheless, the grand occasion goes on without any problems, until Hans proposes to Anna at the reception. They ask for the queen's blessing to marry, but Elsa refuses and is suspicious of the sudden union. The siblings fight, and Elsa has an icy emotional outburst that releases a volley of sharp icicles across the ballroom! Devastated and afraid, Elsa runs away, leaving a snowy wake in her path. But Anna refuses to let her sister run away. With help from Kristoff (Jonathan Groff), a rough mountain man; his sidekick Sven, a reindeer; and a talking snowman, Olaf (Josh Gad), they set off to bring Elsa back. When they find her, Elsa becomes angry and orders them to leave. Anna resists, and Elsa accidentally strikes her again and freezes her heart. Only an "act of true love" can keep Anna's heart from freezing solid forever. Who will save Anna? Will Elsa return to Arendelle to thaw the city and rule over her kingdom?

STARRING:
Kristen Bell,
Idina Menzel,
Jonathan Groff,
Alan Tudyk, and
Josh Gad

BOX OFFICE:
$1.2 billion

DID YOU KNOW?
This is the first time the bond of sisterly love is the focus of a Disney film rather than the traditional prince-and-princess happily-ever-after ending.

MUSIC:
Kristen
Anderson-
Lopez
and
Robert Lopez

Saw it! ☐ Rating: ☆☆☆☆☆

Date: ___/___/_____ With: _____

Notes: _____

_____

109

77

THE WIZARD OF OZ

DIRECTOR:
Victor Fleming

RELEASE DATE:
August 25, 1939

RATED:

G

General
Audiences

RUNTIME:
1 hour,
42 minutes

The Wizard of Oz is arguably the most popular film ever! The original movie is based on the book, *The Wonderful Wizard of Oz*, written by L. Frank Baum and published in 1899.

THE STORY

After Dorothy and her little dog Toto are swept up by a tornado, they are magically transported to the Land of Oz. There, Dorothy meets Glinda (Billie Burke) the good witch and learns that only the Wizard of Oz can send her home to Kansas. On her way to see the Wizard, she stumbles across three characters also in need of the Wizard's help. The tale of this unlikely group of friends who overcome obstacles in search of the Wizard is timeless, and the lessons we learn from this film are still relevant today.

We all need courage to persevere, and like the Cowardly Lion (Bert Lahr), if we're afraid to do something and we don't try, we'll never know if we are capable of doing it. While poor Scarecrow (Ray Bolger)thinks he isn't intelligent, he is able to think on his feet when needed. And caring for one another is what friends do—just ask the Tin Man (Jack Haley).

WHY IT'S FAMOUS

One of the most important messages in *The Wizard of Oz* is simple: "There's no place like home." Growing up, we sometimes think our friends have it so much better than we do. Hopefully, we don't have to travel all the way to Oz to understand that the yellow brick road leads right to the people who love us most: our family.

This film is also a classic "because, because, because" of the wonderful songs and script lines that have become part of our daily language. The famous line "Lions and tigers and bears, oh my!" is chanted by Dorothy, Tin Man, Scarecrow, and Cowardly Lion as they walk through the bewitched forest on their way to the Emerald City in search of the great and powerful Wizard of Oz.

Watch *The Wizard of Oz* and see how many songs, classic lines, and examples of human virtues you recognize!

STARRING:
Judy Garland, Ray Bolger, Bert Lahr, and Jack Haley

BOX OFFICE:
$23.3 million

MUSIC:
Harold Arlen

DID YOU KNOW?
The ruby slippers worn by Dorothy in the film are on permanent display at the Smithsonian museum in Washington, D.C. In 2014, the suit worn by the Cowardly Lion sold at auction for $3.1 million.

Saw it! ☐ Rating: ☆☆☆☆☆

Date: ___/___/_____ With: _____

Notes: _____

_____

SPACE JAM

DIRECTOR:
Joe Pytka

RELEASE DATE:
November 15, 1996

RATED:
PG
for some mild cartoon language

RUNTIME:
1 hour, 28 minutes

WHY IT'S FAMOUS

Warner Bros. produced its first technically-enhanced movie with *Space Jam,* which features classic Looney Tunes cartoon characters mixed with live action stars Michael Jordan, Bill Murray, Larry Bird, Charles Barkley, and Patrick Ewing.

THE STORY

A young Michael Jordan is shooting hoops with his dad and dreams about playing with the NBA. Fast-forward to Jordan on the baseball field trying to conquer another sport. Later, on the golf course, Jordan is suddenly sucked down a hole into Looney Tunes Land.

Meanwhile, in the cartoon world, Swackhammer (Danny DeVito) is the owner of Moron Mountain, an amusement park planet in peril of being foreclosed. He sends the Nerdlucks, five tiny aliens with big weapons, to kidnap Bugs Bunny and company for a new attraction. Bugs makes a deal to play basketball with them: if they win, they get their freedom. The Nerdlucks harness the talents of star NBA basketball players and become the Monstars, but Bugs, Daffy, Porky Pig, Tweety, and the rest of the Looney Tunes gang are only able to capture Jordan. Let the game begin!

DID YOU KNOW?

The song "I Believe I Can Fly," featured in *Space Jam* and written by R. Kelly, won the Grammy for Best Song Written Specifically for a Motion Picture or for Television.

Saw it! ☐ Rating: ☆☆☆☆☆
Date: ___/___/_____ With: _____
Notes: _____
_____

COOL RUNNINGS

THE STORY

A Jamaican Olympic athlete hopeful, Derice Bannock (Leon), doesn't qualify for the 100-meter event at the trials because his fellow runner, Junior Bevil (Rawle D. Lewis), trips and falls, causing Derice and a few other runners to hit the ground as well. With his dreams for an Olympic run shattered, Derice asks competition organizer Coolidge (Winston Stona) for a second chance, but he's denied. Looking at an old photo in Coolidge's office, Derice asks who the stranger standing next to his gold medal-winning father is. Irving Blitzer (John Candy) was an Olympic bobsled medalist, but he had his medals stripped after he was caught cheating. Derice realizes he can still become an Olympic athlete—as a bobsledder! He contacts Irv about putting together a Jamaican bobsled team to compete in the Winter Olympics in Calgary, Canada. This makes no sense to the others, but Derice and Irv try to recruit for the team, and they end up with Sanka Coffie (Doug E. Doug), Junior Bevil, and Yul Brenner (Malik Yoba).

DID YOU KNOW?

Disney's sports comedy film about the 1988 Olympic bobsled team from Jamaica is loosely based on a true story.

DIRECTOR:
Jon Turteltaub

RELEASE DATE:
October 1, 1993

RATED:

PG

for mild language and brief violence

RUNTIME:
1 hour, 38 minutes

Saw it! ☐ Rating: ☆☆☆☆☆

Date: ___ / ___ / _____ With: _____

Notes: _____

80

THE KARATE KID

DIRECTOR:
John G. Avildsen

RELEASE DATE:
June 22, 1984

RATED:

PG

for adult
situations/
language,
violence

RUNTIME:
2 hours,
6 minutes

THE STORY

Daniel LaRusso (Ralph Macchio) moves from New Jersey to Los Angeles with his mother. In a new city and new high school, the mild-mannered teenager faces a group of bullies who study karate at the Cobra Kai Dojo. The sensei at Cobra Kai teaches his pupils a vicious form of karate. After getting beat up regularly by Johnny Lawrence (William Zabka) and his group of thugs for dating Johnny's ex-girlfriend, Ali Mills (Elisabeth Shue), Daniel decides it's time to take matters into his own hands.

Mr. Miyagi (Pat Morita), the janitor at Daniel's apartment complex, seems like a peculiar old man at first—he catches flies with chopsticks! He shocks Daniel one day when he intervenes and single-handedly defeats Daniel's teenage attackers, revealing his superior karate skills. Daniel asks the handyman to teach him to fight. Miyagi refuses and instead offers to

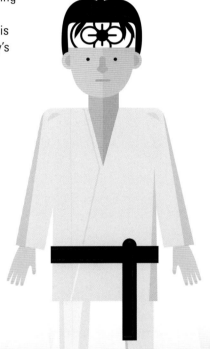

go with Daniel to the Cobra Kai Dojo and show him how to resolve the conflict peacefully. However, sensei Kreese (Martin Kove), scoffs at their peaceful offer. After seeing this, the wise old man agrees to teach Daniel how to defend himself so he can face Johnny at the All-Valley Karate Tournament using a different method of martial arts, one that requires a balance of mind and spirit. The process is slow and involves boring tasks that Miyagi considers essential for muscle memory. "Wax on, use the left. Wax off, use the right," he tells a frustrated Daniel while he makes him clean his car. Daniel wants to quit and thinks Miyagi is just using him to do his chores. As the lessons continue, Daniel starts to understand how he can apply the principles he's learned to his daily life—especially with Ali.

At the tournament, Daniel surprises everyone and makes it to the semi-finals. But one of Kreese's students knocks Daniel out of the competition with an illegal kick to the knee. Johnny is practically declared the winner, except that Daniel has one more surprise under his belt. Will Daniel's bullies finally learn to respect him?

UP NEXT

Also see *The Karate Kid, Part II* (1986) and *The Karate Kid, Part III* (1989). A remake of *The Karate Kid* starring Jaden Smith was released in 2010.

STARRING:
Ralph Macchio,
William Zabka,
Elizabeth Shue,
Pat Morita, and
Martin Kove

BOX OFFICE:
$90.8 million (domestic)

SCREEN-PLAY WRITTEN BY:
Robert Mark Kamen

DID YOU KNOW?
The director of *The Karate Kid* also directed *Rocky* (1976).

Saw it! ☐ Rating: ☆☆☆☆☆

Date: ___/___/_____ With: _____

Notes: _____

_____

81

RUDY

DIRECTOR:
David Anspaugh

RELEASE DATE:
October 22, 1993

RATED:

PG

for mild language

RUNTIME:
1 hour, 54 minute

This inspirational sports film is based on a true story about the life of Daniel "Rudy" Ruettiger, who played football at the University of Notre Dame in 1975.

THE STORY

Rudy (Sean Astin) refuses to accept what everyone tells him about his college prospects: He has neither the grades nor the athletic build to play for the Fighting Irish. But this doesn't stop him from following his dream. After graduating from high school, Rudy and his best friend Pete (Christopher Reed) work at a steel mill. A tragic accident kills Pete, the only one who encouraged Rudy's dream. Against his family's will, Rudy leaves for South Bend, Indiana. He enrolls at Holy Cross Junior College across the way from Notre Dame and improves his grades with help from D-Bob (Jon Favreau), a tutor who discovers that Rudy is dyslexic. After working hard for two years, he applies and is accepted to Notre Dame. Now all he has to do is get on the football team as a walk-on. Rudy sleeps in the groundskeeper's office on a cot and is allowed to practice with the team. All he wants is to wear the uniform and play one game so his name will be on the team's roster. This is a tall order considering he is "5-foot nothin'" and weighs "a hundred and nothing."

DID YOU KNOW?

In 2006, *Rudy* was ranked the 54th-most inspiring film of all time in the American Film Institute's "AFI's 100 Years...100 Cheers" series.

Saw it! ☐ Rating: ☆☆☆☆☆

Date: ___/___/_____ With: _____

Notes: _____

_____

4 ACADEMY AWARDS

CHARIOTS OF FIRE

This British historical drama is based on the true story of two Olympic runners, Eric Liddell (Ian Charleson) and Harold Abrahams (Ben Cross), who competed in the 1924 games in Paris.

THE STORY

In a flashback from Harold Abrahams's memorial service, we're taken to his first day at Cambridge University as a privileged English-Jewish student just after World War I. Showing off, Abrahams impresses everyone by accomplishing the Trinity Great Court Run, completing a lap around the quad in the time it takes for the clock to strike the noon bells. Liddell is a Christian, born of Scottish missionaries in China. They both have the gift of speed, but also have something to prove—their worth to society and to themselves. Their personalities clash, but on the track they both focus on winning and earn spots on the British Olympic team. However, they both face obstacles, too. How these young men resolve their issues and then go on to leave an indelible impression on British history is a lesson worth taking to heart.

451

DID YOU KNOW?

Eric Liddell went back to do missionary work in China. He died under Japanese captivity after they invaded China. He passed away a few months before liberation in 1945.

DIRECTOR:
Hugh Hudson

RELEASE DATE:
March 30, 1981 (UK); April 9, 1982 (USA)

RATED:
PG
for adult situations/language

RUNTIME:
1 hour, 59 minutes

Saw it! ☐ Rating: ☆☆☆☆☆
Date: ___/___/_____ With: _____
Notes: _____
_____

83

FIELD OF DREAMS

DIRECTOR:
Phil Alden
Robinson

**RELEASE
DATE:**
May 5, 1989

RATED:

PG

for thematic
elements and
some language

RUNTIME:
1 hour,
47 minutes

THE STORY

Ray Kinsella (Kevin Costner) trades his city life for a quiet farm in Iowa. One day, he hears a voice say, "If you build it, he will come." He hears the voice several more times and suddenly understands what it's telling him. He needs to build a baseball field on his land. His wife Annie (Amy Madigan), is skeptical about this harebrained idea, but she supports her husband.

Ray follows his dream and bulldozes the cornstalks to make way for a baseball diamond. After the work is finished, Ray sees an old-time uniformed baseball player come out of the cornfield and onto the field. It's Shoeless Joe Jackson (Ray Liotta). Ray searches out author Terence Mann (James Earl Jones) and an older doctor, Moonlight Graham (Burt Lancaster), who also played baseball, and takes them back to the farm to join the rest of the ghosts on the field.

Everyone thinks he's crazy, and Ray starts to doubt himself. Then something magical happens out on the field that convinces everyone that pursuing a dream is sometimes worth the risks.

DID YOU KNOW?

The Chicago White Sox scandal of 1919 is a true event. Accused of throwing games against the Cincinnati Reds to fix the World Series, the team was banned for life from baseball.

Saw it! ☐ Rating: ☆☆☆☆☆
Date: ___/___/_____ With: _____
Notes: _____
_____

REMEMBER THE TITANS

THE STORY

In this adaptation of a true story from 1971, Coach Boone (Denzel Washington) is placed at T.C. Williams High School after the school board adopts the state's integration plan. Coach Bill Yoast (Will Patton), a white man, is demoted to assistant coach to make room for the new system; a black coach is needed to coach the newly integrated football team. Yoast feels humiliated and wants to quit, but the white players also threaten to quit, so he swallows his pride and stays on. Boone is threatened by the administration—if he loses a single game, he'll be fired! Resistance to desegregration is evident in the racial tensions among the players, who train exceptionally hard because there is so much riding on their first season as a team. The monumental task of bringing this new team together to win is now on Boone's shoulders. Can he do it?

WHY IT'S FAMOUS

This movie brings us to the edge of our seats as we see how racial prejudice melts away, and the newly formed bond among the players results in a history-making season.

DID YOU KNOW?

The scene where a brick flies through Coach Boone's window is partially true. It wasn't a brick, but a toilet seat that was flung at his window.

DIRECTOR:
Boaz Yakin

RELEASE DATE:
September 29, 2000

RATED:

PG

for thematic elements and some language

RUNTIME:
1 hour, 53 minutes

Saw it! ☐ Rating: ☆☆☆☆☆

Date: ___/ ___/ _____ With: _____

Notes: _____

_____

85 SEABISCUIT

DIRECTOR:
Gary Ross

RELEASE DATE:
July 25, 2003

RATED:
PG-13
for some sexual situations and violent sports-related images

RUNTIME:
2 hours,
20 minutes

This beautiful biographical film is based on the 2001 best-selling novel by Laura Hillenbrand.

THE STORY

Red Pollard (Tobey Maguire) is abandoned by his parents during the Great Depression. He grows up with a horse owner who uses him to maintain his stables and, angry with his lot in life, takes his frustrations out in boxing matches. He gets injured and ends up blind in one eye. Charles Howard (Jeff Bridges) is a self-made wealthy man who becomes a stable owner. He meets Tom Smith (Chris Cooper), an eccentric horse trainer with a knack for training reluctant horses. Charles hires Tom to find him a horse and train it to win. He chooses Seabiscuit, a small, lazy, stubborn horse with racehorse pedigree. Now they need a jockey. Although Red understands Seabiscuit, he's too tall for a jockey. The three men work together to produce a race-worthy horse that, against all odds, goes on to race War Admiral, a Triple Crown winner. In the process, Seabiscuit becomes a hero for the heartbroken in 1930s America with his inspiring story.

DID YOU KNOW?
The Triple Crown of Thoroughbred Racing is the most coveted title and consists of winning three races: the Kentucky Derby, the Preakness Stakes, and the Belmont Stakes.

Saw it! ☐ Rating: ☆☆☆☆☆
Date: ___/___/_____ With: _____
Notes: _____
_____

A LEAGUE OF THEIR OWN

This movie is a fictionalized version of the origins and development of the All-American Girls Professional Baseball League (AAGPBL).

THE STORY

In 1943, when most of the men were called to fight during World War II, Major League Baseball was on the verge of shutting down. Team owners got together to find a solution, and Walter Harvey (Gary Marshall), candy magnate and owner of the Chicago Cubs, persuaded them to finance a women's league. Jimmy Dugan (Tom Hanks), a former Cubs player, is recruited to coach one of the new all-girl teams. Ball player Dottie Hinson (Geena Davis) and her sister Kit Keller (Lori Petty) are brought from Oregon to Chicago for the tryouts. There ends up being four teams: the Rockford Peaches, Racine Belles, Kenosha Comets, and the South Bend Blue Sox.

WHY IT'S FAMOUS

The women played baseball while their husbands were away at war, and nobody thought the league would amount to much—but it did. And how the players managed to overcome the barriers women face in sports both then and now is the very heart of this story.

DID YOU KNOW?

The AAGPBL survived even after the men returned from the war. The women continued to play baseball until 1954. *A League of Their Own* was selected for preservation in the United States National Film Registry in 2012.

DIRECTOR:
Penny Marshall

RELEASE DATE:
July 1, 1992

RATED:
PG
for language

RUNTIME:
2 hours,
8 minutes

Saw it! ☐ Rating: ☆☆☆☆☆

Date: ___ / ___ / _____ With: _____

Notes: _____

_____

MIRACLE

DIRECTOR:
Gavin O'Connor

RELEASE DATE:
February 6, 2004

RATED:
PG
for language and some rough sports action

RUNTIME:
2 hours,
15 minutes

WHY IT'S FAMOUS

The 1980 Winter Olympic Games were held in Lake Placid, New York. *Miracle* recounts the true story about how the underdog United States hockey team's coach Herb Brooks was selected, how the Olympic team was formed, and what it took for the men's hockey team to make it to the medal round against the Soviets in the 1980 Winter Olympic Games.

THE STORY

Herb Brooks (Kurt Russell) is a former Olympian and the University of Minnesota's head coach. He interviews with the U.S. Olympic Committee (USOC) to be the hockey team's coach and proposes his own training program for the men. The team would be facing the Soviets, who were a force in the sport. Coach Brooks does something unorthodox; he picks 26 players, regardless of the tryouts held in Colorado Springs, and disregards the USOC's recommendations. College rivalries heat up during the intense practices, but Brooks puts an end to the arguments with a rigorous practice routine. Eventually the team starts racking up the wins, leading to the gold medal rounds against the heavy favorites: the Soviet and the Finnish teams. Do they win gold?

DID YOU KNOW?
"Herbies" are named after Coach Herb Brooks. These punishing wind sprints were his preferred drill!

Saw it! ☐ Rating: ☆☆☆☆☆
Date: ___/ ___/ _____ With: _____
Notes: _____
_____

BEND IT LIKE BECKHAM

THE STORY

In this fictional comedy drama, Jesminder "Jess" Bhamra (Parminder Nagra) is the 18-year-old daughter of traditional Punjabi parents living in the suburbs of London. Jess's parents only expect two things from her: to learn to cook a traditional Indian meal and to marry an Indian boy. However, Jess is obsessed with playing soccer, a sport that respectable Indian girls don't play. Jess resorts to hiding her love of soccer from her parents since they have banned her from playing. Kicking the ball around with the boys at the park one day, Juliette Paxton (Keira Knightley) notices Jess's impressive skills and recruits her to play with the Hounslow Harriers, a local women's team. Jess joins the team and develops a crush on Joe, the team's coach. That would be all right except Joe is Irish, and he can't date his players. Also, Juliette likes him too. Complicated? You bet!

Jess continues to play soccer with one goal in mind: to get a scholarship to attend the prestigious Santa Clara University in California. Can her parents' old traditions coexist with Jess's new ones?

DID YOU KNOW?

Parminder Nagra wasn't a soccer player. She went to boot camp to learn a tough Brazilian method that teaches flashy moves. After a private screening of this film, David Beckham told the actress she did a good job.

DIRECTOR:
Gurinder Chadha

RELEASE DATE:
April 12, 2002 (UK);
August 1, 2003 (USA)

RATED:
PG-13
for language and sexual content

RUNTIME:
1 hour, 52 minutes

Saw it! ☐ Rating: ☆☆☆☆☆

Date: ___/___/_____ With: _____

Notes: _____

_____

89

THE SANDLOT

DIRECTOR:
David M. Evans

RELEASE DATE:
April 7, 1993

RATED:
PG
for some language and kids chewing tobacco

RUNTIME:
1 hour,
41 minutes

THE STORY

This is not a typical sports film about kids becoming so good at baseball that they beat all the other teams. In fact, no other teams play in *The Sandlot*.

In the summer of 1960, Scotty Smalls (Tom Guiry) and his just-remarried mother move to a new town near Los Angeles. The adolescent finds new friends at the local sandlot, where eight players need a ninth man to complete the team. Perfect, right? Wrong. Smalls can't play baseball to save his life. He's so bad at sports, he doesn't even know who Babe Ruth is (he thought he was a girl!). To fit in with the team, he asks his stepdad (Denis Leary) to teach him to throw and catch. His stepdad is an avid baseball fan who collects priceless memorabilia, but they never find the time to play. Benny "The Jet" Rodriguez (Mike Vitar) is the best player on the neighborhood team and takes Smalls under his wing. He teaches him what he needs to know about baseball and gets him a spot on the team.

During a particularly hot and dusty day, the boys join in on other summertime rituals, like going to the local pool and challenging each other to kiss the cute lifeguard, Wendy Peffercorn (Marley Shelton). Though they try to fool her into kissing one of them, they end up getting kicked out of the pool. Back at the sandlot, the boys are playing ball, and they accidentally hit their only ball behind the fence where a huge and vicious dog they call "The Beast" lives. They are all too scared to get it back, but Smalls sees his chance to be a hero. He runs home to his stepdad's office, grabs a ball—which is signed by Babe Ruth—out of its case, and runs back to the field to save the day! Except that this ball also goes flying over the fence. They have to retrieve *that* ball. But how will they get around The Beast?

UP NEXT

This cherished coming-of-age movie inspired two more: *The Sandlot 2* (2005) and *The Sandlot 3* (2007).

STARRING:
Tom Guiry,
Denis Leary,
Mike Vitar, and
Patrick Renna

BOX OFFICE:
$33.8 million

MUSIC:
David Newman

DID YOU KNOW?

If you don't know what PF Flyers are, you will after you see the sneakers worn by Benny Rodriguez in this movie. The boys in *The Sandlot* have always been cool.

Saw it! ☐ Rating: ☆☆☆☆☆
Date: ___/___/_____ With: _____
Notes: _____
_____

90

DEAD POETS SOCIETY

1 ACADEMY AWARD

DIRECTOR:
Peter Weir

RELEASE DATE:
June 9, 1989

RATED:
PG
for language, substance use, and thematic elements

RUNTIME:
2 hours, 8 minutes

THE STORY

On the first day of school at Welton Academy, Professor John Keating (Robin Williams) tells the all-boy class to call him "O Captain, My Captain!" He stands on the desks and inspires the class to *carpe diem*, meaning "seize the day!" Neil Perry (Robert Sean Leonard), Knox, Richard, Todd (Ethan Hawke), Meeks, Pitts, and Charlie take the professor's message to heart; they don't have to follow their parents' wishes nor submit to school rules. The boys resurrect the historic Dead Poets Society after they find out their teacher used to be a member of the club. The boys meet in secret and discuss what they really want for themselves, rather than what their parents expect. However, Neil is one of Welton Academy's most prized students, and his parents expect him to go to Harvard University. But Neil wants to be an actor and gets involved in a school play. Shocked, Neil's dad pulls him out of school to enroll him in military school. The boy commits suicide (offscreen) that night. Keating is blamed for the tragedy and gets fired. As Professor Keating collects his things from the classroom, the students rise on their desks and say to him, "O Captain, My Captain!"

Dead Poets Society inspires young adults to follow their dreams and continues to resonate with viewers today. Watch the film, and then ask yourself: Was Keating a good professor?

Saw it! ☐ Rating: ☆☆☆☆☆

Date: ___/___/_____ With: _____

Notes: _____

_____

PRETTY IN PINK

THE STORY

Pretty in Pink stars Molly Ringwald as Andie Walsh in a role written specifically for her by John Hughes. Andie is a teenager who wears the wrong clothes, comes from a broken home, and works at the local mall—a combination that would certainly wreak havoc on any teenager's self-esteem. However, Andie is feisty and proud and won't conform to anyone's idea of what she should wear or who she should be. Moreover, she doesn't let the fact that she's poor get in the way of conquering her crush, Blane McDonnagh (Andrew McCarthy), a preppy boy at her school. He's a rich kid whose decision to become friends with Andie is questioned by his ultra-snobbish friend, Steff McKee (James Spader), who calls her "a mutant." Stuck in the "friend zone" is Duckie (Jon Cryer), Andie's good friend who constantly tries to get her attention with humor and clownish behavior.

DID YOU KNOW?

The ending of *Pretty in Pink* was reshot because teen test audiences didn't like that Andie ended up with Duckie in the original version.

WHY IT'S FAMOUS

This movie was written by John Hughes, who was considered the "teen-pic maestro" at the time with certified hits such as *Sixteen Candles* (1984) and *The Breakfast Club* (1985). The messages about Andie's security and self-confidence still inspire teenagers today.

DIRECTOR:
Howard Deutch

RELEASE DATE:
February 28, 1986

RATED:
PG-13
for adult situations/ language

RUNTIME:
1 hour, 36 minutes

Saw it! ☐ Rating: ☆☆☆☆☆
Date: ___/___/_____ With: _____
Notes: _____

SCHOOL OF ROCK

DIRECTOR:
Richard Linklater

RELEASE DATE:
October 3, 2003

RATED:
PG-13
for some rude humor and drug references

RUNTIME:
1 hour,
48 minutes

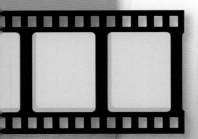

THE STORY

Dewey Finn (Jack Black) is living out his dream of playing in a rock band. His dream is shattered when the guitarist takes a stage dive into the audience and the crowd doesn't even try to catch him. His band, No Vacancy, has also had enough of his over-the-top antics on stage and kicks him out of the band. Washed up and out of a job, the scruffy musician needs to pay his rent but hasn't had a gig for months. His roommate, Ned Schneebly, used to be in a band, but now has a regular job as a substitute teacher, and although he sympathizes with Dewey's situation, he gives him an ultimatum—pay the rent or move out. But rock 'n' roll is Dewey's life, and he doesn't know what else to do.

The phone rings with a call for Ned; the prestigious Horace Green prep school needs a substitute teacher. After hearing this, the proverbial light bulb clicks on in Dewey's head! He poses as

Ned and takes the job. However, instead of teaching the precocious fifth graders English or history, Dewey secretly instructs them on classic rock and how to play instruments so they can make their own band, complete with a manager, Summer Hathaway (Miranda Cosgrove), costume designer, and groupies. Obviously, this does not sit well with principal Rosalie "Roz" Mullins (Joan Cusack), who discovers Dewey's false identity and his plans to have the kids participate in a battle of the bands.

Meanwhile, Ned gets a check in the mail from Horace Green and discovers what Dewey has been up to. Dewey is trying to convince his buddy to not tell anybody about his impersonation scheme when Patty, Ned's girlfriend (Sarah Silverman), walks in on their conversation and hears about the elaborate deception. She calls the police, and Dewey's plan starts to fall apart. Or, does it?

WHY IT'S FAMOUS

School of Rock is a comedy with a serious undertone. The film's ability to reach both kids and adults with lessons about being passionate about something and pursuing it no matter what has made this a favorite family movie that's fun and entertaining to watch.

STARRING:
Jack Black, Miranda Cosgrove, Mike White, and Joan Cusack

BOX OFFICE:
$131.2 Million

MUSIC:
Craig Wedren

DID YOU KNOW?
Andrew Lloyd Webber (*Phantom of The Opera, Jesus Christ Superstar*) bought the rights to *School of Rock* and announced that a musical is in production.

Saw it! ☐ Rating: ☆☆☆☆☆
Date: ___/___/_____ With: _____
Notes: _____
_____

MEAN GIRLS

DIRECTOR:
Mark Waters

RELEASE DATE:
April 30, 2004

RATED:
PG-13
for sexual content,
language, and
some teen
partying

RUNTIME:
1 hour,
37 minutes

In the movie *Mean Girls*, Cady Heron (Lindsay Lohan) shows us that there may be a remote possibility for all girl cliques to coexist peacefully in the largest social experiment that has ever existed—high school.

THE STORY

Cady moves to the suburbs from Africa, where she was homeschooled by her zoologist parents, and enrolls in Evanston Township High School in Illinois. She becomes friends with the goth-like Janis

(Lizzy Caplan) and Damian (Daniel Franzese), who is gay. They explain the social hierarchy on campus to Cady. The Plastics are the popular group and are led by Regina George (Rachel McAdams), Gretchen (Lacey Chabert), and Karen (Amanda Seyfried). One day, Regina eyes Cady and invites her to sit with her group at lunch. Janis jumps up and tells Cady to do it, thinking that she can spy on the Plastics and get some gossip that will bring down the vile girls' group once and for all. However, Cady has little experience navigating the treacherous high school social scene, and she thinks the Queen Bee actually likes her. Cady gradually changes her personality and adopts the Plastics' superficial and spiteful attitude. Things take a turn when Cady develops a crush on Regina's ex-boyfriend, Aaron Samuels (Jonathan Bennett), and the alpha girl gets jealous. To show her who's boss, Regina steals back her old boyfriend from Cady, humiliating her in the process. Things start to get ugly after Cady pulls a series of stunts to get revenge on Regina, essentially turning herself into the new Queen Bee. She causes a riot at school, but Ms. Norbury (Tina Fey), Cady's math teacher, hauls all of the girls into the gym and tries to make them understand that they are all at fault in creating this mess. Will Cady be able to turn things around?

STARRING:
Lindsay Lohan, Rachel McAdams, Lacey Chabert, Amanda Seyfried, and Tina Fey

BOX OFFICE:
$129 million

DID YOU KNOW?
The script was written by Tina Fey (*Saturday Night Live*, *30 Rock*), and based on the non-fiction book by author Rosalind Wiseman, *Queen Bees and Wannabes: Helping Your Daughter Survive Cliques, Gossip, Boyfriends, and Other Realities of Adolescence* (2002).

SCREEN-PLAY WRITTEN BY:
Tina Fey

Saw it! ☐ Rating: ☆☆☆☆☆

Date: ___/___/_____ With: _____

Notes: _____

_____

94

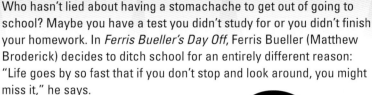

FERRIS BUELLER'S DAY OFF

DIRECTOR:
John Hughes

RELEASE DATE:
June 11, 1986

RATED:
PG-13
for adult situations/ language

RUNTIME:
1 hour, 43 minutes

Who hasn't lied about having a stomachache to get out of going to school? Maybe you have a test you didn't study for or you didn't finish your homework. In *Ferris Bueller's Day Off*, Ferris Bueller (Matthew Broderick) decides to ditch school for an entirely different reason: "Life goes by so fast that if you don't stop and look around, you might miss it," he says.

THE STORY

Ferris is the typical popular high school slacker. Addressing the camera (which is called "breaking the fourth wall" in film speak), the high school senior narrates his bold day off. He convinces his girlfriend, Sloane Peterson (Mia Sara), and his gloomy best friend, Cameron (Alan Ruck), to join him. Bueller fast-talks Cameron into borrowing his dad's cherished 1961 fire-engine-red Ferrari 250 GT convertible, and they take it on an unforgettable joyride around Chicago.

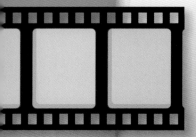

They visit the Sears Tower (renamed the Willis Tower in 2009), gawk at masterpieces at the Art Institute, watch a Cubs game at Wrigley Field, and crash a parade float, where Bueller grabs the microphone and sings "Twist and Shout" with a marching band backing him up. They bamboozle their way into a fancy restaurant and have lunch. As they're leaving, they almost get caught by Ferris's father! Meanwhile, suspicions arise about Bueller's absence when his teacher (portrayed by Ben Stein) is taking attendance and repeats in a now-famous monotone voice, "Bueller? Bueller? Anyone, anyone?" The school principal, Edward Rooney (Jeffrey Jones), has had it with Bueller and his cocky attitude. Even Bueller's sister, Jeanie (Jennifer Grey), is mad that he's able to get away with everything. Rooney heads to the rogue teenager's home, determined to catch Bueller in the act and punish the trickster. The truant student's antics become more and more incredible as the infamous day off progresses. How will Ferris Bueller save the day—and his high school diploma?

FUN FACT

Ben Stein was a speech writer for former U. S. Presidents Richard Nixon and Gerald Ford.

STARRING:
Matthew Broderick, Mia Sara, Alan Ruck, Jeffrey Jones, and Jennifer Grey

BOX OFFICE:
$70.1 million

DID YOU KNOW?

John Hughes intentionally featured Chicago sites and landmarks as a tribute to the city where he grew up.

SCREEN-PLAY WRITTEN BY:
John Hughes

Saw it! ☐ Rating: ☆☆☆☆☆

Date: ___/___/_____ With: _____

Notes: _____

_____

SPELLBOUND

DIRECTOR:
Jeffrey Blitz

RELEASE DATE:
June 27, 2003

RATED:
G
General
Audiences

RUNTIME:
1 hour,
37 minutes

Spellbound follows eight children between the ages of 10 and 14 as they prepare to compete in the 1999 Scripps National Spelling Bee held in Washington, D.C.

THE STORY

Nupur Lala comes from a family of Indian descent who believes that in America, if you work hard, you will succeed. Angela Arenivar is from a small town in Texas. She taught herself how to spell because her parents immigrated from Mexico and barely speak English. Ashley White lives in the housing projects in Washington, D.C. and gets help from her teachers. Neil Kadakia has a doting father

and professional coaches and courses to help him master his spelling skills.

April DeGideo's parents are also consumed with helping her study words. Ted Brigham is from Missouri, and his above-average intelligence makes him stand out. Emily Stagg is from a wealthy Connecticut family and studies spelling while also juggling riding and choir lessons. Harry Altman makes faces when trying to spell a word, and he tells jokes.

WHY IT'S FAMOUS

Imagine trying to learn all the words in a dictionary. That's what contestants have to do for the annual Scripps National Spelling Bee. The preparation, commitment, and willpower shown by the students in this documentary are simply amazing! Who wins this spelling bee? I can tell you this: After you watch *Spellbound*, the clear winner will be you!

STARRING:
Angela Arenivar, Ubaldo Arenivar, and Jorge Arenivar

BOX OFFICE:
$5.5 million

DID YOU KNOW?
Webster's Third New International Dictionary is the official dictionary of the Scripps National Spelling Bee. It has 476,000 word entries.

SCREEN-PLAY WRITTEN BY:
Jeffrey Blitz

Saw it! ☐ Rating: ☆☆☆☆☆
Date: ___/___/_____ With: _____
Notes: _____
_____

96

MARCH OF THE PENGUINS

DIRECTOR:
Luc Jacquet

RELEASE DATE:
July 22, 2005

RATED:
G
General Audiences

RUNTIME:
1 hour, 20 minutes

THE STORY

Imagine living in Antarctica. Sounds cold, right? To film *March of the Penguins*, a camera crew was stationed in the sub-zero climate for over a year! They documented the emperor penguin migration from the ocean to its arctic mating ground.

The footage captured during the months of filming in the harshest and coldest climate on earth (sometimes at -80 degrees!) reveals the struggles the emperor penguins endure to produce their young every year, including walking hundreds of miles to a particular area in the Antarctic where they settle to have their family. While the mothers go back to the ocean in search of food, the males sacrifice comfort, food, and experience loneliness to ensure their single egg safely hatches into a chick.

DID YOU KNOW?

Emperor penguins can grow to be 4 feet tall, and they can hold their breath underwater for up to 20 minutes.

WHY IT'S FAMOUS

March of the Penguins was a very successful film because it showed nature in its true habitat—not one fabricated in a movie studio or enhanced by special effects. Filming in an environment like the Antarctic hadn't been done like this before, and it presented a true test for the camera crew, who had to wear six layers of clothing to film for only three hours each day!

You'll also have newfound respect for these tall, flightless birds after watching this film. The next time you see emperor penguins at the local zoo, you'll understand that they are amazing creatures!

Saw it! ☐ Rating: ☆☆☆☆☆
Date: ___/___/_____ With: _____
Notes: _____
_____

SUPER SIZE ME

THE STORY

Morgan Spurlock decided to eat McDonald's for a month and make a documentary about the experiment. He graduated from New York University's film program in 1993, and he was inspired to make this movie by a news story about two teenage girls suing McDonald's for making them fat. Spurlock wanted to find out if this could really happen. He made some rules to follow from February 1 to March 2, 2003. He had to eat breakfast, lunch, and dinner only at McDonald's; supersize his meal when it was offered; and consume every item on the menu at least once during the 30 days.

Spurlock started his experiment weighing 185 pounds at 6'2" tall. He incorporated an average American's walking regimen of 5,000 steps, or 2 miles, per day. In this film you can see the physical transformation he undergoes after just 30 days of his "McDiet." His liver shows toxic signs equal to that of a binge-drinker and he develops heart palpitations, among other negative side effects. Throughout the documentary, he is supervised by a cardiologist, a gastroenterologist, and a general practitioner. He also has a nutritionist and a personal trainer.

How much weight did Spurlock gain, and how long did it take him to get back to his original self? Watch the film to find out.

DID YOU KNOW?

McDonald's phased out their Super Size program the same year this documentary was released.

DIRECTOR:
Morgan Spurlock

RELEASE DATE:
May 21, 2004 (Canada); June 11, 2004 (USA)

RATED:
PG-13
for thematic elements, a graphic medical procedure, and some language

RUNTIME:
1 hour, 40 minutes

Saw it! ☐ Rating: ☆☆☆☆☆

Date: ___/___/_____ With: _____

Notes: _____

_____

98

LINCOLN

DIRECTOR:
Steven
Spielberg

**RELEASE
DATE:**
November 16, 2012

RATED:

PG-13

for an intense
scene of war
violence, some
images of carnage
and brief strong
language

RUNTIME:
2 hours,
30 minutes

Pay close attention to this movie. It is long, dense, and contains valuable insights into what it took for the 13th Amendment to become a reality.

THE STORY

In this political drama of epic proportions, we learn that Lincoln (portrayed by British actor Daniel Day-Lewis) was a humble man from even more humble origins. The movie begins in 1865 with Lincoln already in the White House dealing with the imminent end of the Civil War, but there's also a personal battle the president has been fighting. He's afraid the Emancipation Proclamation of 1863 will be repealed by the courts once the war is over. Lincoln

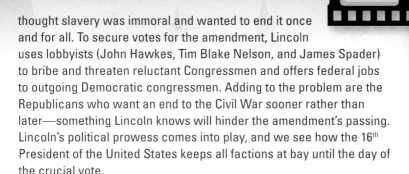

thought slavery was immoral and wanted to end it once and for all. To secure votes for the amendment, Lincoln uses lobbyists (John Hawkes, Tim Blake Nelson, and James Spader) to bribe and threaten reluctant Congressmen and offers federal jobs to outgoing Democratic congressmen. Adding to the problem are the Republicans who want an end to the Civil War sooner rather than later—something Lincoln knows will hinder the amendment's passing. Lincoln's political prowess comes into play, and we see how the 16th President of the United States keeps all factions at bay until the day of the crucial vote.

Meanwhile, Lincoln is also a husband and father. Mary Todd Lincoln (Sally Field) is not happy at the White House—the social demands are too much for her. She is also grieving the loss of one son, while coping with anxiety for her other son, Robert, who left college to serve in the war. How does the Lincoln family hold up during these difficult times?

As the film winds down, a relieved Lincoln is talking with his close advisers, when he is called away to join Mary at Ford's Theatre. "I suppose it's time to go, though I would rather stay," Lincoln says as he walks away.

STARRING:
Daniel Day-Lewis, Sally Field, David Strathairn, Tommy Lee Jones, and James Spader

BOX OFFICE:
$275.2 million

DID YOU KNOW?

DVDs of Steven Spielberg's *Lincoln* were donated to all middle schools and high schools, public or private, in the United States.

MUSIC:
John Williams

Saw it! ☐ Rating: ☆☆☆☆☆

Date: ___/___/_____ With: _____

Notes: _____

_____

99

APOLLO 13

DIRECTOR:
Ron Howard

RELEASE DATE:
June 30, 1995

RATED:

PG

for language and emotional intensity

RUNTIME:
2 hours,
20 minutes

THE STORY

Jim Lovell (Tom Hanks) wasn't supposed to be on Apollo 13, the third scheduled lunar landing of the NASA space program. Command unexpectedly informs him that he will lead the crew on this mission, instead of Apollo 14 as originally planned. The flight surgeon then tells Lovell that all three members of the crew have been exposed to the measles and that Ken Mattingly (Gary Sinise), who has not had the measles before, is at risk of getting sick during the mission.

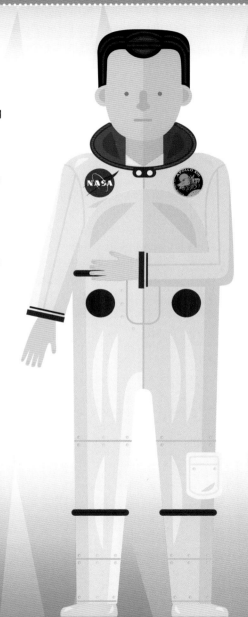

His substitute is Jack Swigert (Kevin Bacon), who joins
Fred Haise (Bill Paxton) and Lovell on the crew.

Once in space, an air tank suddenly explodes and the astronauts'
oxygen supply begins to vent into space. The blast also damages their
electrical source, limiting their power capabilities and putting their
ability to re-enter the Earth's atmosphere at risk. The three men seem
doomed to either freeze to death or run out of oxygen unless they can
repair the craft and steer it back home. Using everything on board,
from a brush to a sock, the engineers fix one thing after another in
a desperate race to get home. On the ground, Flight Director Gene
Kranz (Ed Harris) instructs Mission Control to bring the astronauts
home saying, "Failure is not option."

WHY IT'S FAMOUS

This film retells the true story about the ill-fated Apollo 13
lunar mission in 1970. Astronauts Jim Lovell, Fred Haise, and Jack
Swigert made it back from outer space alive due to their bravery,
ingenuity, and the incredibly bright team on the ground at NASA.

STARRING:
Tom Hanks,
Gary Sinise,
Bill Paxton,
Kevin Bacon,
and Ed Harris

**BOX
OFFICE:**
$355.2 million

**SCREEN-
PLAY
WRITTEN
BY:**
William Broyles Jr.
and Al Reinert

DID YOU KNOW?
The famous quote, "Houston, we have a problem" is actually
a misquote. The original line uttered by Jack Swigert was
"Houston, we've had a problem here."

Saw it! ☐ Rating: ☆☆☆☆☆
Date: ___/___/_____ With: _____
Notes: _____
_____

100

PEARL HARBOR

DIRECTOR:
Michael Bay

RELEASE DATE:
May 25, 2001

RATED:
PG-13
for sustained
intense war
sequences,
images of
wounded,
brief sensuality
and some
language

RUNTIME:
3 hours,
3 minutes

This fictional version of the attack on Pearl Harbor has plenty of explosions and graphic depictions of the horrors of war in order to give you a sense of what it was like to be in the middle of this infamous day in history.

THE STORY

Rafe McCawley (Ben Affleck) and Danny Walker (Josh Hartnett) are childhood friends living in Tennessee in 1923. They grow up and become lieutenants in the U.S. Army Air Corps, where Rafe meets Evelyn Johnson (Kate Beckinsale), a Navy nurse, and falls in love.

However, Rafe is committed to volunteering with the Royal Air Force and soon leaves for England, promising Evelyn he'll come back for her. Evelyn and Danny are transferred to Pearl Harbor, Hawaii. Reports say Rafe was shot down flying over the English Channel, and Danny and Evelyn bond over the loss of their friend. But Rafe didn't die, and when he comes back, he finds his friends are now a couple. Rafe and Danny get into a bar brawl and part ways that night. Little did they know that the next morning, December 7, 1941, they'd be attacked by Japanese bomber planes.

Danny and Rafe jump in their planes and mount a counter offensive against the Japanese. The raid sinks the USS *Arizona*, the USS *Oklahoma*, and several other ships. There are many casualties, and dozens of wounded fill the unprepared hospital. A few days later, both pilots are promoted to captain as the USA declares war on Japan. President Franklin D. Roosevelt (Jon Voight) orders a secret mission to bomb Japan. Danny and Rafe are assigned by Colonel Doolittle (Alec Baldwin) to bomb Tokyo and other Japanese towns. Before they leave, Evelyn tells Rafe a secret that he needs to keep from Danny—at least until they come back from the secret mission. Do they make it back? And what does Evelyn have to hide?

STARRING:
Ben Affleck,
Josh Hartnett,
Kate Beckinsale,
Jon Voight, and
Alec Baldwin

BOX OFFICE:
$449.2 million

DID YOU KNOW?
The Doolittle Raid of Tokyo took place in April of 1942 as retaliation for Pearl Harbor.

MUSIC:
Hans Zimmer

Saw it! ☐ Rating: ☆☆☆☆☆

Date: ___/___/_____ With: _____

Notes: _____

_____

101

HUGO

DIRECTOR:
Martin Scorsese

RELEASE DATE:
November 23, 2011

RATED:

PG

for mild thematic material, some action/peril, and smoking

RUNTIME:
2 hours,
6 minutes

THE STORY

Hugo Cabret (Asa Butterfield) learns to love films from his father, an inventor (Jude Law). Tragically, he becomes an orphan after his father dies in a fire. The only thing left from his father is a broken automaton—a robot—that should be able to write with a pen. Hugo now lives with his uncle in a secret room deep within a magnificent Parisian train station. He learns to fix clocks from his uncle, whose job is to wind and maintain the station's clocks every day. He's also determined to fix the automaton with help from his father's notebook and blueprints, because he's sure his father left a message for him to discover. To do this, Hugo steals toy parts from a bad-tempered store owner, Georges Méliès (Ben Kingsley). Méliès was once a famous French filmmaker, but Hugo is unaware of the grumpy man's past. One day, Méliès catches Hugo stealing a small toy and snatches his notebook as punishment. Hugo follows Méliès home, hoping to take back his notes. When the man leaves, Hugo sneaks in and encounters Isabelle (Chloë Grace Moretz), Méliès's goddaughter. She loves books and saves Hugo's notebook. They become friends and sneak into movies together. Surprisingly, they discover that Méliès was once a highly regarded actor as well. The kids decide to help the once-great cinema star realize that his films are still admired. Will Hugo fix the robot and find out if it has a secret message for him?

This is Martin Scorsese's first family film, and the first time the legendary storyteller used 3-D cameras.

Saw it! ☐ Rating: ☆☆☆☆☆

Date: ___/___/_____ With: _____

Notes: _____

_____

101 TV SHOWS

TO SEE BEFORE YOU GROW UP

After you watch each show, join the fun by using the blanks below each profile to record your own rating.

The suggested age ranges in this book are taken from Common Sense Media or reflect the authors' best recommendations. Be sure to talk with your parents before watching a new show.

The best way to watch TV is with the people you love!

WRITTEN BY SAMANTHA CHAGOLLAN AND ERIKA MILVY
ILLUSTRATED BY NATASHA HELLEGOUARCH

TABLE OF CONTENTS

The shows in this book are divided by genre and listed in random order, so you can start watching wherever you like. Enjoy!

1

SESAME STREET

GENRE:
Educational

AGE:
2+

SEASONS:
47 and counting

MADE BY:
Joan Ganz
Cooney

"Sally, you've never seen a street like
Sesame Street. Everything happens
here. You're gonna love it!"
— The first line in the first episode,
November, 1969

Sesame Street is TV at its finest, funniest, and furriest. Launched in 1969 and still adored today, *Sesame Street* is a groundbreaking show set on a diverse city block where puppets and humans of all ages mingle and learn from one another. The lessons, filled with humor and friendship, aim to help viewers learn to read, count, and understand feelings, relationships, and the world around them. Sidewalk action is interspersed with short, live-action films; animation; and music, plus witty parodies and A-list guest stars that parents love.

The cast includes some adult actors and plenty of kids, but it's Jim Henson's amazing Muppets that steal the show and viewers' hearts. Bert and Ernie, the odd couple of Muppets, show that you can be best friends with someone who is very different from you. Oscar the Grouch lets viewers know it's okay to be cranky sometimes. And Cookie Monster's sugar cravings, Grover's enthusiasm, and Big Bird's curiosity are all things we can relate to.

"Can you tell me how to get, how to get to Sesame Street?" This familiar line from the theme song has comforted generations of kids. The show initially aired on public television and is now available on HBO, so classic songs like Oscar's "I Love Trash," Cookie Monster's "C is for Cookie," and Ernie's "Rubber Ducky," can be sung by a new generation!

STARRING:
Jim Henson's Muppets, and Puppeteers and voice actors like Frank Oz

NETWORK:
PBS, HBO

SPIN-OFFS

Elmo's World
Play with Me Sesame
Journey to Ernie
Bert and Ernie's Great Adventures
Abby's Flying Fairy School
Elmo the Musical

DID YOU KNOW?

The pink, pigtailed puppet Abby Cadabby speaks her own language. She calls it Dragonfly.

Saw it! ☐ Rating: ☆☆☆☆☆
Date: ___/___/_____ With: _____
Notes: _____
_____

2

BILL NYE THE SCIENCE GUY

GENRE:
Educational

AGE:
7+

SEASONS:
5

STARRING:
Bill Nye

With his peppy bow ties and impressively broad areas of expertise, Bill Nye is one of the coolest scientists in our stratosphere. In this classic show, Nye plays the role of the mad scientist and shares his enthusiasm for biology, physics, chemistry, and the natural world with viewers. A variety of creative experiments and upbeat segments make it clear why Nye finds science so fascinating.

The show covers gravity, dinosaurs, biodiversity, sound, the moon, digestion, cells, eyeballs, electricity, and so much more. In one regular feature, "Way Cool Scientist," Nye talks to an expert in the field. "Nifty Home Experiments" show viewers how to "try this at home." "Soundtrack of Science" segments include music videos like "Evolution" sung to the tune of "Revolution" by The Beatles. Vintage film footage, sketches, fake commercials, and kid input also keep the show lively.

Nye has a knack for explaining complex ideas in memorable ways. In one episode, he runs around a soccer field to show how big the solar system is, even jumping in his car and driving to where Pluto would be. Many teachers use Bill Nye segments to introduce science topics to their classes, and young scientists often say it was Bill Nye that made them fans of science.

DID YOU KNOW?

Carl Sagan was Nye's teacher. Nye studied mechanical engineering at Cornell University and took classes with the famous astronomer.

Saw it! ☐ Rating: ☆☆☆☆☆

Date: ___/ ____/ _____ With: _____

Notes: _____

_____

PEPPA PIG

3

Snort along with Peppa and the Pig family in this delightfully silly series where everyone likes to play games and have fun together. Peppa is a cheeky British piggy who plays hide-and-seek with her little brother George Pig. Together they have adventures with her friends Suzy Sheep, Danny Dog, Emily Elephant, Candy Cat, and Rebecca Rabbit. They jump in muddy puddles, go on treasure hunts, fly kites, and take bicycle rides. Peppa also loves to blow raspberries, burp, and of course, snort with her family.

Peppa Pig first aired in 2004, and is still going strong. Each five-minute episode is about friendship, family, laughter, and imagination. Peppa is quite popular—her show is watched and loved in more than 180 countries around the world. The official website is filled with games and print-and-color pages, and includes a separate site for grown-ups with lessons, apps, and activities. Peppa's adventures have even inspired a theme park, Peppa Pig World, in Hampshire, England, where a million visitors each year get to see Peppa's world up close. Visitors can jump in muddy puddles, take a ride on Miss Rabbit's helicopter, and visit Peppa's house. Whether you're palling around with Peppa in Pig World or watching her show, you can be assured it will be lots of snorty fun!

GENRE:
Educational

AGE:
3+

SEASONS:
6 and counting

STARRING:
Lily Snowden-Fine,
John Sparkes,
Alice May,
Morwenna Banks,
Richard Ridings,
and
Oliver May

DID YOU KNOW?
Several different actors voice Peppa as she gets older throughout the series.

Saw it! ☐ Rating: ☆☆☆☆☆

Date: ___ / ___ / _____ With: _____

Notes: _____

_____

4

READING RAINBOW

GENRE:
Educational

AGE:
4+

SEASONS:
21

STARRING:
LeVar Burton

When this show first aired in 1983, some skeptics doubted whether TV was the best forum for encouraging reading. But 155 episodes and 26 Emmys later, *Reading Rainbow* proved that TV and reading do mix.

Produced and hosted by LeVar Burton, the show features interviews with a wide variety of authors, such as Maya Angelou and Pete Seeger. Celebs such as Whoopi Goldberg, Susan Sarandon, Martin Short, Helen Mirren, James Earl Jones, and Run DMC narrate each episode and sometimes make guest appearances. There are field trips and mini documentaries on topics such as dinosaurs, deserts, and recycling. In other segments, kids talk about their favorite books.

Each episode focuses on a theme. In one episode about emotions, LeVar talks about why he feels bad, a film about Koko the Gorilla, who was given a kitten when she felt sad, is shown, and an animated segment has kids reading poems about their feelings.

This long-running multicultural celebration of books features a wide variety of genres, cultures, and formats—making it a true reading rainbow!

DID YOU KNOW?

When the show went off the air, LeVar Burton bought the rights, hoping he could someday launch the series again. While the show hasn't returned to TV, Burton raised over $5 million to create the popular Reading Rainbow Skybrary app, which is filled with interactive books and videos.

Saw it! ☐   Rating: ☆☆☆☆☆
Date: ___/___/_____   With: _____
Notes: _____
_____

MISTER ROGERS' NEIGHBORHOOD

A landmark show, *Mister Rogers' Neighborhood* is a play date with Fred Rogers, a sweet-as-can-be neighbor who talks in the gentlest way. Viewers regularly feel like Mr. Rogers is coming home from work to spend some time with them. He comes through his door and speaks directly to the camera as he changes into his sneakers and cardigan sweater.

Mister Rogers' Neighborhood isn't hip, zany, or loud. It's not action packed or filled with quick cuts, stimulating motion, or flashing colors. Rather, it is an engaging show filled with honest communication and imagination. Rogers brings viewers along on field trips, demonstrates crafts or experiments, and visits with neighbors. One favorite feature is "The Neighborhood of Make-Believe," where viewers watch a toy trolley enter a kingdom populated by puppet characters like Cornflake S. Pecially and Daniel Striped Tiger. Providing a consistent routine for viewers by singing "Won't You Be My Neighbor?" at the beginning of each episode and "It's Such a Good Feeling" at the end, this is as cozy as TV gets!

GENRE:
Educational

AGE:
4+

SEASONS:
31

DID YOU KNOW?

Koko, a famous gorilla that communicates with scientists using American Sign Language, loves watching *Mister Rogers' Neighborhood* in her spare time. When Rogers visited Koko on his show, she knew exactly who he was and took his shoes off, just like he does at the beginning of each episode!

STARRING:
Fred Rogers

Saw it! ☐ Rating: ☆☆☆☆☆

Date: ___/___/_____ With: _____

Notes: _____

_____

6

THE ELECTRIC COMPANY

GENRE:
Educational

AGE:
5+

SEASONS:
6

STARRING:
Morgan Freeman,
Judy Graubart,
Skip Hinnant,
Rita Moreno, and
Jim Boyd

From the Children's Television Workshop comes a *Sesame Street* for the 1970s elementary-school set. Making use of sketch comedy, cartoons, and songs, the show teaches phonics, spelling, and grammar, while entertaining viewers long after they master these skills.

The show features many memorable characters. There's Fargo North, Decoder, a detective who has the ability to decode messages by making sentences out of jumbled words. Comedian Joan Rivers is part of the cast, as is Morgan Freeman, who plays Easy Reader, a smooth soul man who loves reading. Rita Moreno began her career on the show, and her loud holler, "Hey, you guys!" became the show's tagline. Other regular characters include Vincent the Vegetable Vampire, Lorelei the Chicken, and Pandora the Brat. The show even features guest stars such as Oscar the Grouch and Big Bird.

Each show is broken into mini episodes. Live-action skits parody popular soap operas, cooking shows, and monster movies. Whatever segment you love best, you'll finish every episode of *The Electric Company* thinking, "*Power on!*"

DID YOU KNOW?

The Electric Company included a regular segment called "Spidey Super Stories," where Spider-Man catches criminals and speaks through word balloons.

Saw it! ☐ Rating: ☆☆☆☆☆

Date: ___/___/_____ With: _____

Notes: _____

_____

WHERE IN THE WORLD IS CARMEN SANDIEGO?

7

A game show that makes geography fun for everyone, *Where in the World Is Carmen Sandiego?* is an international sensation based on a series of computer games. Contestants, called "gumshoes," are hired by the Acme Crime Detective Agency to track down one of Carmen Sandiego's henchmen.

In each episode, Carmen Sandiego, a "sticky-fingered filcher," and her gang of crooks circle the globe while host Greg Lee challenges three gumshoes to follow the clues and find the thieves. The skits, quizzes, and games are non-stop fun, and the stakes are high for each group of gumshoes—they are competing for a grand prize trip to anywhere in North America.

The show was the first game show to air on PBS, and also the second-longest-running game show for kids in TV history (beaten only by *Double Dare*). It received a Peabody award, several Emmys, and was ranked in the Top 50 Greatest Game Shows of All Time by *TV Guide*. The National Academy of Recording Arts and Sciences also says the show's theme song, written by Sean Altman and David Yazbek, is one of the most recognized TV theme songs in history.

GENRE:
Educational

AGE:
7+

SEASONS:
5

STARRING:
Greg Lee and
Rita Moreno

DID YOU KNOW?

In the early 1990s, borders were changing rapidly, so many episodes ended with a disclaimer saying "all geographic information was accurate as of the date this program was recorded."

Saw it! ☐ Rating: ☆☆☆☆☆
Date: ___/ ___/ _____ With: _____
Notes: _____
_____

8

SCHOOLHOUSE ROCK

GENRE:
Educational

AGE:
5+

SEASONS:
7

MADE BY:
David McCall
and Tom Yohe

*"I'm just a bill. Yes, I'm only a bill.
And I'm sitting here on Capitol Hill.
Well, it's a long, long journey to the capital city."*
—From the lyrics to "I'm Just a Bill"

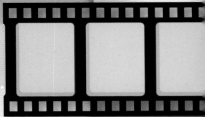

This iconic series was a stroke of educational programming genius. Airing between cartoons on Saturday mornings, the animated shorts feature songs that are so catchy, adults still sing them today. The songs teach concepts by pairing them with memorable characters and catchy lyrics. In "I'm Just a Bill," simple lessons explain how a bill becomes a law.

The program was created by David McCall, an ad man who noticed his son could remember all the lyrics to Beatles' songs but not his multiplication tables. Viewers can watch everything from "My Hero Zero" to "Naughty Number Nine" to learn their multiplication tables. *Grammar Rock* explains word usage and answers questions with songs like "Unpack Your Adjectives," "Lolly, Lolly, Lolly, Get Your Adverbs Here," and "A Noun Is A Person, Place Or Thing." With this show, whatever topic you're interested in, you'll find learning rocks!

SPIN-OFFS

America Rock
Multiplication Rock
Grammar Rock
Science Rock
Money Rock
Scooter Computer and Mr. Chips

DID YOU KNOW?

To coincide with the United States bicentennial in 1976, *Schoolhouse Rock* introduced *America Rock,* with segments on government and American history.

STARRING:
Jack Sheldon,
Darrell Stern,
and
Sue Manchester

NETWORK:
ABC, Disney

Saw it! ☐ Rating: ☆☆☆☆☆
Date: ___ / ___ / _____ With: _____
Notes: _____
_____

9

MYTHBUSTERS

GENRE:
Educational

AGE:
9+

SEASONS:
14

MADE BY:
Peter Rees

"I don't think our death ray is working.
I'm standing right in it and I'm not dead yet."
—Jamie Hyneman

MythBusters is a science show that takes learning out of the lab and into more dramatic settings. Two Hollywood special-effects experts, Jamie Hyneman and Adam Savage, conduct experiments to confirm or debunk urban legends. They use the scientific method, trial and error, and astute problem-solving skills to determine if myths and rumors are factually sound. Each episode results with a conclusion that labels a myth "busted," "plausible," or "confirmed." The humorous duo answers pressing questions: *Can tooth fillings receive radio waves? Can being covered with gold paint actually be deadly? Do frozen chickens cause more damage than thawed chickens when shot at a plane's windshield?*

The action-packed, bizarre experiments are always highly entertaining; there are car crashes, bangs, blasts, and pyrotechnics. Along the way, viewers learn a lot about science, exploring questions like: *exactly how many bacteria do reside on a toothbrush?* The hosts also tackle far-fetched plots from movies (*Can a person be really sucked down by killer quicksand?* Watch to find out!), and even construct the weirdest things. In one episode, Adam and Jamie are left on a deserted island with nothing but a pile of duct tape. They make a series of nifty devices, including a duct-tape canoe to get them home. Join the *MythBusters* as they put these wacky myths to the test!

STARRING:
Jamie Hyneman
and
Adam Savage

NETWORK:
Discovery
Channel

SPIN-OFFS
Head Rush
Search for the Next MythBusters

DID YOU KNOW?
The hosts have worked on special effects for a wide variety of popular movies, including *The Matrix* and *Star Wars* series.

Saw it! ☐ Rating: ☆☆☆☆☆

Date: ___/___/_____ With: _____

Notes: _____

_____

10 THE MUPPET SHOW

Waldorf: These seats are awful.
Statler: Why? Can't you see anything?
Waldorf: That's the problem. I can see everything.

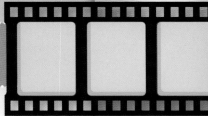

Preschoolers aren't the only people who adore Kermit and the fuzzy puppets from *Sesame Street*. *The Muppet Show* is a variety show in which the puppets do more than sing and dance. They play "real" actors who have off-stage lives and backstage crises. Kermit the Frog, always the most grown-up Muppet, is the producer who oversees the drama-filled cast, including Miss Piggy, a diva with lots of demands. The other Muppets include Fozzie Bear, who frequently performs really bad stand-up; Gonzo the Great, who does stunts; Rowlf the Dog; Scooter; Animal; and the house rock band, Dr. Teeth and The Electric Mayhem. The show features favorite sketches like "Muppet Melodrama," in which Miss Piggy is often in danger; "Pigs in Space," a *Star Trek* spoof; "Muppet Labs," which features Dr. Bunsen Honeydew's latest inventions (with frequent malfunctions); and "Muppet News Flash," an absurd news program.

Many of these skits and parodies are designed to appeal to viewers of all ages. Because of the vaudeville format, there's a great variety of acts, and the breezy pace keeps viewers' attention. Each episode features A-list human guest stars such as Elton John, Gene Kelley, Steve Martin, Harry Bellafonte, Roy Rodgers, and Rudolf Nureyev. The Muppets went on to star in a wildly entertaining collection of popular movies, and in 2015, a new take on the old series began airing on TV.

STARRING:
Puppeteers:
Jim Henson,
Frank Oz, and
Richard Hunt

NETWORK:
ITV

SPIN-OFFS

Muppet Babies
The Great Muppet Caper
The Muppets Take Manhattan
The Jim Henson Hour
Muppet Treasure Island
The Muppet Christmas Carol
Muppets from Space

DID YOU KNOW?
Kermit is the only Muppet character to appear on both *Sesame Street* and *The Muppet Show*.

Saw it! ☐   Rating: ☆☆☆☆☆
Date: ___ / ___ / _____   With: _____
Notes: _____
_____

11

FRAGGLE ROCK

GENRE:
Puppets

AGE:
6+

SEASONS:
5

MADE BY:
Jim Henson

Mokey Fraggle: It was rapturous!
Red Fraggle: Is rapturous the same as boring?
Wembley Fraggle: I don't think so.

Those who are hankering for more Muppets can let the music play (clap, clap)! *Fraggle Rock* introduces Fraggles, Doozers, and Gorgs, all new furry species created by Jim Henson. These cave-dwelling creatures inhabit a rock formation behind a hole in a garage that belongs to an eccentric inventor named Doc. The Fraggles call Doc's workshop "outer space," and try to avoid the "silly creatures," or humans, that live there. The Fraggles, Doozers, and Gorgs live in a complex society. Most Fraggles play a lot and work a little, while the tiny Doozers work a lot and play a little. Outside of Fraggle Rock, a family of giant Gorg trolls stomp carelessly, as they attempt to rule the universe, despite being simple farmers.

It's a loopy mix of characters, but they all depend on each other. Every episode uses a light touch to present themes of connection, responsibility, and teamwork. Story lines address identity, social conflict, prejudice, and the environment, but *Fraggle Rock* is also a silly musical with loads of energy and humor for both adults and kids. This show is a joy to watch—whether you're dancing your cares away down at Fraggle Rock or watching in your living room.

SPIN-OFFS

Fraggle Rock: The Animated Series
Jim Henson's Doozers

STARRING:
Gerard Parkes,
Karen Prell, and
Kathryn Mullen

NETWORK:
CBC, HBO

DID YOU KNOW?
The Fraggles were originally known as Woozles.
Jim Henson changed the name to avoid confusion with the
woozles in A.A. Milne's Winnie the Pooh stories.

Saw it! ☐ Rating: ☆☆☆☆☆
Date: ___/___/_____ With: _____
Notes: _____
_____

12

THE BRADY BUNCH

GENRE:
Sitcom

AGE:
7+

SEASONS:
5

MADE BY:
Sherwood
Schwartz

"All day long at school I hear how great Marcia is at this or how wonderful Marcia did that! Marcia, Marcia, Marcia!"
—Jan Brady

It's oh-so-1970s and more than a little corny, but this story of a lovely lady, a handsome fellow, and their blended family is a pioneering sitcom. Rather than presenting divorce and stepparents as something to be feared, the show features a family that makes building new relationships seem fun and easy. *The Brady Bunch*, which ran from 1969–1974, tells the story of a father with three sons who marries a mother of three girls. Robert Reed played Mike Brady, a successful architect in Southern California, and Florence Henderson played Carol Brady. She runs their large suburban home with the help of their wise-cracking, live-in housekeeper, Alice Nelson. The kids include Greg, the eldest; Peter, the mischievous one; and Bobby, the annoying little brother. There's also Marcia, who's super popular; Jan, who's jealous of her popular sister; and Cindy, the baby of the family.

During the show's five seasons, the kids' ages ranged from 7–18 years old. By including boys and girls of all ages, the show appeals to a wide audience and addresses almost any issue you can think of, from sibling rivalry, popularity, and independence to honesty and competition. And they also encounter some not-so-typical comic situations—like finding out that the only reason a talent agency wants to make you into a rock star is because you fit inside an ornate gold matador suit! Whatever episode you watch, this show is sure to give you lots of groovy giggles!

STARRING:
Robert Reed, Florence Henderson, Ann B. Davis, Barry Williams, Maureen McCormick, Christopher Knight, Eve Plumb, Mike Lookinland, and Susan Olsen

NETWORK:
ABC

SPIN-OFFS
The Brady Kids
The Brady Bunch Variety Hour
The Brady Girls Get Married
A Very Brady Christmas
The Bradys

DID YOU KNOW?
While there was often a camera in the Brady bathroom, the network censors never allowed the toilet to be shown.

Saw it! ☐ Rating: ☆☆☆☆☆

Date: ___ / ___ / _____ With: _____

Notes: _____

_____

13

BOY MEETS WORLD

GENRE:
Sitcom

AGE:
10+

SEASONS:
7

STARRING:
Ben Savage,
Rider Strong,
Danielle Fishel,
and
William Daniels

Growing up is never easy, but having true friends makes it easier. This show follows average kid and all-around good guy Cory Matthews from middle school through college. With his best friend, Shawn Hunter, by his side, Cory navigates friendships, school, and crushes. Free spirit Topanga Lawrence is Cory's super smart classmate, but could she be so much more?

Over seven seasons, the friends tackle being grounded, first kisses, bullying, and of course…prom. Even though things may not always go Cory's way, the relationships he depends on help him—and the viewers—learn valuable and relatable life lessons.

While the show wasn't raved about by critics, and never soared in the ratings, a generation of teens grew up devoted to Cory and his friends, and laughed and cried with them all the way to the series finale in 2000.

SPIN-OFFS
Girl Meets World

DID YOU KNOW?
Much of the show was filmed at John Marshall High School, where movies including *Pretty in Pink*, *Grease*, *Transformers*, and *Raiders of the Lost Ark* were filmed.

Saw it! ☐ Rating: ☆☆☆☆☆
Date: ___/___/_____ With: _____
Notes: _____
_____

GOOD TIMES

Even though the Evans family is poor and goes through plenty of hardships, they always manage to find the good times. Living in the projects of Chicago, James and Florida Evans do everything they can to make a good life for their three children, J.J., Michael, and Thelma. Michael is the scholarly one in the family—he learns all he can about African-American history, and later gets involved in politics. J.J. is the artistic one—he hopes to be an artist someday. Thelma is the voice of reason.

In the mid 1970s, *Good Times* was one of the first sitcoms to feature an African-American cast, providing a glimpse into the American family that audiences hadn't seen before. The issues the Evans struggle with, such as finding work and stretching every dollar to make ends meet, were familiar to many families at the time. Audiences could relate to the show—and laugh along with it too.

GENRE:
Sitcom

AGE:
10+

SEASONS:
6

STARRING:
Esther Rolle,
John Amos,
Jimmie Walker,
Ralph Carter,
BernNadette
Stanis, and
Ja'net DuBois

DID YOU KNOW?
As J.J., Jimmie Walker made his catchphrase, "DY-NO-MITE,"
a true pop-culture phenomenon!

Saw it! ☐ Rating: ☆☆☆☆☆
Date: ___ / ___ / _____ With: _____
Notes: _____
_____

15

THE FRESH PRINCE OF BEL-AIR

GENRE:
Sitcom

AGE:
11+

SEASONS:
6

MADE BY:
Andy Borowitz
and Susan
Borowitz

"Now this is a story all about how my life got flipped, turned upside down, And I'd like to take a minute, just sit right there, I'll tell you how I became the Prince of a town called Bel-Air..."
—From the classic theme song rapped by Will Smith

Will Smith stars in this fish-out-of-water series, playing a fictionalized version of himself as a teenager sent to live with his wealthy aunt and uncle and their three kids in Bel-Air, California. The new digs are meant to help Will get a better education and stay out of trouble, but the family ends up learning a thing or two about life from Will too.

The Fresh Prince provides much needed positive portrayals of African-American family life. Uncle Phil is a gruff-but-caring lawyer with experience fighting for civil-rights and lots of real-world lessons to share, while Aunt Viv is a career-minded mother and doctor. Carlton, their conservative, preppy son, couldn't be more different than Will. Ashley, the youngest daughter, connects more with the newest member of the family; in one episode, Will encourages her to quit violin and take up the drums after she reveals she doesn't enjoy playing it. Older sister Hilary is a shallow valley girl. The sarcastic butler, Geoffrey, and Will's friend, Jazz, add humor. The series also features a stellar list of guest stars including Whoopi Goldberg, Chris Rock, Dr. Dre, Kareem Abdul-Jabbar, BB King, Isaac Hayes, Queen Latifah, Oprah Winfrey, and many more.

This beloved show combines classic sitcom jokes with serious topics like racial profiling, robbery, and Will's relationship with his dad. Throughout the series, Smith's comedic timing and charisma shine. If you like watching him flash his famous movie-star smile, you'll love watching his career get started on the small screen.

STARRING:
Will Smith,
James Avery,
Janet Hubert,
Alfonso Ribeiro,
Karyn Parsons,
Tatyana Ali,
Joseph Marcell,
and
Daphne Reid

NETWORK:
NBC

DID YOU KNOW?

In 1994, President Donald Trump guest starred as himself. He was interested in buying the Banks' estate, but they decided not to sell.

Saw it! ☐ Rating: ☆☆☆☆☆

Date: ___/___/_____ With: _____

Notes: _____

_____

16

THE WONDER YEARS

GENRE:
Sitcom

AGE:
12+

SEASONS:
6

STARRING:
Fred Savage,
Dan Lauria,
Alley Mills,
Olivia d'Abo,
Jason Hervey,
Danica McKellar,
Josh Saviano,
and
Daniel Stern

This charming dramedy follows Kevin Arnold as he tackles growing up, from his first pimple to his first car. The show began airing in 1988, but it's set during the late 1960s, an era when values were changing and Americans faced political strife. The show also broke ground with an off-screen narrator who puts a lyrical spin on the wonders of childhood.

Fred Savage gives an impressive, authentic, often touching performance as Kevin, a sweet, slightly twerpy kid. Winnie Cooper, who goes from friend to girlfriend and back a few times during the span of the series, lives next door. Kevin's obnoxious older brother, Wayne, takes pleasure in tormenting Kevin and his nerdy best friend Paul. Sister Karen is a hippie who butts heads with their gruff father, a Korean War veteran. Mom Norma softens his edges.

While some episodes share plot points with other shows (school dances, dates, sports teams, math tests, cool kids, ethical dilemmas), *The Wonder Years* approaches these issues with nuanced humor, a thoughtful perspective, and high-quality storytelling.

DID YOU KNOW?

Danica McKellar, the actress who played Winnie, wrote a series of books to encourage girls to study math. *Math Doesn't Suck: How to Survive Middle School Math Without Losing Your Mind or Breaking a Nail* is the first title in the series.

Saw it! ☐ Rating: ☆☆☆☆☆

Date: ___ / ___ / _____ With: _____

Notes: _____

_____

BEWITCHED

17

Darrin Stephens thinks he's marrying an average girl—until his wife Samantha tells him on their honeymoon that she has a little secret…she's a witch! She promises Darrin she won't use her magical powers at home, but as their life together begins, Samantha finds it impossible to refrain from casting a few spells to help her family.

Their home on Morning Glory Circle in Westport, Connecticut is the home of many magical shenanigans. Samantha's mother, Endora, is also a witch and not particularly fond of her mortal son-in-law. Nosy neighbor Gladys Kravitz is always suspicious of Samantha, but she can never quite catch her crafting a spell. Darrin's boss Larry Tate is a frequent visitor, along with Samantha's identical cousin, Serena (also played by Elizabeth Montgomery). Most episodes feature Samantha casting a spell that somehow goes wrong. But she and Darrin are always able to solve the problem together, proving that love is a special kind of magic!

GENRE:
Sitcom

AGE:
7+

SEASONS:
8

STARRING:
Elizabeth Montgomery, Dick York, Dick Sargent, and Agnes Moorhead

DID YOU KNOW?

The opening credits were created by the famous animation team Hanna-Barbera, who developed *The Flintstones*, *The Jetsons*, *Scooby-Doo*, and *The Smurfs*!

Saw it! ☐ Rating: ☆☆☆☆☆

Date: ___/___/_____ With: _____

Notes: _____

_____

18

GILLIGAN'S ISLAND

GENRE:
Sitcom

AGE:
7+

SEASONS:
3

STARRING:
Bob Denver,
Alan Hale, Jr.,
Jim Backus,
Natalie Schafer,
Tina Louise,
Russell Johnson,
and
Dawn Wells

Originally airing in the mid 1960s, *Gilligan's Island* is a light-hearted, goofy comedy about castaways marooned on a deserted island. A skipper and his first mate, Gilligan, take five passengers sight seeing. But a tropical storm ruins what is meant to be "a three-hour tour," and the crew and the passengers must band together to survive.

The castaways send signals to passing boats and planes. They even make a raft. But invariably there's a snag, and it's usually due to one of Gilligan's bumbling blunders. When the survivors include everyone from a professor to a movie star, tensions can rise. But the crew and passengers work together to craft the comforts of home using bamboo, coconuts, and other island materials. With snazzy thatched-roof huts, cozy hammock beds, tropical drinks, a radio built from coconuts, and even a pedal-powered car, viewers can't help but think surviving on this island looks less like a shipwreck and more like a vacation!

SPIN-OFFS
The New Adventures of Gilligan

DID YOU KNOW?
Actor Alan Hale went to great lengths to audition for the role of the skipper. To get there he rode horseback, hitchhiked, took an airplane, and made the last leg of the trip in a taxi!

Saw it! ☐ Rating: ☆☆☆☆☆
Date: ___ / ___ / _____ With: _____
Notes: _____
_____

DIFF'RENT STROKES

Millionaire widower Phillip Drummond promises his housekeeper he will take care of her sons, no matter what. So when she passes away, he adopts 8-year-old Arnold and 12-year-old Willis. Moving into the 30th floor penthouse with their new guardian and new sister, 13-year-old Kimberly, is a big change for Arnold and Willis, but they come to love their new lifestyle. Calling them his sons and treating them like his own children, Mr. Drummond—along with his housekeeper Mrs. Garrett—helps Arnold and Willis learn some important lessons.

As the smart and lovable Arnold, Gary Coleman is the star of the show. He was 10 years old when the show started filming in 1978; Gary had caught producers' attention in a number of commercials, and the show was created with him in mind.

A popular show when it debuted, *Diff'rent Strokes* was one of the first shows to feature an interracial family, and the sitcom became known for episodes that tackled dramatic topics, such as racism and kidnapping. Through it all, laughter and love keep this unique family strong, no matter what differences they have to overcome.

SPIN-OFFS
The Facts of Life

DID YOU KNOW?
Future superstar Janet Jackson appears as Willis's girlfriend Charlene Duprey in several seasons of the show. Her hit single "Control" debuted while the show was still airing.

20

ALL IN THE FAMILY

GENRE:
Sitcom

AGE:
12+

SEASONS:
9

STARRING:
Carroll
O'Connor,
Jean Stapleton,
Rob Reiner, and
Sally Struthers

All in The Family revolves around a typical working class family from the 1970s. In each episode, Archie Bunker's outspoken bigotry clashes with his son-in-law, Mike Stivic's, liberal views. Archie's wife, Edith, can be a little dense—but she is also the moral and kind voice in the family. Gloria, Mike's wife and Archie and Edith's daughter, acts as the peacemaker.

Widely considered to be one of the most groundbreaking shows ever aired, *All in The Family* brought conversations about the current affairs of the 1970s into viewers' living rooms. Debates about politics, social change, race relations, and the changing roles of men and women are only some of the hot-button topics that producer Norman Lear served up at the Bunker family table.

All in the Family still stands as a prime-time example of how TV can entertain and educate all at the same time.

SPIN-OFFS

Archie Bunker's Place
Maude
The Jeffersons

DID YOU KNOW?

Producer Norman Lear said his father inspired many of Archie's best insults. "Meathead," "Dingbat," and "Stifle" were all things Lear heard his father say.

Saw it! ☐ Rating: ☆☆☆☆☆

Date: ___ / ___ / _____ With: _____

Notes: _____

_____

THE GOLDBERGS

21

Follow 11-year-old Adam Goldberg as he documents his crazy childhood with a totally rad video camera. Set in "1980-something" in suburban Pittsburgh, *The Goldbergs* is the story of super geek and pop-culture fan Adam and his family, which includes mother Beverly, who believes her kids can do anything and will protect them at all costs; hardworking Murray, a dad who enjoys walking around in his underwear; confident middle brother Barry; popular older sister Erica; and of course, Adam's best friend and grandpa, Pops, who gives good advice and doesn't take anything too seriously.

Getting (and keeping) a girlfriend, learning how to do magic, auditioning for a part in the school play, and getting lost at a Phillies game are just some of the hurdles Adam tries to overcome with the help (and sometimes hindrance) of his parents and siblings. *The Goldbergs* has been praised by critics and viewers alike for bringing back life in the 1980s in such a colorful—and hysterical—fashion.

GENRE:
Sitcom

AGE:
14+

SEASONS:
4 and counting

STARRING:
Wendi McLendon-Covey,
Sean Giambrone,
George Segal,
and
Jeff Garlin

DID YOU KNOW?

Every season, the show does an episode inspired by a famous 80s movie. So far, *The Goonies*, *Ferris Bueller's Day Off*, and *A Christmas Story* have all been featured.

Saw it! ☐ Rating: ☆☆☆☆☆

Date: ___/___/_____ With: _____

Notes: _____

_____

22

THE DICK VAN DYKE SHOW

GENRE:
Sitcom

AGE:
7+

SEASONS:
5

MADE BY:
Carl Reiner

"It just so happens that you don't
know me as well as I know me, because
I'm with myself almost constantly."
—Rob Petrie

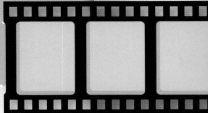

You may already know Dick Van Dyke from his movie roles in *Mary Poppins* and *Chitty Chitty Bang Bang*, but during the same time, this enormously talented actor, singer, dancer, and all-around funnyman was starring in a lovable sitcom.

The Dick Van Dyke Show was created by comic genius Carl Reiner and was partly based on his experience as a writer for *Your Show of Shows*, a variety show starring Sid Caesar. Van Dyke stars as Rob Petrie, head writer for a TV variety show. Mary Tyler Moore plays his wife, Laura, who wears capri pants and matches wits with Rob. They are vulnerable and loving characters who also stress out and obsess about little things, which leads to delightfully silly situations. In one great episode, Rob is convinced they brought the wrong baby home from the hospital. In another, he's convinced he's allergic to his family.

Rob and his staff spend the day writing skits, cracking jokes, mocking their producer, and trying to keep the show's difficult star happy. Much of *The Dick Van Dyke Show* takes place behind the scenes of a popular TV show where witty, creative people manage celebrities under the pressure of exhausting deadlines and show-biz kookiness. This sitcom feels fresher than others from the era because Rob and Laura are smart and sophisticated—and so is their humor.

SPIN-OFFS
The Dick Van Dyke Show Revisited

STARRING:
Dick Van Dyke,
Mary Tyler
Moore,
Rose Marie,
Morey
Amsterdam,
and
Larry Mathews

NETWORK:
CBS

DID YOU KNOW?
The network censors objected to Mary Tyler Moore wearing pants, and required her to wear dresses in most scenes—at least for the first few episodes!

Saw it! ☐   Rating: ☆☆☆☆☆

Date: ___ / ___ / _____ With: _____

Notes: _____

_____

23

FAMILY MATTERS

GENRE:
Sitcom

AGE:
8+

SEASONS:
9

STARRING:
Reginald
VelJohnson,
Jo Marie Payton,
Darius McCrary,
Kellie Shanygne
Williams, and
Jaleel White

Carl Winslow, a Chicago police officer, lives in the suburbs with his wife, Harriette, and their children, Eddie, Laura, and Judy. Carl tries his best to keep his family strong by teaching his kids to work hard and have good values. He's the dad everyone wishes they had, with the perfect mix of wisdom, reason, discipline, and humor.

But there's one character that can make him lose his good humor—the bumbling super geek, Stephen Urkel. Sporting his glasses, suspenders, and high-waisted pants, Urkel is about the most annoying neighbor you could ever have, even though he always means well. He never stops professing his love for Laura, trying to be friends with Eddie, or annoying Carl. He's guilty of accidentally burning down the local teen hangout, waking up the entire neighborhood while serenading Laura, and somehow knocking both Carl and Eddie off the roof. But through all the antics and misadventures, the Winslows—and Steve Urkel—show us that family really does matter.

DID YOU KNOW?

Originally, Urkel was written to be in just one episode; but the audience reaction was so positive that he was written in as a regular. He also made guest appearances on *Step by Step*, *Full House*, and *Meego*.

Saw it! ☐ Rating: ☆☆☆☆☆
Date: ___/___/_____ With: _____
Notes: _____

3RD ROCK FROM THE SUN

What if aliens landed on Earth, aka the third rock from the sun? Unlike the scary aliens we fear at the movies, the aliens that land on this show are ridiculous, utterly perplexed, and totally harmless.

John Lithgow plays Dick Solomon, the innocent commander who leads an expedition to Earth. He and his crew assume human forms and masquerade as a (very weird) family. Solomon assumes the form of a middle-aged man, but he's the youngest alien in his crew. Meanwhile Tommy, the eldest alien, assumes the body of a teenager, and has to deal with teen issues. The other "family members" are Sally, the second-in-command security officer, and Harry, the dim-witted communications officer.

Throughout the series, the gang tries to fit in, not blow their cover, and learn what they can about the human condition. Just like humans, these lovable aliens stumble through Earthling emotions. Whatever form they take, the crew on *3rd Rock* offers an unconventional, smart alternative in this down-to-earth sitcom.

GENRE:
Sitcom

AGE:
14+

SEASONS:
6

DID YOU KNOW?

3rd Rock from the Sun: The Official Report On Earth is a fictional book written by the Solomons about observations made during their stay on Earth.

STARRING:
John Lithgow,
Kristen Johnston,
French Stewart,
Joseph Gordon-Levitt,
and
Jane Curtin

Saw it! ☐ Rating: ☆☆☆☆☆

Date: ___ / ___ / _____ With: _____

Notes: _____

_____

25
THE ADVENTURES OF OZZIE & HARRIET

GENRE:
Sitcom

AGE:
6+

SEASONS:
14

STARRING:
Ozzie Nelson,
Harriet Nelson,
David Nelson,
and
Ricky Nelson

Started as a radio show in 1952, *The Adventures of Ozzie & Harriet* eventually became the longest-running live-action sitcom on American television. With over 434 episodes, this all-American show became the gold standard for family television.

Essentially playing themselves, the Nelson family used their own real lives—even their home and their neighbors—as inspiration for new episodes. Ozzie is a bandleader and musician, and Harriet is his "girl singer;" their sons Ricky and David grow up in front of the cameras over the course of the show.

The show is known for depicting America in the "good old days," when every house had a white picket fence, your neighbors were your best friends, and all your spare time was spent at the the malt shop in town. It's a true classic and will always be remembered as a snapshot of the ideal 1950s American family.

DID YOU KNOW?
The show blurred the lines between reality and fiction. When real-life Ricky wanted to become a drummer, the show featured an episode with the same theme. The teen's character performed the song "I'm Walkin,'" and Ricky sold a million real-life records that week!

SPIN-OFFS
Ozzie's Girls

Saw it! ☐ Rating: ☆☆☆☆☆
Date: ___/___/_____ With: _____
Notes: _____
_____

iCARLY

iCarly is a show within a show. Webcasting from her makeshift, third-floor loft studio, Carly and her best friends, Sam and Freddie, accidentally create a show that becomes an online sensation and an international hit.

Carly is laid back, smart, and gifted with the ability to get out of nearly any sticky situation. She's also super-smart and pretty laid-back. Her best friend and co-host, Sam, comes from a slightly unusual family and loves to eat. Freddie, who lives across the hall, is the tech-producer for the show. He's got a crush on Carly, and he's close with Carly's older brother and legal guardian, Spencer.

Set in Seattle, the show deals with typical teen adventures, such as boyfriends, detention, mean teachers, and talent shows. The webcast adds another layer to the show, as Carly, Sam, and Freddie host contests, interview guests, and answer fan questions. The *iCarly* crew always keeps it funny!

The show was a favorite of the Kids' Choice and Teen Choice Awards, and was nominated for an Emmy for Outstanding Children's Program five times. As the first show to include content kids wrote in the scripts, *iCarly* is definitely a part of TV history too. iThink you are absolutely going to want to see *iCarly*!

SPIN-OFFS

Sam & Cat

DID YOU KNOW?

Every episode title starts with "i," such as "iMust Have Locker 239" and "iMight Switch Schools."

GENRE:
Sitcom

AGE:
8+

SEASONS:
6

STARRING:
Miranda Cosgrove, Jerry Trainor, Jennette McCurdy, and Nathan Kress

Saw it! ☐ Rating: ☆☆☆☆☆

Date: ___ / ___ / _____ With: _____

Notes: _____

_____

27

ROSEANNE

GENRE:
Sitcom

AGE:
13+

SEASONS:
9

MADE BY:
Matt Williams
and
Roseanne Barr

Dan: Are you ever
sorry we got married?
Roseanne: Every second
of my life.
Dan: Me too.
Roseanne: You are, really?
Dan: [thinks] Nah.
Roseanne: OK,
me neither, then.

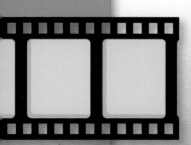

With nine seasons, four Emmys, three Golden Globes, four American Comedy Awards, a Peabody, and great ratings, *Roseanne* was a groundbreaking show. It was one of the first series about a struggling, working-class family, where both parents worked outside the home. It was also one of the first series to take a female perspective.

Roseanne is a big, brassy, hardworking woman with an in-your-face personality and a quick wit. The comedy follows the Conners, a loving couple with three kids. But *nothing* is sugar coated; the family fights and bickers, the parents yell at their kids, and the kids yell back. And these aren't just silly sitcom misunderstandings; the characters fight about important topics. But with all the stress, tension, and chaos, *Roseanne* manages to be a truly funny show.

Roseanne works on an assembly line and goes on to have a series of menial jobs, while her husband, Dan, works in construction. Roseanne's sister, Jackie, flounders to find a decent job and a suitable relationship. Daughter Darlene is a tomboy who refuses to conform to society's definition of a proper young lady. Her older sister Becky is an overachiever, but also a bit of a rebel, and eventually runs away with her biker boyfriend. DJ is the youngest. Paychecks are precarious, and money is always a concern. All the characters are cynical and sarcastic, but they also show each other real affection and loyalty, while cracking jokes and making fun of one another.

STARRING:
Roseanne Barr,
John Goodman,
Laurie Metcalf,
Sara Gilbert,
Michael Fishman,
Alicia Goranson,
and
Sarah Chalke

NETWORK:
ABC

DID YOU KNOW?
Roseanne was filmed on the same stage as *Gilligan's Island*, *Mary Tyler Moore*, and *That 70s Show*!

Saw it! ☐ Rating: ☆☆☆☆☆
Date: ___/___/_____ With: _____
Notes: _____
_____

28

EVERYBODY HATES CHRIS

GENRE:
Sitcom

AGE:
12+

SEASONS:
4

STARRING:
Tyler James Williams,
Terry Crews,
Tichina Arnold,
Tequan Rich-mond,
Imani Hakim,
and
Vincent Martella

Like *The Wonder Years*, this show is narrated by an adult version of the main character, a plucky boy in middle school. But this show is about an urban African-American family, rather than a suburban white family, and the edgier tone reflects their difficult experiences.

Throughout the series, comedian Chris Rock brings his cynical sense of humor to his memories of childhood. And there's often a funny disparity between what young Chris tells his parents and what adult Chris Rock confesses to viewers.

Chris's strict parents, Julius and Rochelle, reprimand their kids, but they strive to keep them safe and honest while helping them steer clear of the crime that surrounds them. Chris's parents send him to a safer school two hours away, but whether he's there or in his neighborhood, his moral compass is always spinning as he encounters bullies, thieves, and police, as well as typical teen concerns. Some story lines include heavy topics, but Chris Rock's commentary always keeps each episode playful and fun. And lines like "I'll slap da caps off ya knees!" make the other characters just as memorable.

DID YOU KNOW?
The show is set in the 1980s, even though Chris Rock actually grew up the 1970s, because there were already so many shows set in the 1970s.

Saw it! ☐ Rating: ☆☆☆☆☆
Date: ___/___/_____ With: _____
Notes: _____
_____

THE ANDY GRIFFITH SHOW

29

Premiering in 1960, *The Andy Griffith Show* earned its place in TV history as the perfect depiction of life in a sleepy, small town in middle America.

The show follows widowed sheriff Andy Taylor and his young son, Opie, as they live their lives in the fictional town of Mayberry, North Carolina. It's Andy's job to deal with the town's troublemakers, and he always doles out justice fairly. Whatever the crime at hand, there are also plenty of laughs along the way, especially when bumbling deputy Barney is involved. Since not much crime happens in Mayberry, Andy has plenty of time on his hands to reflect and offer advice to the locals. He also loves taking Opie fishing and spending quiet evenings at home on the porch. Extremely popular throughout its eight-season run, *The Andy Griffith Show* influenced a generation of viewers, and has been on the air, between prime time and syndication, for more than 50 years!

SPIN-OFFS

Gomer Pyle, U.S.M.C
Mayberry R.F.D.

GENRE:
Sitcom

AGE:
6+

SEASONS:
8

DID YOU KNOW?

Unlike other sitcoms of its time, *The Andy Griffith Show* was filmed on location, rather than in a studio.

STARRING:
Andy Griffith,
Ron Howard,
and
Don Knotts

Saw it! ☐   Rating: ☆☆☆☆☆
Date: ___/___/_____   With: _____
Notes: _____
_____

30

MODERN FAMILY

GENRE:
Sitcom

AGE:
13+

SEASONS:
8 and counting

MADE BY:
Christopher
Lloyd and
Steven Levitan

"I've always said that if my son thinks of me as one of his idiot friends, I've succeeded as a dad."
—Phil Dunphy

Today families may look a little different than they did 50 or 100 years ago. *Modern Family* highlights these differences for laughs, and the result is a thought provoking show for parents and kids who like to watch quality TV together.

Featuring smart writing and an A-list cast, *Modern Family* is a clever, goofy, character-based comedy. The show follows three very different households in the Pritchett family. Jay Pritchett is a curmudgeonly father of two adult children and a new baby, a stepfather, *and* a grandfather. His second wife, Gloria, a wise, strong-willed Colombian, is younger than Jay's own daughter and has a precocious son, Manny, from a previous marriage. Jay's eldest son, Mitchell, is married to Cam, and they have a daughter, Lily, whom they adopted from Vietnam. Mitchell's sister Claire is married to Phil Dunphy, and they have three kids: Haley, the popular one; Alex, the smart one; and Luke, the weird one.

This loving and hilariously imperfect brood represents a wide variety of marriage and parenting styles. Siblings Claire and Mitchell are tightly wound and rigid like their dad, while their partners Phil, Cam, and Gloria have much more fun-loving personalities. It's a lot to keep track of, but the memorable characters make it easy to get to know this family. With this show, 12 characters + 1 modern family = lots of laughs!

STARRING:
Ed O'Neill,
Sofía Vergara,
Julie Bowen,
Ty Burrell,
Jesse Tyler Ferguson,
Eric Stonestreet,
Sarah Hyland,
Ariel Winter,
Nolan Gould,
Rico Rodriguez,
and
Aubrey Anderson-Emmons

NETWORK:
ABC

DID YOU KNOW?
Each season of *Modern Family* features a vacation. The family has been to Disneyland, a dude ranch, Hawaii, and Las Vegas—and none of the trips have gone quite as planned!

Saw it! ☐ Rating: ☆☆☆☆☆

Date: ___/___/_____ With: _____

Notes: _____

_____

31

THE JEFFERSONS

GENRE:
Sitcom

AGE:
11+

SEASONS:
11

STARRING:
Isabel Sanford,
Sherman
Hemsley,
Marla Gibbs,
Roxie Roker,
Franklin Cover,
and
Paul Benedict

A spin-off of *All in The Family*, *The Jeffersons* follows the Bunkers' African-American neighbors who, as the theme song says, "moved on up" from Queens to Manhattan. George Jefferson, the owner of an expanding chain of dry-cleaning stores, was the thorn in racist Archie Bunker's side. Now George boasts about being rich, and much of the show's comedy comes from his tantrums. He's a small man with an arrogant, combative disposition. But his wife Louise is feisty, and knows how to stand up to her husband. There is also their housekeeper, Florence the wise-cracking maid, who often ridicules her boss, and other eccentric characters, such as British neighbor Harry Bentley.

The show frequently addresses issues of class and race, such as a prosperous African-American family being stereotyped as disadvantaged. Families watching this show will also want to take time to talk about the uncensored use of racial expletives. But mostly, there's lots of light humor with typical sitcom misunderstandings.

Over 30 years after it first aired, it's still great to watch a show that features African-Americans and doesn't traffic in stereotypes, leading the way for everyone to "move on up."

DID YOU KNOW?
George's neighbors, Helen and Tom Willis, were one of the first interracial couples on TV.

SPIN-OFFS
Checking In

Saw it! ☐ Rating: ☆☆☆☆☆
Date: ___ / ___ / _____ With: _____
Notes: _____
_____

FRESH OFF THE BOAT

32

One of the first prime-time shows to feature an Asian-American family, *Fresh Off the Boat* is based on actor/writer Eddie Huang's experiences growing up. Eddie's Taiwanese family relocates from Washington DC's Chinatown to Orlando, Florida in the 1990s to pursue the American Dream. But it's not as easy to fit in as they thought it would be.

The show begins when Eddie is 11 years old. Everyone in the family is trying to make friends, win the respect of their new neighbors, and fit in with the community. Eddie's mother, Realtor and go-getter Jessica, runs the show, while dad Louis manages the family restaurant with spotty success. Eddie is a cool, confident guy who loves Biggie Smalls and rap. He wants his first school dance to be as awesome as a John Hughes movie, but sometimes his strict parents get in the way.

Fresh Off the Boat is a hit with viewers, and was nominated for a slew of awards. The series pushes viewers to think about race, but this isn't just must-see TV because it's an important show—it's also hilarious to watch!

DID YOU KNOW?

The real Eddie Huang is a famous chef who owns BaoHaus, a Taiwanese bun restaurant in New York City.

GENRE:
Sitcom

AGE:
12+

SEASONS:
3 and counting

STARRING:
Randall Park, Constance Wu, and Hudson Yang

Saw it! ☐ Rating: ☆☆☆☆☆
Date: ___ / ___ / _____ With: _____
Notes: _____
_____

33

THE PARTRIDGE FAMILY

GENRE:
Sitcom

AGE:
7+

SEASONS:
4

MADE BY:
Bernard Slade

"C'mon, get happy!"
—From the classic theme song

If you liked *The Brady Bunch*, *The Partridge Family* is even groovier! This 1970s show is full of bell-bottom jeans, guitars, and eye-popping color schemes. The Partridges aren't just a family; they're a pop band fronted by shaggy-haired teen-heartthrob Keith Partridge. Also in the family band are headstrong Laurie, sarcastic Danny, the younger Chris and Tracy, and their single mom Shirley Partridge.

The show and the music offer fluffy fun. The family band tours in their iconic painted school bus, while girls chase behind after Keith. Life on the road often produces memorable mishaps, including the gang bathing in tomato juice when a skunk sprays them before a gig, or the kids trying to play matchmaker for their mother and their manager, Ruben. While the TV band's catchy songs were mostly lip-synced, their music was popular in real life and often played on the radio. Their hit song "I Think I Love You" reached Number 1 on the charts in 1970. Fan crushes, sibling rivalry, high-school shenanigans, coping with fame, and the band's career kept the show humming along for four happy seasons.

SPIN-OFFS

Partridge Family 2200 A.D.
Thanksgiving Reunion with The Partridge Family and My Three Sons

STARRING:
Shirley Jones, David Cassidy, Danny Bonaduce, Susan Dey, Suzanne Crough, Brian Forster, and Dave Madden

NETWORK:
ABC

DID YOU KNOW?
Real life mirrored art when teen heartthrob David Cassidy played fictional teen heartthrob Keith Partridge. Girls were gaga for both.

Saw it! ☐ Rating: ☆☆☆☆☆
Date: ___/___/_____ With: _____
Notes: _____
_____

34

PUNKY BREWSTER

GENRE:
Sitcom

AGE:
8+

SEASONS:
4

STARRING:
Soleil Moon
Frye,
George
Gaynes,
and
Cherie
Johnson

At just 8 years old, perky Penelope "Punky" Brewster is an orphan. Luckily, she meets Henry Warnimont, an elderly widower who's a bit grumpy, but grows to love Punky. Her best friend is 8-year-old Cherie Johnson, who lives upstairs with her grandmother Betty. She also loves to hang out with her friend Allen, who's a bit of a geek, and Margaux, who comes from a very wealthy family.

With her colorful wardrobe and persistently optimistic attitude, Punky looks at life through a rainbow-colored lens. Whether she's going fishing with Henry, having a sleepover with Cherie and Margaux, or going on an adventure with her dog, Brandon, Punky uses her "Punky Power" to brave any trouble that arises. And even though he's never raised a child, Henry does his best to be the kind of foster parent that Punky can be proud of. They may not have a family like everyone else's, but Punky and Henry prove that loyalty and love are what make a family work, as they teach each other about kindness, friendship, and making the best of any difficult situation.

SPIN-OFFS
It's Punky Brewster

DID YOU KNOW?
Candace Cameron (who plays D.J. in *Full House*) is in an episode of *Punky Brewster* as Punky's new neighbor.

Saw it! ☐ Rating: ☆☆☆☆☆
Date: ___/___/_____ With: _____
Notes: _____
_____

WHO'S THE BOSS?

35

One of the most popular sitcoms of the 1980s, *Who's The Boss?* tells the story of a retired baseball player, Tony Micelli, and his daughter, Samantha, who come to live with a wealthy family in Connecticut. Tony applies to be busy advertising-executive Angela Bower's live-in housekeeper, and while at first she is thrown off by the idea of a guy cleaning her house, Angela warms to the idea once she sees how Tony gets along with her mom, Mona, and her son, Jonathan.

Over eight seasons, as Sam and Jonathan grow up, Tony and Angela create their own kind of family, even though they're not married. Tony's laid-back cool balances Angela's stricter, more uptight parenting style, and together, they make the perfect match. Together the family tackles big and small questions: *Will Sam be the next prima ballerina? Will Jonathan gain the confidence he needs? Is that a little romance brewing between Tony and Angela?* And *who really IS the boss in this family?* You'll have to watch to find out!

DID YOU KNOW?

Versions of *Who's the Boss?* have been produced in several countries around the world, including England, France, Germany, Mexico, Italy, and Russia.

SPIN-OFFS

Living Dolls
Charmed Lives

GENRE:
Sitcom

AGE:
8+

SEASONS:
8

STARRING:
Tony Danza,
Judith Light,
Alyssa Milano,
Danny Pintauro,
and
Katherine
Helmond

Saw it! ☐ Rating: ☆☆☆☆☆
Date: ___/ ___/ _____ With: _____
Notes: _____
_____

36 HAPPY DAYS

GENRE:
Sitcom

AGE:
7+

SEASONS:
11

MADE BY:
Gary Marshall

"Eyyy"
—Fonzie

A nostalgic depiction of the 1950s, *Happy Days* was a long-running series that began airing in 1974. The show follows a group of all-American teenagers who hang out at Arnold's Drive-In, dance to the jukebox, and navigate dating, parents, and high school—while trying to appear as cool as possible.

Ron Howard plays Richie Cunningham, a wholesome, freckle-faced kid who is part of a typical, middle-class, suburban family. Throughout the series, he tries to balance being a good kid with being a socially successful teen. Since the show ran for almost a decade, its focus transformed from a charming look at youth culture to a broader comedy with more antics and bigger laughs. Richie hangs out with his best friends Potsie, Ralph, and a greaser named Fonzie. While the show revolves around Richie, his family, and friends, Fonzie, played by Henry Winkler, is the breakout star. Always wearing his white T-shirt and black leather jacket, Fonzie is the tough guy with a heart of gold. His success with the ladies is legendary, and his magical ability to whack a jukebox and make it play earns him a mythic reputation as the coolest of the cool. Though the show discusses difficult topics like racism and the Cold War, these subjects are addressed with a light touch. In this feel-good show, jokes and one-liners are always the priority.

STARRING:
Ron Howard,
Marion Ross,
Anson Williams,
Tom Bosley,
Henry Winkler,
Don Most, and
Erin Moran

NETWORK:
ABC

SPIN-OFFS

Laverne & Shirley
Blansky's Beauties
Mork & Mindy
Out of the Blue
Joanie Loves Chachi
The Fonz and the Happy Days Gang

DID YOU KNOW?

The Fonz became so popular that after the first few seasons, the network considered renaming the show *Fonzie's Happy Days* or *Fonzie*.

Saw it! ☐ Rating: ☆☆☆☆☆

Date: ___ / ___ / _____ With: _____

Notes: _____

37

MALCOLM IN THE MIDDLE

GENRE:
Sitcom

AGE:
13+

SEASONS:
7

STARRING:
Bryan Cranston,
Jane Kaczmarek,
and
Frankie Muniz

Malcolm has a photographic memory and an IQ of 165. But even a super-smart 10-year-old kid can have a dysfunctional family. His mom, Lois, is a teeny bit overbearing, while his dad, Hal, is a tad clueless. Malcolm is the middle child, and he and his family live in a typical American suburban neighborhood.

The show doesn't have a "laugh track," and it frequently allows the characters to "break the fourth wall" and address viewers directly through the camera. Malcolm's monologues give viewers insight into his "aha" moments and more details about his lovable and quirky family. He goes through what every American kid navigates: bullies, babysitting, pranks, and parental injustices. But he's also trying to contend with what it means to be a genius and how it sometimes stinks to be good at everything. Through it all, the family's unpredictable hijinks are hysterical.

The show received rave reviews and several Emmys at a time when everyone thought the classic sitcom was dead. A surprise hit, the show is now a time capsule for American family life in the early 2000s, and definitely deserves a spot on your must-see list!

DID YOU KNOW?
Malcolm's family doesn't have an official last name. It was briefly mentioned as "Wilkerson" in the pilot episode, but it was never used again. Producers jokingly referred to them on set as the "Nolastname" family.

Saw it! ☐ Rating: ☆☆☆☆☆
Date: ___/___/_____ With: _____
Notes: _____
_____

LEAVE IT TO BEAVER

38

A black-and-white series that premiered in 1957, *Leave It to Beaver* is about a young boy and his family. Beaver's mom, June, is the perfect 1950s mom; she's constantly dressed up in high heels and pearls, even when she's cleaning the house, and she always seems to have a plate of cookies and milk available for the kids. Beaver's dad, Ward, works hard and doles out fair, reasonable discipline to his boys. Wally, Beaver's older brother, is a popular jock who often defends his little brother.

Leave It to Beaver was one of the first prime-time shows to be told from a kid's perspective. But *Leave It to Beaver* is truly a show about family; in most episodes, Beaver or Wally has a problem that June and Ward help with. Their adventures are captured with a sense of fun, and the show has proven to stand the test of time, with many fans, new and old, loving *Leave It to Beaver*.

DID YOU KNOW?

Theodore is called "Beaver" by his family because when Wally was younger, he tried saying "Theodore," and it came out sounding like "Beaver!"

GENRE:
Sitcom

AGE:
6+

SEASONS:
6

STARRING:
Barbara
Billingsley,
Jerry Mathers,
Hugh Beaumont,
and
Tony Dow

Saw it! ☐ Rating: ☆☆☆☆☆

Date: ___/___/_____ With: _____

Notes: _____

_____

39

FAMILY TIES

GENRE:
Sitcom

AGE:
11+

SEASONS:
7

MADE BY:
Gary David
Goldberg

"Mom, I need to reevaluate my life. Do you have a minute?"
—Mallory Keaton

The *Family Ties* premise gives traditional sitcoms a funny switcheroo. In the Keaton household, parents Steven and Elyse hope to share their liberal values with their kids, but instead they always seem to butt heads with their conservative son. While it's always light-hearted, this series demonstrates the clash between ideology from the 1960s and the 1980s.

Alex P. Keaton, the sweater-vest-and-tie-wearing teenager played by Michael J. Fox, gives the show its charm. Much of the plot revolves around Alex's plans to attend an Ivy League college and take over the world. He often mocks his sister, Mallory, who's more interested in boys and shopping than school and power. There's also youngest sister, Jennifer, and in the fifth season, Elyse gives birth to baby Andy. Amidst the comedy (much of it related to Alex's high-strung nature), the show tackles a lot of serious topics.

Unlike other 1980s sitcoms, *Family Ties* relies more on wit and character-based humor than punch lines, slapstick, and corny comedy. And viewers can rest easy knowing, while the Keatons clash over politics or quirks in personality, these family ties are strong enough to withstand any differences.

STARRING:
Meredith Baxter,
Michael Gross,
Michael J. Fox,
Justine Bateman,
Tina Yothers,
and
Brian Bonsall

NETWORK:
NBC

DID YOU KNOW?
The Keaton parents, Elyse and Steven, were originally conceived as the show's focus, but Michael J. Fox's charisma and humor stole the show.

Saw it! ☐ Rating: ☆☆☆☆☆

Date: ___/___/_____ With: _____

Notes: _____

_____

40

FULL HOUSE

GENRE:
Sitcom

AGE:
7+

SEASONS:
8

STARRING:
John Stamos,
Bob Saget,
Dave Coulier,
Candace
Cameron Bure,
Jodie Sweetin,
Mary-Kate Olsen,
Ashley Olsen,
and
Lori Loughlin

When Danny Tanner's wife dies in a tragic accident, he suddenly needs help raising his three daughters, D.J., Stephanie, and Michelle. His brother-in-law Jesse and best friend Joey move in, and the three men do their best to advise, guide, and support the three girls. And they have a whole lot of fun along the way!

Cool Uncle Jesse is a musician, Joey is a stand-up comedian, and Danny is a sportscaster who later becomes a morning talk-show host. The smart and practical D.J. (whose nickname is short for Donna Jo) is the oldest daughter. She's best friends with her next-door neighbor, Kimmy Gibbler. Sarcastic middle daughter Stephanie is a wee bit nosy, with a talent for snooping in her sister's business, and prone to exclaiming catchphrases like "How rude!" and "Hot dog!" Youngest daughter Michelle, played by famous twins Mary-Kate and Ashley Olsen, also has a ton of memorable catchphrases, including "You got it, dude!" and "You're in big trouble, mister!"

This show is a classic 1980s sitcom! Three men trying to take care of three growing girls leads to a bunch of misadventures and misunderstandings, but the bond between this family is truly touching.

SPIN-OFFS
Fuller House

DID YOU KNOW?
Though the show is set in San Francisco, it was filmed in Los Angeles. Only the opening credits and one episode in season eight were shot in San Fran!

Saw it! ☐ Rating: ☆☆☆☆☆
Date: ___/___/_____ With: _____
Notes: _____
_____

THE FACTS OF LIFE

The Facts of Life was one of the longest running sitcoms of the 1980s. Over nine seasons, the girls who live at Eastland Academy—a boarding school for girls—go through everything together, from falling in love to learning to drive. There's Blair, the rich, bratty girl; Jo, the tough girl from the Bronx; Natalie, the wide-eyed innocent one; and Tootie, the youngest who loves her roller skates. Watching over them is housemother Mrs. Garrett—former housekeeper from *Diff'rent Strokes*. She always has a hug and some seasoned advice to offer the girls.

  The Facts of Life was also known for its more serious episodes, which tackle topics like drug abuse, eating disorders, and peer pressure. Through it all, the Eastland girls show us that friendship is the key to taking the bad with the good and being happy as you learn the facts of life.

GENRE:
Sitcom

AGE:
11+

SEASONS:
9

STARRING:
Charlotte Rae,
Lisa Whelchel,
Kim Fields,
Mindy Cohn,
and
Nancy McKeon

DID YOU KNOW?

Two modern movie stars appeared on *The Facts of Life:* George Clooney and Molly Ringwald. And both were fired from the show!

Saw it! ☐ Rating: ☆☆☆☆☆
Date: ___/___/_____ With: _____
Notes: _____
_____

42

THE ADDAMS FAMILY

GENRE:
Sitcom

AGE:
8+

SEASONS:
2

STARRING:
Carolyn Jones,
John Astin,
Jackie Coogan,
Ted Cassidy,
Blossom Rock,
Ken Weatherwax,
and
Lisa Loring

As *The Addams Family's* memorable theme song explains, "they're creepy and they're kooky, mysterious and spooky, they're all together ooky…" *The Addams Family* was a refreshingly weird alternative to the sugary, all-American families of retro TV.

Inspired by characters created by *New Yorker* cartoonist Charles Addams, the black-and-white sitcom follows a ghoulish family and their eerie friends, including a butler who looks like Frankenstein; Cousin Itt, who is covered in hair; and a helpful, disembodied hand named Thing. The characters are as weird as can be, but the audience knows they mean no harm. Despite their macabre tastes, the family loves and supports one another. And they're kind to strangers, even if their hospitality might include scary touches like a bed of nails. This spooky series was short lived, but many years later it's still beloved by those who wandered into the Addams family's weird world.

DID YOU KNOW?
To make Cousin Itt's voice, the producer spoke gibberish into a tape recorder and played it back at a higher speed.

SPIN-OFFS

Addams Family Values
Addams Family Reunion
The Addams Family Broadway Musical
The New Addams Family

Saw it! ☐ Rating: ☆☆☆☆☆
Date: ___ / ___ / _____ With: _____
Notes: _____
_____

THE MUNSTERS

43

The Munsters might seem like a copycat of *The Addams Family*, but in fact, the two series about ghoulish families aired at the same time, and *The Munsters* drew a larger audience. Both shows are a send-up of the corny all-American sitcoms of the previous decade. The characters differ though; the Addams are spooky and ooky humans, while the Munsters are actually supernatural.

Herman Munster is a lumbering, clumsy Frankenstein-style monster prone to temper tantrums. He drives a hearse and works as a gravedigger. His wife, Lily, manages the family and the household—sometimes with the help of a little magic. The couple, who married over a hundred years ago, live in a crumbling Victorian house on Mockingbird Lane with their son, Eddie; Lily's father, Sam Dracula; and Lily's niece, Marilyn. Like the Addams family, the Munsters don't understand why others are frightened of them, which of course means funny shenanigans ensue. The show's makeup and costumes are wonderfully fun, and the ghoulish humor tickles instead of chills the bones.

SPIN-OFFS

The Munsters Today
Munster, Go Home!
The Mini-Munsters
The Munsters' Revenge
Here Come the Munsters

GENRE:
Sitcom

AGE:
8+

SEASONS:
2

STARRING:
Fred Gwynne,
Yvonne De Carlo,
Al Lewis,
Pat Priest, and
Butch Patrick

Saw it! ☐ Rating: ☆☆☆☆☆
Date: ___/___/_____ With: _____
Notes: _____
_____

44

I LOVE LUCY

GENRE:
Sitcom

AGE:
6+

SEASONS:
6

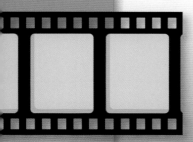

MADE BY:
Lucille Ball and
Desi Arnaz

DID YOU KNOW?
I Love Lucy has never *not* been on TV. New episodes ran from 1951 to 1957 on CBS, and it has aired in syndication ever since.

"Lucy, you got some 'splainin' to do!"
—Ricky Ricardo

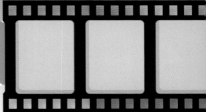

People can't help going nuts for *I Love Lucy!* Many say it's the best sitcom of all time. While other black-and-white TV shows from the 1950s might seem stale or corny today, the comic genius of Lucille Ball has made her show a favorite for over 50 years.

The show featured Lucy and her real-life husband, Desi Arnaz, as Ricky Ricardo, a famous Cuban entertainer. William Frawley and Vivian Vance played Fred and Ethel Mertz, the Ricardos' best friends and neighbors. But the real star was Lucy's brilliant physical comedy. In one famous episode, Lucy and Ethel bet their husbands that going to work is easier than staying at home. They take a job in a chocolate factory but can't keep up with the assembly line that just keeps going faster and faster. When things go haywire, the chocolates start stacking up. They try stuffing them in their hats—and even in their mouths. The scene is totally ridiculous and unforgettably funny.

Many episodes centered on Lucy trying to trick or plead with Ricky into letting her do or buy something. But the show is also about friendship and being yourself, even when you're a bit of an odd ball. In the show, Lucy's cockamamie schemes often wind up backfiring. But hilarity always ensues! No laugh track needed.

In real life, Lucille Ball was a pioneering comedienne with an unsurpassed talent for slapstick and funny faces. But she was more than a clown. She was also a successful businesswoman and the first woman in television to lead a production company.

STARRING:
Lucille Ball,
Desi Arnaz,
William Frawley,
and
Vivian Vance

NETWORK:
CBS

SPIN-OFFS
The Lucy–Desi Comedy Hour
The Lucy Show
Here's Lucy
Life with Lucy

Saw it! ☐ Rating: ☆☆☆☆☆
Date: ___/___/_____ With: _____
Notes: _____
_____

45

SAVED BY THE BELL

GENRE:
Sitcom

AGE:
9+

SEASONS:
4

STARRING:
Mark-Paul
Gosselaar,
Mario Lopez,
Dustin Diamond,
Lark Voorhies,
Tiffani Theissen,
and
Elizabeth
Berkley

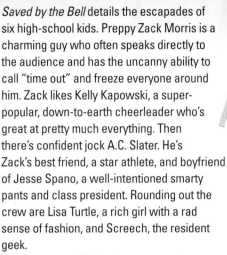

Saved by the Bell details the escapades of six high-school kids. Preppy Zack Morris is a charming guy who often speaks directly to the audience and has the uncanny ability to call "time out" and freeze everyone around him. Zack likes Kelly Kapowski, a super-popular, down-to-earth cheerleader who's great at pretty much everything. Then there's confident jock A.C. Slater. He's Zack's best friend, a star athlete, and boyfriend of Jesse Spano, a well-intentioned smarty pants and class president. Rounding out the crew are Lisa Turtle, a rich girl with a rad sense of fashion, and Screech, the resident geek.

Everyone can find a character to relate to, and the crew's shenanigans are pretty hilarious. Favorite episodes include the gang pairing off into husband-and-wife teams for home-ec class, the students taking Mr. Belding's place as the principal, and a telethon at the friends' favorite diner. *Saved by the Bell*'s wild popularity make it one for the yearbooks!

DID YOU KNOW?
The set the show was filmed on still exists. It has also been used in shows like *That's So Raven* and *iCarly!*

SPIN-OFFS
Saved by the Bell: The College Years
Saved by the Bell: The New Class

Saw it! ☐ Rating: ☆☆☆☆☆
Date: ___ / ___ / _____ With: _____
Notes: _____
_____

WELCOME BACK, KOTTER

46

In this 1970s series, Gabe Kotter returns to the inner-city high school of his youth to teach a group of unruly, remedial students called the "Sweathogs."

Based on star Gabe Kaplan's real-life experience as a student in a Brooklyn, New York school, the show features a variety of characters, all based on Kaplan's classmates; wise-cracking ladies' man Vinnie Barbarino is the leader of the pack, while Arnold Horshack is the jokester. Freddie "Boom Boom" Washington is the jock of the group, and Juan Epstein is small in stature but tough in nature. Kotter's job is to teach this group of "Sweathogs" more than just what's in the lesson plan; he also helps them sort out bad grades, disagreements, and their futures.

Welcome Back, Kotter features then-rising star John Travolta. Lunch boxes, action figures, and comic books were all created featuring the show's characters and punchlines. It's no wonder the show was such a hit; the Sweathogs and Mr. Kotter show us how some wise guys can actually learn some valuable (and hilarious) lessons from a great teacher.

GENRE:
Sitcom

AGE:
9+

SEASONS:
4

STARRING:
Gabe Kaplan, Marcia Strassman, John Travolta, Ron Palillo, Robert Hegyes, and Lawrence Hilton-Jacobs

DID YOU KNOW?

This show made the catchphrase "up your nose with a rubber hose" popular. It was one of Vinnie's many colorful comebacks.

Saw it! ☐ Rating: ☆☆☆☆☆
Date: ___ / ___ / _____ With: _____
Notes: _____
_____

47

GET SMART

GENRE:
Action & Adventure

AGE:
10+

SEASONS:
5

STARRING:
Don Adams,
Barbara Feldon,
and
Edward Platt

Forever trying to foil the international organization of evil, KAOS, bumbling secret agent Maxwell Smart is always a split second away from disaster. Also known as Agent 86, Smart is on the case with Agent 99, his clever partner. Together they tackle villains and foil schemes working for CONTROL, a secret government agency in Washington, DC. They are aided by canine agent Fang—also known as Agent K-13—who loves to play with rubber ducks and turtlenecks.

The adventures of the agents always include a number of silly gadgets and secret weapons disguised as everyday objects like a ping-pong paddle, a cheese sandwich, or even an umbrella. There are secret passwords, top-secret documents, and dastardly villains. Whether they're protecting a princess, going undercover in outrageous disguises, or fighting off killer robots, with these spies, there is truly never a dull moment!

DID YOU KNOW?

Throughout its 138 episodes, the show features more than 50 different objects that are actually concealed phones, including Agent Smart's shoe phone!

Saw it! ☐ Rating: ☆☆☆☆☆
Date: ___/___/_____ With: _____
Notes: _____
_____

H2O: JUST ADD WATER

In *H2O: Just Add Water*, three best friends on the Gold Coast of Australia discover they have superpowers—whenever they come into contact with water, they transform into mermaids! This makes everyday life a bit more complicated, and the girls have to rely on each other to keep their new identities a secret.

Rikki, the new girl in town, can raise the temperature of water; Emma can freeze water; and Cleo can manipulate water into whatever form she wants. Lewis, Cleo's friend and science lover, tries to help the girls discover more about their powers, including how and why this happened to them.

Other than their new tails and scales, the girls are just like other 16-year-olds; they have to babysit their younger siblings, navigate the social hurdles of being invited (or uninvited) to parties, and try to avoid the humiliation of found diaries and botched karaoke parties.

H2O: Just Add Water has inspired fans all over the world. Exploring an underwater world through the eyes of magical mermaids? Who wouldn't love these fish tales!

SPIN-OFFS
Mako: Island of Secrets

DID YOU KNOW?
When wet, each mermaid tail weighs over 80 pounds! The actresses trained with experts to learn how to swim in their costumes.

GENRE:
Action & Adventure

AGE:
7+

SEASONS:
3

STARRING:
Cariba Heine,
Claire Holt,
and
Phoebe Tonkin

Saw it! ☐   Rating: ☆☆☆☆☆
Date: ___/___/_____   With: _____
Notes: _____
_____

49

DOCTOR WHO

GENRE:
Action &
Adventure

AGE:
10+

SEASONS:
26 and counting

MADE BY:
Sydney
Newman

"Do you wanna come with me? 'Cause if you do, then I should warn you, you're gonna see all sorts of things. Ghosts from the past; aliens from the future; the day the Earth died in a ball of flame; It won't be quiet, it won't be safe, and it won't be calm. But I'll tell you what it will be: the trip of a lifetime."
—The Ninth Doctor

Have you ever wished you could travel through space and time? With *Doctor Who*, you can! Doctor Who, an alien from the planet Gallifrey, travels in his stolen time-machine, or TARDIS, which stands for Time And Relative Distance In Space, and just happens to be camouflaged as a blue British call box from the 1950s.

The Doctor is passionately curious about Earth and humans. He travels through space and time trying to right wrongs, help others, and combat monsters and villains. He never uses a gun, but he does have a sonic screwdriver.

Twelve different actors have portrayed the Doctor; since Time Lords reincarnate, the Doctor takes on a new body (and perhaps some new personality quirks too) whenever he comes back from a "fatal" injury. Doctor Who typically has a human companion with him on his adventures, although sometimes he may bring a humanoid alien too. This companion helps remind Doctor Who of his "moral duty"—and sometimes causes trouble for him too.

The adventures of the Doctor are immensely popular, both in the UK and internationally. The show has inspired novels, video games, museum exhibits, and toys— even a pinball game! More than 800 episodes have been broadcast since the original show started in 1963, and there is no reason to think the Doctor's adventures will be ending anytime soon!

SPIN-OFFS

Torchwood
Totally Doctor Who
The Sarah Jane Adventures

STARRING:
Matt Smith,
Peter Capaldi,
and
Jenna Coleman

NETWORK:
BBC

DID YOU KNOW?
The show's popularity is so much a part of pop culture that the word *TARDIS* is now included in the Shorter Oxford English Dictionary!

Saw it! ☐ Rating: ☆☆☆☆☆
Date: ___ / ___ / _____ With: _____
Notes: _____
_____

50

BATMAN

GENRE:
Action &
Adventure

AGE:
9+

SEASONS:
3

MADE BY:
Based on
the characters
created by Bob
Kane and Bill
Finger

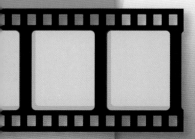

"Quick! To the Batmobile!"
—Batman

Almost everyone knows about Batman: the legend, the comic book, the blockbuster films. But way back in the 1960s, the cape crusader and his sidekick, Robin, appeared in a campy live-action TV series that was way more light-hearted than the intense encounters the Dark Knight faces today. Starring Adam West as a squeaky-clean Batman and Burt Ward as Robin, the wide-eyed boy wonder, the series aired on ABC from 1966 to 1968.

Unlike other superheroes, Batman doesn't have any superpowers. He's just super awesome and super smart. Mix in an arsenal of super cool bat-gadgets and secret identities, and the show gets really exciting. The villains are criminals with goofy names like The Joker, The Penguin, Cat Woman, and Egg Head. Fight scenes are sprinkled with words like *KLONK, KAPOW, POWIE, THWACK*, and *VRONK*! Modern satires like *Austin Powers* mimic *Batman's* absurdity, like when the villain plots the hero's elaborate and totally escapable death. In one episode, Batman is attacked by an exploding shark, but he's saved by the Boy Wonder and a can of shark repellent. In another over-the-top pickle, Mr. Freeze tries to turn Batman and Robin into giant Sno-Cones. The series appeals to all ages; adults and older kids will appreciate the humor, while younger kids will love the candy-coated, high-octane action.

SPIN-OFFS
Batman: The Animated Series
The Batman

STARRING:
Adam West,
Burt Ward,
Alan Napier, and
Neil Hamilton

NETWORK:
ABC

DID YOU KNOW?
Robin the Boy Wonder exclaimed over 300 creative variations of "Holy," including "Holy Trampoline," "Holy Unknown Flying Object," and "Holy Fate-Worse-than-Death!"

Saw it! ☐ Rating: ☆☆☆☆☆
Date: ___/___/_____ With: _____
Notes: _____
_____

51

THUNDERBIRDS

GENRE:
Action & Adventure

AGE:
7+

SEASONS:
2

STARRING:
Peter Dyneley,
Shane Rimmer,
Matt
Zimmerman,
Ray Barrett,
David Holliday,
Sylvia Anderson,
and
David Graham

Premiering in 1965, and set in 2065, this British sci-fi series features human-like puppets as the Tracys, a family who created the top-secret organization International Rescue (IR). IR is dedicated to saving human lives, with the help of their hi-tech machines, Thunderbirds.

Former astronaut Jeff Tracy has five adult sons. Scott pilots Thunderbird 1, a hypersonic rocket; Virgil pilots Thunderbird 2, a supersonic carrier; Alan and John pilot Thunderbird 3, a spacecraft, and Thunderbird 5, the space station; and Gordon pilots Thunderbird 4, a submersible. Lady Penelope Creighton-Ward, who leads a group of secret agents connected to IR and drives a pink Rolls Royce, and an engineer named Brains also join in the Thunderbird adventures. Together, they rescue those in need and save the world, all the while showcasing the amazing abilities of their machinery. Whether they are rescuing soldiers from a blazing pit, saving solarnauts from deadly radiation, or stopping the detonation of an atomic bomb, the Tracys are on the case. Viewers are sure to find this show totally FAB!

SPIN-OFFS
Thunderbirds Are Go

DID YOU KNOW?
The Tracy brothers are named after five of the "Original 7" American astronauts: Alan Shepard, Gordon Cooper, John Glenn, Scott Carpenter, and Virgil Grissom.

Saw it! ☐ Rating: ☆☆☆☆☆

Date: ___/___/_____ With: _____

Notes: _____

_____

MACGYVER

MacGyver is a secret agent who refuses to carry a gun—but he's so smart that he doesn't need it to outwit the bad guys. He just needs his trusty Swiss Army knife, a roll of duct tape, good ol' scientific logic, and his uncanny ability to use everyday items to create extraordinary solutions. The fact that he speaks a bunch of languages and knows everything there is to know about chemistry, technology, and physics helps too.

MacGyver can rig pretty much anything—shorting out a missile timer with a paper clip, making dynamite with salt and sugar, using a paper map as both a sled and a hot-air-balloon patch, and even fixing a blown fuse with a wad of chewing gum. While his missions are always harrowing, MacGyver's level-headed calm helps him avert danger and bring the bad guys to justice.

MacGyver's ability to make something out of nothing has become known in popular culture as "MacGyvering" it.

GENRE:
Action & Adventure

AGE:
11+

SEASONS:
7

STARRING:
Richard Dean Anderson and Dana Elcar

DID YOU KNOW?

Saturday Night Live did a parody skit of the show called "MacGruber," which went on to become a feature film in 2010.

Saw it! ☐ Rating: ☆☆☆☆☆
Date: ___/___/_____ With: _____
Notes: _____
_____

53 BUFFY THE VAMPIRE SLAYER

GENRE:
Action & Adventure

AGE:
13+

SEASONS:
7

MADE BY:
Joss Whedon

"Sure. We saved the world. I say we party. I mean, I got all pretty."
–Buffy Summers

Sarah Michelle Gellar plays Buffy, a high-school student who discovers she's the "chosen one" tasked with protecting the world from vampires and demons. Besides being an awesome slayer, Buffy is a regular teenage girl with regular problems. She befriends Xander, the witty, geeky kid who offers comic relief, and Willow, a shy straight-A student with magical powers. They call themselves the "Scooby Gang," because they work together to battle the forces of evil—something that happens often since Sunnydale High School sits on top of a portal to the demon world. Total bummer!

While the episodes are often grisly, the show works on many levels. Story lines include a tumultuous relationship with a vampire, Willow's journey into witchcraft, and Buffy meeting other slayers. One part supernatural adventure, and one part comedy (with a lot of romantic drama mixed in), the series is about more than winning the war against demons. It's about surviving being a teenager, which can be just as monstrous.

SPIN-OFFS
Angel

STARRING:
Sarah Michelle Gellar, Nicholas Brendon, Alyson Hannigan, Charisma Carpenter, and Anthony Stewart Head

NETWORK:
The WB, UPN

DID YOU KNOW?
Buffy the Vampire Slayer has become a legitimate area of academic study known as Buffy Studies. Books, conferences, and dissertations have examined the show from the perspective of philosophy, religion, gender, linguistics, and more.

Saw it! ☐ Rating: ☆☆☆☆☆
Date: ___/___/_____ With: _____
Notes: _____
_____

54

WONDER WOMAN

GENRE:
Action & Adventure

AGE:
7+

SEASONS:
3

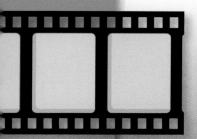

MADE BY:
William Moulton Marston and Stanley Ralph Ross

"No one can resist the golden lasso. It binds all who are encircled and compels them to tell the truth!"
—Wonder Woman

During World War II in the 1940s, Major Steve Trevor crashes his plane on Paradise Island in the Bermuda Triangle. He is discovered by an Amazon princess, Diana, who's compelled to return to America with him to fight against the Nazis and help the United States win the war. And so Wonder Woman is born!

Based on the wildly popular comic-book character, Wonder Woman is practically unstoppable. With bullet-deflecting bracelets, a boomerang tiara, a lasso of truth, and an invisible jet at her disposal, who can defeat her? Disguised as Major Trevor's secretary, Diana Prince keeps her Wonder Woman superpowers a secret, but twirls to transform into her alter ego whenever evil needs to be defeated—or whenever Steve is in trouble. Recovering stolen secrets from the Nazis, thwarting bank robbers, and diverting hijacked missiles are all in a day's work for Wonder Woman.

The first season of the TV series closely followed the comic books, but when the series moved to its second and third seasons, the setting was updated to the 1970s. The series went on to air in syndication throughout the 1980s, and was popular with viewers of all ages, who enjoyed the campy fun of the show. The theme song says: "Wonder Woman! All the world is waiting for you and the powers you possess! In your satin tights, fighting for your rights and the old red, white, and blue!" Surely, this is a show to salute!

STARRING:
Lynda Carter
and
Lyle Waggoner

NETWORK:
ABC, CBS

DID YOU KNOW?
Wonder Woman's metal bracelets are made from a material called "Feminum"!

Saw it! ☐ Rating: ☆☆☆☆☆

Date: ___/___/_____ With: _____

Notes: _____

_____

55

STAR TREK

GENRE:
Action & Adventure

AGE:
8+

SEASONS:
3

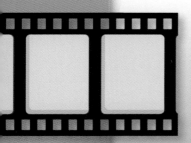

MADE BY:
Gene Roddenberry

"Space, the final frontier. These are the voyages of the starship Enterprise. Its five-year mission: to explore strange new worlds, to seek out new life and new civilizations, to boldly go where no man has gone before."
—Captain Kirk in the opening sequence

Probably the most iconic science-fiction TV show of our time, *Star Trek* is a must-see for anyone who is curious what the future might hold. Exploring new galaxies and planets and discovering new life forms are the sci-fi elements that draw viewers in. But it's the relationships between the members of the crew and creatures from other planets that lie at the heart of the show.

Star Trek's optimistic glimpse into the future shows a world where exploration is valued and all things are possible. With cool gadgets like the universal translator, handheld communicators, and the phaser gun, Captain Kirk and his crew inspired the imaginations of viewers all over the world—so much so, that many of these "far-fetched" imaginary gadgets now exist today!

Though the show never had particularly high ratings, it did have legions of dedicated and vocal fans called "Trekkies," who enthusiastically supported the show and demanded to see more of its characters. So while the original series only lasted for three seasons, the *Star Trek* world evolved into numerous full-length movies, spin-off TV series, and most recently, a reboot series of movies that reimagines the original characters.

The adventures of the starship *Enterprise* are now legendary, and the show is considered a cult classic; Captain Kirk, Mr. Spock, and the rest of the crew are so well known that viewers of all generations are boldly going where no one has gone before!

SPIN-OFFS

Star Trek: The Next Generation
Star Trek: Voyager
Deep Space Nine
Enterprise
Star-Trek: Discovery

STARRING:
William Shatner,
Leonard Nimoy,
DeForest Kelley,
Nichelle Nichols,
James Doohan,
and
George Takei

NETWORK:
NBC

DID YOU KNOW?
NASA is working on making the warp-drive technology featured in *Star Trek* real!

Saw it! ☐ Rating: ☆☆☆☆☆
Date: ___ / ___ / _____ With: _____
Notes: _____
_____

56

MIGHTY MORPHIN' POWER RANGERS

GENRE:
Action & Adventure

AGE:
7+

SEASONS:
3

STARRING:
Richard Steven Horvitz,
Ed Neil,
David Yost,
David J. Fielding,
Amy Jo Johnson,
and
Thuy Trang

Do you have the Power in you? The Power Rangers phenomenon began in 1993 with the debut of the *Mighty Morphin' Power Rangers*. The show is adapted from the Japanese TV series *Super Sentai*, and uses much of the original Japanese footage. Episodes revolve around a team of five "teenagers with attitude" recruited by the wizard Zordon. He morphs them into superheroes with amazing abilities to fight against a witch named Rita Repulsa and the evil Lord Zedd. Each Ranger possesses a colorful, tight-fitting suit, a superhuman skill, and a special weapon.

It's not all teamwork and drop kicks though. These tough teens can never use their powers for their own personal gain or show their powers to the public, or they risk losing their abilities.

While these teens are dealing with the normal trials and tribulations of other high schoolers, they also have to worry about saving the universe. Football and cheerleading tryouts, getting good grades, and having crushes are all mixed up with navigating force fields, fighting super-sized monsters, and avoiding timeholes. Intergalactic battles, epic fights, and zippy dialogue are the hallmarks of the *Power Rangers*, making any time spent with them a whole lot of spacey, colorful fun!

DID YOU KNOW?
Fans who can't get enough *Power Rangers* attend the annual convention known as the Power Morphicon!

Saw it! ☐ Rating: ☆☆☆☆☆

Date: ___/ ___/ _____ With: _____

Notes: _____

_____

GOOSEBUMPS

Based on the best-selling horror book series of the same name, *Goosebumps* is a collection of spooky stories about kids who find themselves in supernatural situations. For readers who loved R.L. Stine's original *Goosebumps* books, several titles were transformed into episodes, including such frightful tales as "Return of the Mummy," "The Girl Who Cried Monster," "Let's Get Invisible," and "Ghost Beach."

Ready to get thrilled and chilled? Each creepy installment of the TV show offers some spine-tingling twists, from chasing monsters to a haunted summer camp and a magical mask with questionable powers. The kids in each episode have to follow the clues to solve these mystical mysteries and overcome their darkest fears, while viewers are along for the ride. "Viewer beware, you're in for a scare!" says the narrator, warning viewers of the scary tales ahead. Sometimes gross and goofy, sometimes thrillingly terrifying, the *Goosebumps* adventures are sure to leave you delightfully frightened. Some braveness required!

GENRE:
Action & Adventure

AGE:
10+

SEASONS:
4

STARRING:
R.L. Stine

DID YOU KNOW?
The man in black carrying a briefcase in the opening sequence is author R.L. Stine.

Saw it! ☐ Rating: ☆☆☆☆☆
Date: ___/___/_____ With: _____
Notes: _____
_____

58

THE TWILIGHT ZONE

GENRE:
Action &
Adventure

AGE:
10+

SEASONS:
5

MADE BY:
Rod Serling

"You're traveling through another dimension, a dimension not only of sight and sound but of mind. A journey into a wondrous land whose boundaries are that of imagination. That's the signpost up ahead: your next stop, the Twilight zone!"
—From the opening narration of the show

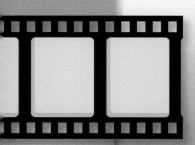

What happens when regular people are affected by extraordinary circumstances? They have entered the Twilight Zone! Each episode tells a different tale; unlike other shows that tell the story of a group of characters over time, this show features a completely new story and new characters in every episode. The only constant is narrator and creator Rod Serling, who introduces and closes each episode with some wise insights for viewers. Several well-known actors appear on the show, including William Shatner and Leonard Nimoy of *Star Trek*, movie stars Burt Reynolds and Robert Redford, and funny lady Carol Burnett.

Supernatural events, encounters with aliens, robots who seem human, time travel, and glimpses into the future are all reality in *The Twilight Zone*. Each episode's characters learn a valuable moral lesson in the end; most endings are a surprise or contain a twist the viewers wouldn't see coming.

Unlike anything else that was on air at the time, the show mixed fantasy, reality, and unpredictability, which made viewers tune in each week. Who would star in this week's episode? Would it be set in space or in someone's backyard? Which parts would be fantastic, and which would be so real you knew it could happen to you? Once you get a glimpse of the "fifth dimension," you'll want to see everything!

STARRING:
Rod Serling

NETWORK:
CBS

SPIN-OFFS
The Twilight Zone (1985)
The Twilight Zone (2002)

DID YOU KNOW?
Ray Bradbury, the great sci-fi author, wrote an episode of *The Twilight Zone.*

Saw it! ☐ Rating: ☆☆☆☆☆
Date: ___/___/_____ With: _____
Notes: _____
_____

59

SCOOBY-DOO, WHERE ARE YOU!

GENRE:
Animated
Adventure

AGE:
5+

SEASONS:
2

MADE BY:
William Hanna
and
Joseph Barbera

"And I would have gotten away with it, too, if it wasn't for you meddling kids."
—Classic Scooby-Doo villains

Long before Ghostbusters, a group of teenage friends and their dog Scooby-Doo chased ghosts, vampires, witches, and other spooky creatures in this Saturday morning cartoon. Four California high-school students drive around in a groovy green van called The Mystery Machine to solve mysteries. The supernatural spooks they chase always turn out to be regular human villains in disguise.

Shaggy is the slacker beatnik who has a scruffy goatee and says "like" a lot. Scooby-Doo is his dog, and together they're a lazy, cowardly, and comically hungry crime-solving duo. The rest of the gang includes Velma, the brainy one, who is always losing her glasses; Fred, the blond, handsome one, who wears an ascot and looks a little like a Ken doll; and the fashionable redhead Daphne, whose nickname is "Danger Prone Daphne," since she often needs rescuing. Together the gang works to prove what at first appears to be supernatural mysteries are actually simple hoaxes. Along the way, there are always chills, thrills, and plenty of laughs. The show premiered in 1969, following *The Archies; Scooby-Doo* mimicked *The Archies* simple cartoon style to appeal to the same teen audience. Today the biggest draws are still the silly, sweet Scooby-Doo and the fun of watching the gang solving a mystery in every episode. *Zoinks!*

STARRING:
Don Messick,
Casey Kasem,
Frank Welker,
Nicole Jaffe,
Stefanianna
Christopherson,
and
Heather North

NETWORK:
CBS, ABC

SPIN-OFFS
A Pup Named Scooby-Doo
The New Scooby-Doo Movies
Scooby's All-Star Laff-A-Lympics
Scooby-Doo Goes Hollywood
What's New, Scooby-Doo?
Scooby-Doo! Mystery Incorporated

DID YOU KNOW?
The show's theme song has been covered by a number of famous artists, including Matthew Sweet, Third Eye Blind, The B-52s, and Billy Ray Cyrus.

Saw it! ☐   Rating: ☆☆☆☆☆
Date: ___/ ___/ _____ With: _____
Notes: _____
_____

60

POPEYE THE SAILOR

GENRE:
Animated
Adventure

AGE:
5+

SEASONS:
2

STARRING:
Jack Mercer,
Mae Questel,
and
Jackson Beck

Popeye, the sailor man, has been guzzling spinach for over 85 years. He and his gangly gal pal Olive Oyl have appeared in comic strips, books, cartoons, radio segments, movie shorts, and films. When the old movie shorts from the 1930s, 1940s, and 1950s were broadcast on TV in the 1960s, viewer enthusiasm prompted a new series of made-for-television cartoons. The iconic characters remained the same, with Popeye getting out of a pickle by guzzling his spinach and brandishing his biceps in each episode.

The series is a mash-up of styles, plotlines, and spoofs. There are moments of Loony-Tunes-style hijinks and slapstick, and lots of fanciful elements, including shape-shifting and invisibility. The story lines range from competitions to more imaginative concepts, like when Popeye's prehistoric ancestors discover spinach. Other episodes feature arch-enemy Brutus putting Popeye in a machine that turns him into a baby. There are also Egyptian tombs, sunken treasure, fortune tellers, and bull fighting. But through it all, Popeye always wears his bright white navy duds, and manages to save the day!

DID YOU KNOW?
Popeye's love of spinach inspired adults and children to eat more spinach during the Great Depression!

Saw it! ☐ Rating: ☆☆☆☆☆

Date: ___ / ___ / _____ With: _____

Notes: _____

_____

SPEED RACER

61

Go, Speed Racer, Go! Speed Racer is just 18, and while he may be the youngest driver on the circuit, he's got the talent to go, go, go far.

Based on the Japanese manga series *Mach GoGoGo, Speed Racer* first came to American TV screens in 1967. Speed Racer drives the Mach 5, a super sweet race car that's said to be modeled after three real-life speed mobiles: the Aston Martin, the Ford GT40, and the Ferrari Testarossa. Speed's girlfriend, Trixie, a helicopter and airplane pilot, often accompanies him on his adventures, as does his brother, Spritle, and his pet chimpanzee, Chim-Chim. Masked Racer X drives Car 9 (also called the Shooting Star). He's an excellent driver, yet remains a mystery to Speed.

Speed always tries to do the right thing, whether he's competing in a race against Captain Terror and his Car Acrobatic Team, trying to defeat international spies, or foiling an assassination attempt. Speed's adventures are never short on fun or intrigue, and the style of the animation is colorful and bright, much like the manga series it's based on. Once you get hooked on the adventures of Speed Racer and his friends, you'll be pulling for him to win every race and defeat every villain.

GENRE:
Animated
Adventure

AGE:
6+

SEASONS:
1

STARRING:
Peter Fernandez,
Katsuji Mori,
and
Jack Grimes

DID YOU KNOW?

Trixie's name in the original Japanese series is Michi Shimura, which is why her shirt has an *M* on it.

Saw it! ☐ Rating: ☆☆☆☆☆

Date: ___ / ___ / _____ With: _____

Notes: _____

_____

62 RUGRATS

GENRE:
Animated
Adventure

AGE:
6+

SEASONS:
10

STARRING:
Elizabeth Daily,
Christine
Cavanaugh,
Kath Soucie,
and
Cheryl Chase

How much trouble can four babies get into when their parents aren't looking? It depends on how big their imaginations are! Tommy Pickles is a baby with a few great friends and a whole lot of big ideas. Along with his pals Chuckie and twins Phil and Lil, Tommy has a ton of adventures. Everyday stuff gets way more exciting through the babies' eyes, whether they are listening to tall tales from Tommy's Grandpa, avoiding naughty girl Angelica's attempts to scare them, or tackling vertigo on the big kids' slide. They always find a way to make everything into an adventure from their own unique point of view.

Inspired by their two small sons, creators Gábor Csupó and Arlene Klasky thought it would be cool to imagine what babies would say if they could talk and explore why they do all the silly things they do every day. While originally planned to appeal to kids, the show eventually became a hit with adults too. *Rugrats* was such a popular show that it inspired several specials, three feature films, and a bunch of cool collectibles, including pajamas, games, toys, and comics. No matter what age you are, you'll go gaga for this show!

DID YOU KNOW?
Until *SpongeBob SquarePants* came along, *Rugrats* was the longest running cartoon on Nickelodeon!

Saw it! ☐ Rating: ☆☆☆☆☆
Date: ___/___/_____ With: _____
Notes: _____
_____

POKÉMON

Based on a super-popular Japanese video game, the anime series *Pokémon* is a worldwide phenomenon. The series follows 10-year-old Ash, who can't wait to become a Pokémon (or Pocket Monster) master. Ash's main Pokémon is Pikachu, a small, yellow, mouse-like creature who has the power to attack its adversaries with electricity. Training for the Pokémon league, Ash and Pikachu gradually learn to trust one another, as they battle other Pokémon and their masters. Along the way, they make new friends, like gym leaders Misty and Brock, artist Tracey, and Pokémon coordinator May. Ash and his friends find new adventures in every episode, whether they are traveling through Neon City, where everyone is sleep-deprived and cranky, or journeying through the Orange Islands, making new friends and meeting mysterious creatures. There is always excitement to be found and more tests to be passed on Ash's way to becoming a master.

Pokémania recently surged again when the Pokémon Go app took the world by storm. With 19 seasons, you've got plenty of episodes to start watching. Gotta go catch 'em all!

SPIN-OFFS
Pokémon Chronicles
Pokémon Origins

DID YOU KNOW?
Pokémon legend states that Pikachu's name comes from a mash-up of two Japanese words: *pika* for the sound made when electricity sparks, and *chu* for the squeaky noise a mouse makes.

GENRE:
Animated
Adventure

AGE:
6+

SEASONS:
19 and counting

STARRING:
Ikue Otani,
Rodger Parsons,
and Sarah
Natochenny

Saw it! ☐ Rating: ☆☆☆☆☆
Date: ___/___/_____ With: _____
Notes: _____
_____

64

SPIDER-MAN AND HIS AMAZING FRIENDS

GENRE:
Animated
Adventure

AGE:
6+

SEASONS:
3

MADE BY:
Stan Lee,
Jack Kirby,
and
Steve Ditko

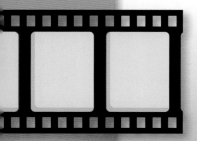

"Firestar,
honey,
I lava you."
—Iceman

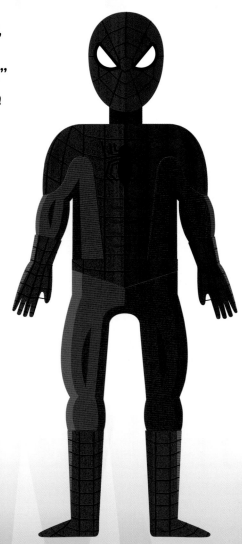

Are your Spidey senses tingling? They should be—Spider-Man and his friends Iceman and Firestar are here to save the day! Fighting villains across the globe, these Spider-Friends combine their superpowers to create a team to fight bad guys. By day, Peter Parker, Bobby Drake, and Anjelica Jones are all college students at Empire State University, living together with Peter's Aunt May. But when evil shows up, the three friends use their superpowers to defeat the supervillains.

This show introduces us to some awesome characters in the Marvel world, including Lightwave, who can control light, and Videoman, who is made of energy from a video arcade. Other more familiar X-Men also appear in the series, including Professor X, Magneto, Cyclops, Storm, and Wolverine. Together, the Spider-Friends try to foil the evil plots of the Beetle, the Shocker, the Chameleon, Electro, Green Goblin, and Mysterio. There's even an episode narrated by creator Stan Lee, and another that features a cameo from Marvel icon Iron Man.

Although *Spider-Man and His Amazing Friends* was only on TV for three seasons, the adventures of the Spider-Friends are definitely worth checking out. They're not just superheroes saving the planet; they're also good friends who have fun hanging out together whether they're battling a supervillain or goofing around at a superhero costume party.

STARRING:
Dan Gilvezan,
Frank Welker,
and
Kathy Garver

NETWORK:
NBC

DID YOU KNOW?

The Marvel character Human Torch was not available for this series due to legal issues, so the Marvel team created Firestar, a brand new character with similar powers.

Saw it! ☐ Rating: ☆☆☆☆☆

Date: ___/___/_____ With: _____

Notes: _____

_____

65 FOSTER'S HOME FOR IMAGINARY FRIENDS

GENRE:
Animated
Adventure

AGE:
7+

SEASONS:
6

STARRING:
Sean Marquette,
Grey Griffin,
and
Keith Ferguson

Have you ever wondered what happened to your old imaginary friends once you outgrew them? Chances are, they're living at Foster's Home for Imaginary Friends, an adoption center for outgrown imaginary pals.

The series revolves around eight-year-old Mac, who initially thinks he's outgrown Blooregard Q. Kazoo, a security blanket also known as Bloo, but later realizes he doesn't want to be without him. Mac talks old Madame Foster, proprietor of the Home, into letting Bloo stay there forever, as long as he comes to visit every day. During these visits, Mac encounters all kinds of castoff imaginary friend creatures waiting to be adopted by kids who can't think up their own imaginary friends, including Coco, an airplane-bird-palm tree hybrid who lays colorful eggs; Eduardo, a huge purple guy with horns and big teeth (who's actually kind of shy); and Wilt, a tall, red basketball player with just one arm. A world where kids and imaginary friends can stay together is pretty awesome, and you'll love seeing what kind of shenanigans Mac, Bloo, and the rest of the crew get into!

DID YOU KNOW?

Creator Craig McCracken, who also developed *The Powerpuff Girls*, reportedly got the idea for *Foster's* after adopting a shelter dog.

Saw it! ☐ Rating: ☆☆☆☆☆
Date: ___/ ___/ _____ With: _____
Notes: _____
_____

AVATAR: THE LAST AIRBENDER

66

What if you were the only one who could save the world? That's what 12-year-old Aang is faced with when he realizes he is the chosen one and must fight to fix his war-torn world. There are four nations: The Fire Nation, The Water Tribes, The Earth Kingdom, and the Air Nomads. "Benders" of each nation can control, or bend, their own element through a combination of innate talent and magic. An Avatar is the only one who can bend all four elements, and there's only one Avatar in the whole world: Aang.

When we meet Aang, he has just been discovered hibernating in an iceberg by young Waterbender Katara and her elder brother Sokka from the Southern Tribe. Aang learns the world is out of balance since the Fire Nation attacked 100 years ago, sparking a global war. Together, they train to bend the elements and experience incredible adventures as they try to destroy the Fire Lord.

Aang's journey is spellbinding, with new twists and turns in every episode. The inspiring characters, intricate plots, and unique magical universe make *The Last Airbender* a must-see on your TV show list!

GENRE:
Animated Adventure

AGE:
8+

SEASONS:
3

STARRING:
Zach Tyler,
Mae Whitman,
and
Jack DeSena

DID YOU KNOW?

Each bending style is based on a different style of Chinese martial arts, including *tai chi* and *ba gua*.

SPIN-OFFS

The Legend of Korra

Saw it! ☐   Rating: ☆☆☆☆☆

Date: ___ / ___ / _____   With: _____

Notes: _____

_____

67

TEENAGE MUTANT NINJA TURTLES

GENRE:
Animated
Adventure

AGE:
7+

SEASONS:
10

MADE BY:
Kevin Eastman
and
Peter Laird

"Turtle power! They're the world's most fearsome fighting team! They're heroes in a half-shell, and they're green!"
—From the classic theme song

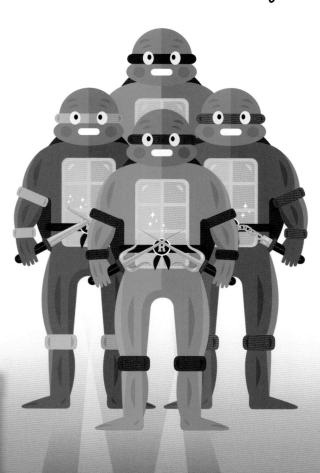

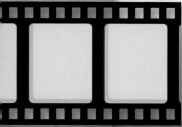

Creators Kevin Eastman and Peter Laird were starving artists when they came up with the idea for the *Teenage Mutant Ninja Turtles* comic book. That first issue sold for just $1.50, but it's now worth thousands of dollars! The popularity of the characters soon inspired a TV show.

A group of teenagers who loves pizza and hanging out sounds pretty normal, but the Teenage Mutant Ninja Turtles are anything but normal! The four ninja warriors fell into a sewer and were exposed to some gnarly toxic sludge that transformed them from regular turtles into super humanoid turtles. Named after four legendary Renaissance artists, Leonardo, Donatello, Raphael, and Michelangelo are out to save the world from evil. Their sensei Yoshi, aka Splinter, raised the four turtles like sons, and taught them everything they know about martial arts. Splinter, a humanoid rat, was also exposed to the same toxic sludge. The martial-arts master has a lifelong feud with Shredder, who is determined to destroy him. The Turtles often team up with Channel 6 news reporter April O'Neill as they battle Shredder and other villains, including Krang, a disembodied brain from Dimension X who wants to take over the world.

The show inspired several films, including the two recent hits starring Megan Fox. A new generation is discovering what many already know about *TMNT*. These four turtles aren't just fearless ninja warriors, they're pretty funny guys too. Cowabunga! Let's kick some shell!

STARRING:
Cam Clarke,
Townsend
Coleman,
Barry Gordon,
and
Rob Paulsen

NETWORK:
CBS

DID YOU KNOW?

The TMNT inspired a live musical tour, called Coming Out of Their Shells. The musical was sponsored by Pizza Hut—of course!

Saw it! ☐ Rating: ☆☆☆☆☆

Date: ___/___/_____ With: _____

Notes: _____

_____

68 THE POWERPUFF GIRLS

GENRE:
Animated
Adventure

AGE:
8+

SEASONS:
6

STARRING:
Cathy Cavadini,
Elizabeth Daily,
and
Tara Strong

By combining sugar, spice, and everything nice, Professor Utonium thought he was concocting three perfect little girls. But somehow a little Chemical X got added to the mix, creating the Powerpuff Girls: Blossom, Bubbles, and Buttercup.

With superpowers that help them save Townsville from evil, the Powerpuff Girls often face off against supervillain monkey Mojo Jojo, who is always scheming to take over the world or destroy the Powerpuff Girls. Blossom, the pink leader of the Powerpuff Girls, uses her smarts and element of "everything nice" to outwit enemies. Bubbles, the blue-loving sweetheart, uses her element of sugar, of course. Buttercup, who's signature color is green, uses her element of spice to fight any foe.

DID YOU KNOW?

The Powerpuffs are known by different names around the world. In Italy, they are called Lolly, Dolly, and Molly. In Latin America they're known as Bombón, Burbuja, and Bellota (or Chocolate, Bubble, and Acorn).

Whether they're confronting a zombie magician, mixing it up with the Gangreen Gang, or accidentally creating a monster, Blossom, Bubbles, and Buttercup prove girls can be strong and feminine at the same time, fighting crime with style, class, and their signature Powerpuff flair!

Saw it! ☐ Rating: ☆☆☆☆☆
Date: ___/ ___/ _____ With: _____
Notes: _____
_____

DEXTER'S LABORATORY

69

Dexter is a boy-genius with a secret lab in his house, where he invents all kinds of super cool stuff. He's always trying to keep big sister Dee Dee out of his lab, and competes with his equally genius next-door neighbor, Mandark, who has his own much larger at-home lab.

As a serious scientist, Dexter is constantly creating new experiments and inventions that create havoc. Whether he's traveling back in time to understand the origin of fire, transforming his sister into a giant or a monster, or making a "mom-droid" robot to take over for his sick mom, Dexter's ridiculously smart brain is constantly coming up with new ideas. But even though this kid is a genius, he's a lot like every other kid—he would love to keep his sister out of his room, avoid detention, and when he can, save planet Earth from a horrifyingly destructive meteor storm.

When he's not saving the world, Dexter likes going to his favorite restaurant, Burrito Palace; throwing snowballs with his dad; and of course, trying to outsmart Mandark. Dexter is totally relatable and fun to watch, with clever dialogue, great animation, and zingy jokes. You'll love this modern classic cartoon!

DID YOU KNOW?

Dexter has an accent because, as creator Genndy Tartakovsky has said, "all well-known scientists have accents!"

GENRE:
Animated
Adventure

AGE:
7+

SEASONS:
5

STARRING:
Christine
Cavanaugh,
Kath Soucie,
and
Jeff Bennett

Saw it! ☐ Rating: ☆☆☆☆☆

Date: ___/___/_____ With: _____

Notes: _____

_____

70

THE SMURFS

GENRE:
Animated
Adventure

AGE:
4+

SEASONS:
9

MADE BY:
Peyo

"Now, now! We all need to smurf down!"
—Brainy Smurf

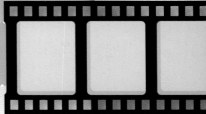

Originally based on a Belgian comic strip by artist Peyo, *The Smurfs* became a TV series in 1981 and quickly rose to international fame. With their tiny mushroom houses, blue skin, white hats, and special Smurf language, the smurfs are "smurftastic!"

There are a bunch of smurfs who live in Smurf Village. Many have an adjective as their first name, such as Grouchy Smurf, Brainy Smurf, Clumsy Smurf, and Lazy Smurf. Others have a job as their first name, such as Actor Smurf or Farmer Smurf. While most Smurfs are boys, there is one girl amongst them: the beautiful blonde Smurfette. There's also Papa Smurf, a 543-year-old Smurf who takes care of everyone in Smurf Village with a magical touch. Evil wizard Gargamel is always trying to catch the smurfs for devious purposes, such as turning them into gold. Gargamel's mischievous cat, Azrael, is often lurking nearby too. When the Smurfs aren't trying to escape from danger, they celebrate being Smurfs with Olympic-style Smurfic Games!

The Smurfs are always getting into trouble, and their silly adventures are fun to watch. For a smurfing good time, you should definitely smurf over to your screen and watch *The Smurfs*!

SPIN-OFFS
The Smurfs Movie
The Smurfs 2

STARRING:
Don Messick,
Lucille Bliss, and
Paul Winchell

NETWORK:
NBC

DID YOU KNOW?
The Smurf language uses the word *smurf* in place of nouns, verbs, and adjectives. So have yourself a smurftastic smurf!

Saw it! ☐ Rating: ☆☆☆☆☆

Date: ___/___/_____ With: _____

Notes: _____

_____

71

ADVENTURE TIME

GENRE:
Animated
Adventure

AGE:
10+

SEASONS:
7 and counting

MADE BY:
Pendleton
Ward

"What time is it?
Adventure time!"
—Finn

DID YOU KNOW?

Each episode takes about four months to animate; the animation is done in South Korea, and then the episode comes back to the United States for review before it airs.

In a strange and magical world, Finn and Jake, a boy and his best friend (who happens to be a dog that can change his appearance), protect The Land of Ooo. In their many amazing adventures, they encounter Princess Bubblegum, The Ice King, Marceline the Vampire Queen, and even a Lumpy Space Princess.

Through their adventures, such as tracking down the Gut Grinder, helping Donny the grass ogre (who's kind of obnoxious), and trying to get the Crystal Eye out of a dank dungeon, Finn and Jake encounter incredible creatures and places—from a phantom called the Fear Feaster to a robot who throws pies. Lady Rainicorn, a rainbow-bellied unicorn who speaks Korean, is a fan favorite. Finn and Jake even travel into the belly of a monster to save someone, only to discover a party of bears inside. Unlike most cartoon characters, Finn ages with each season, so viewers can watch him grow and change.

This animated world may be a bit strange, but *Adventure Time* has been praised by critics for its imaginative storytelling, unique humor, and delightful dialogue. This is a show that's adored by kids, teens, and adults alike.

Creator Pendleton Ward has said the show was inspired by the uber-popular fantasy role-playing game Dungeons & Dragons. It started out as a 7-minute film that quickly went viral. After several years, the series has won a ton of awards, including Emmys, Annies, Kids' Choice and Teen Choice awards, and there's even been talk of a future feature film!

STARRING:
Jeremy Shada
and
John DiMaggio

NETWORK:
Cartoon
Network

Saw it! ☐ Rating: ☆☆☆☆☆

Date: ___/___/_____ With: _____

Notes: _____

_____

72

THE GUMBY SHOW

GENRE:
Animated
Adventure

AGE:
4+

SEASONS:
Hundreds
of episodes
created over
40 years

MADE BY:
Art Clokey

*"If you've got
a heart, then
Gumby's a part
of you."
— From the
classic theme*

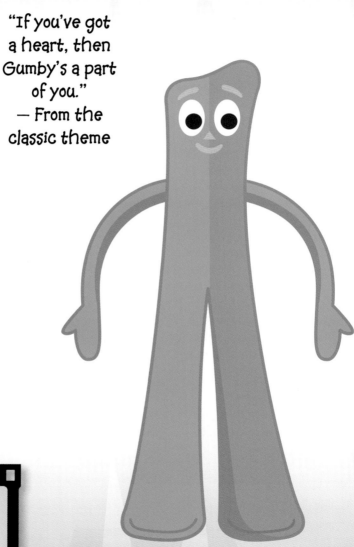

The Gumby Show was the very first Claymation show on TV. It first aired in the 1950s and 1960s and then returned in the 1980s. Starring a bendy green boy named Gumby and his orange horse Pokey, *Gumby* is tremendously low-tech—which is exactly what makes it worth watching. The show turns shape-shifting clay into art in motion and stimulates the imagination. *Gumby's* creator, Art Clokey, was a pioneer in Claymation, the process of carefully moving and taking thousands of photographs of clay figures to create an animated movie or TV show. The craftsmanship on *Gumby* lead to *Bob the Builder, Shaun the Sheep, Wallace and Gromit,* and loads of other shows.

Despite being stretchy, green, and cut from a slab of clay, Gumby is an average boy with parents, friends, and a few enemies—the notorious Blockheads. Gumby even plays in a band called The Clayboys. But it's hard to ignore what makes him unique. Gumby can stretch himself tall or flatten himself out whenever he needs. Cooler still, he and Pokey can walk in and out of books and get in on the action. In each episode they embark on weird adventures and learn all kinds of important life lessons. Throughout the series, Gumby models everyday heroism in big and small ways. Viewers will find enjoying this show isn't a stretch. In fact, most people don't just say they like Gumby, they say they love him!

SPIN-OFFS
Gumby Adventures
Gumby: The Movie

STARRING:
Dal McKennon,
Norma
MacMillan,
Bobby
Nicholson,
and
Art Clokey

NETWORK:
NBC

DID YOU KNOW?
Art Clokey's father, who had a large cowlick in his hair, inspired Gumby's appearance.

Saw it! ☐   Rating: ☆☆☆☆☆

Date: ___/___/_____   With: _____

Notes: _____

_____

73

THE SIMPSONS

GENRE:
Animated
Comedy

AGE:
12+

SEASONS:
27 and counting

MADE BY:
Matt Groening

"Ay, caramba!"
—Bart Simpson

You could watch a different episode of *The Simpsons* every week for 10 years and never get bored! This animated family sitcom has fart gags, absurdist humor, and cartoon slapstick right alongside political humor, social satire, and high-brow cultural references. The show ushered in the trend of creating cartoons for adults, but *The Simpsons* is loved by all ages, and it's miles above the rest in originality and quality of its writing.

Created by Matt Groening in 1987, the yellow-skinned Simpsons never age. Each week they face similar problems; Parents Homer and Marge deal with marriage, home, and money problems, while their children, Bart, Lisa, and Maggie, deal with sibling rivalry, crushes, detention, and grades. Many of the crises are caused by Homer, who is a lovable but lazy, irresponsible, and unreasonable family man. Like a dog, Homer is loyal, devoted, and loving— but lacks common sense or impulse control. Marge, with her bright blue beehive hairdo, tries to manage the chaos but sometimes loses her temper. 10-year-old Bart is an impish troublemaker; 8-year-old Lisa is a precocious, politically correct, straight-A student; and after 30 years, 1-year-old Maggie is still crawling and sucking her pacifier. The family may seem dysfunctional, but don't have a cow, man! Underneath the antics, *The Simpsons* shines with strong family values.

SPIN-OFFS

Futurama
The Simpsons Movie

STARRING:
Dan Castellaneta,
Julie Kavner,
Nancy Cartwright,
Yeardley Smith,
Harry Shearer,
and
Hank Azaria

NETWORK:
Fox

DID YOU KNOW?
Doh! Homer's utterance of surprised disappointment is now listed in the *Oxford English Dictionary*.

Saw it! ☐ Rating: ☆☆☆☆☆
Date: ___/___/_____ With: _____
Notes: _____
_____

74

SHAUN THE SHEEP

GENRE:
Animated
Comedy

AGE:
5+

SEASONS:
4

STARRING:
John Sparkes,
Justin Fletcher,
Richard Webber,
Kate Harbour,
and
Jo Allen

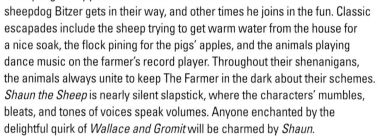

From Aardman Animations, the awesome folks who created *Wallace and Gromit, Shaun the Sheep* is a Claymation masterpiece. In this charming series, Shaun is the chief sheep at Mossy Bottom Farm in northern England. He's the sharpest sheep in the flock, so he tends to hatch plots, draw diagrams, and call the shots. Shaun and his flock are particularly captivated by human activities and the gadgets and gizmos they use to enjoy life on the farm. Each 7-minute episode includes several stories that involve the animals attempting to copy human behavior. Sometimes the sheepdog Bitzer gets in their way, and other times he joins in the fun. Classic escapades include the sheep trying to get warm water from the house for a nice soak, the flock pining for the pigs' apples, and the animals playing dance music on the farmer's record player. Throughout their shenanigans, the animals always unite to keep The Farmer in the dark about their schemes. *Shaun the Sheep* is nearly silent slapstick, where the characters' mumbles, bleats, and tones of voices speak volumes. Anyone enchanted by the delightful quirk of *Wallace and Gromit* will be charmed by *Shaun.*

SPIN-OFFS
Shaun the Sheep Movie

DID YOU KNOW?
Claymation is a painstaking process. *Shaun the Sheep* animators produce just two to three minutes of footage every week.

Saw it! ☐ Rating: ☆☆☆☆☆
Date: ___/___/_____ With: _____
Notes: _____
_____

THE NEW TOM AND JERRY SHOW

75

Tom and Jerry started as theatrical short films, winning seven Academy Awards for Animated Short Film. But the films that won all those awards never made it to TV. When the cartoons first aired in 1965, they were in a heavily edited and toned-down form. The efforts of Tom the cat to catch Jerry the mouse represent some of the most violent humor in theatrical animation. There are plots involving hammers and firecrackers. Tom and Jerry even whack each other with baseball bats, brooms, and bricks.

Tom and Jerry's battles all but vanished in the kinder, gentler 1970s. In *The New Tom and Jerry Show*, which premiered in 1975, Tom and Jerry are best friends who work together to fight villains and solve mysteries. This classic cat-and-mouse duo surely belongs in the Cartoon Hall of Fame.

DID YOU KNOW?

The Simpsons' show-within-a-show, *The Itchy and Scratchy Show*, is a parody of *Tom and Jerry*.

SPIN-OFFS

The Tom and Jerry Show
The Tom and Jerry Comedy Show
Tom and Jerry Kids

GENRE:
Animated Comedy

AGE:
5+

SEASONS:
1

STARRING:
Henry Corden,
Kathy Gori,
Don Messick,
Alan Oppenheimer,
Joe E. Ross,
and
Hal Smith

Saw it! ☐ Rating: ☆☆☆☆☆
Date: ___/___/_____ With: _____
Notes: _____
_____

76

THE FLINTSTONES

GENRE:
Animated
Comedy

AGE:
5+

SEASONS:
6

MADE BY:
William Hanna
and Joseph
Barbera

"Yabbadabba-
doo!"
—Fred
Flintstone

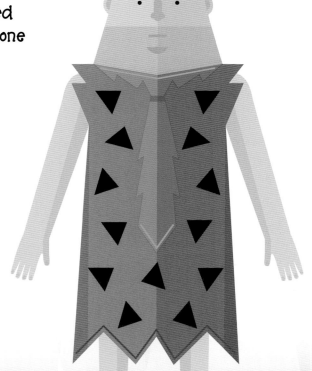

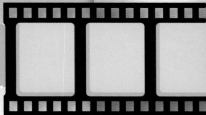

A 1960s cartoon about a prehistoric family might sound like a perplexing premise for a show, but the unique concept hit the funny bones of kids and adults alike. Inspired by *The Honeymooners*, the hugely popular sitcom from the 1950s, *The Flintstones* was TV's first primetime, animated sitcom. Like Ralph Kramden of *The Honeymooners*, Fred Flintstone is an average working-class man who is quick to holler at his wife, Wilma, and his loyal best friend Barney Rubble. The Flintstones have a pet dinosaur named Dino and a baby named Pebbles. The Rubbles, their neighbors, have a son named Bamm-Bamm.

The best jokes are the crazy gadgets, appliances, tools, and cars the residents of Bedrock use each day. A shower is a woolly mammoth spraying water from its trunk, and a laundry machine is a pelican with a throat full of sudsy water. Birds with long beaks serve as hedge clippers, record-player needles, and even the inner mechanics of a camera. These animals often make disgruntled one-liners about their jobs as appliances or tools.

Fred is grouchy when he punches in as brontocrane operator at the Slate Rock and Gravel Company, but when he finishes another day and comes home to his family—or bowls a strike—he does a happy dance that's prehistorically adorable! Watch a few episodes, and you too will be cheering "Yabbadabba-doo!"

STARRING:
Alan Reed,
Jean Vander Pyl,
Mel Blanc, and
Bea Benaderet

NETWORK:
ABC

SPIN-OFFS
The Man Called Flintstone
The Pebbles and Bamm-Bamm Show
The Flintstones
The Flintstones in Viva Rock Vegas

DID YOU KNOW?
The cereals Fruity Pebbles and Cocoa Pebbles are named after The Flintstone's baby daughter, Pebbles.

Saw it! ☐ Rating: ☆☆☆☆☆
Date: ___/___/_____ With: _____
Notes: _____
_____

77

SPONGEBOB SQUAREPANTS

GENRE:
Animated
Comedy

AGE:
6+

SEASONS:
10 and counting

STARRING:
Tom Kenny,
Bill Fagerbakke,
Rodger
Bumpass,
Clancy Brown,
Carolyn
Lawrence, and
Mr. Lawrence

SpongeBob, the star of this bonkers show, is overflowing with energy, optimism, and naiveté. He lives in an underwater pineapple in Bikini Bottom with his pet snail, Gary. His best friend is a pink starfish named Patrick, who's not the brightest starfish in the sea. SpongeBob gleefully works as a fry cook at the Krusty Krab, and he's exuberant about his work and Krabby patties. An ever-loyal employee, he also often helps his boss, the miserly Mr. Krabs. His grumpy neighbor Squidward Tentacles also works at the Krusty Krab, but hates it there. He also hates SpongeBob and Patrick.

Some episodes feature fantastical story lines; in one episode Squidward gets stuck in a freezer for 2,000 years and travels through time. Sometimes the plots are more ordinary; in another episode Patrick invents a board game and wants his friends to play. In many episodes, Plankton, the dastardly owner of The Chum Bucket, a second-rate seafood restaurant, schemes to steal the secret recipe for Krabby patties. Blending all these elements together into an underwater brew of creativity, this kooky show somehow manages to be both sincere and satiric, as well as innocent and weird.

DID YOU KNOW?
Stephen Hillenburg, the creator of the show, used to be a marine biologist.

SPIN-OFFS
The SpongeBob SquarePants Movie
The SpongeBob Movie: Sponge Out of Water

Saw it! ☐   Rating: ☆☆☆☆☆
Date: ___/___/_____   With: _____
Notes: _____
_____

THE BUGS BUNNY SHOW

78

Chomping confidently on a carrot with ears held high, Bugs Bunny is more than a TV character. He's an institution, and his silly spirit pervades popular culture.

In this entertaining series, Bugs Bunny presents three new cartoons in each episode. He also "educates" audiences with silly facts about animals and humans. The cartoons feature characters like Sylvester Cat, Tweety Bird, Daffy Duck, Porky Pig, Road Runner and Wile E. Coyote, Speedy Gonzales, and of course, Bugs Bunny. Each of the animated critters has their own silly personality. Elmer Fudd has been 'hunting wabbits' for 85 years. Bugs Bunny always outsmarts him—and usually humiliates him. Likewise, the Road Runner always evades his predator, Wile E. Coyote. Together, the gang throws themselves into the slapstick comedy they're known for.

The Bugs Bunny Show's hijinks appeal to both young and old. This show is a classic with timeless comedy and sophisticated concepts. Plus puddy tats, wascawwy wabbits, and a pantless pig!

SPIN-OFFS

The Bugs Bunny/ Road Runner Hour
The Bugs Bunny/Looney Tunes Comedy Hour
The Looney Tunes Show
Baby Looney Tunes

GENRE:
Animated Comedy

AGE:
7+

SEASONS:
3

DID YOU KNOW?
Tweety, the cute yellow bird, was originally pink—and named Orson!

STARRING:
Mel Blanc,
June Foray,
Stan Freberg,
Hal Smith,
and
Daws Butler

Saw it! ☐ Rating: ☆☆☆☆☆
Date: ___/___/_____ With: _____
Notes: _____
_____

79

ANIMANIACS

GENRE:
Animated
Comedy

AGE:
7+

SEASONS:
5

MADE BY:
Tom Ruegger

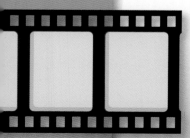

"We protest you calling us 'little kids.'
We prefer to be called 'vertically-
impaired pre-adults.'"
—Yakko

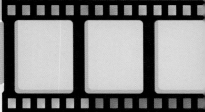

What happens when a bunch of animated characters are too zany for regular cartoons? Meet the Animaniacs: a group of characters that bring a bunch of silly, mischievous fun to each and every episode.

Executive produced by Hollywood superstar Steven Spielberg, *Animaniacs* is an animated variety show, where each episode features skits with different characters. There's Yakko, Dot, and Wakko Warner, who have been locked away in the Warner Bros. water tower until now. Pinky and the Brain are mice that are always plotting world domination. Pesto, Squit, and Bobby make up the Goodfeathers, a team of New York pigeons who obsess over Martin Scorsese. Rita and Runt, a cat and dog that like to sing, just want to find a good, loving home.

With its irreverent humor, clever catchphrases, and smart recurring gags, the *Animaniacs* is a barrel of laughs. References to Hollywood movies and parodies of popular shows, such as *Power Rangers* and *Friends*, make the show appealing to both kids and adults. With so many characters in the *Animaniacs* gang, there's an endless array of possibilities to entertain you each season. Whether you're watching the Warners spend the night in Dracula's Transylvanian castle or admiring Pinky and Brain's use of Merlin's book of magic to take over the world, you're bound to enjoy the wacky antics of *Animaniacs*!

STARRING:
Rob Paulsen,
Tress MacNeille,
and
Jess Harnell

NETWORK:
Fox Kids,
The WB

DID YOU KNOW?
Kooky, crazy Wakko, Yakko, and Dot are based on creator Tom Ruegger's three kids!

Saw it! ☐ Rating: ☆☆☆☆☆

Date: ___/___/_____ With: _____

Notes: _____

_____

80

HEY ARNOLD!

GENRE:
Animated
Comedy

AGE:
7+

SEASONS:
5

STARRING:
Lane Toran,
Spencer Klein,
Jamil
Walker Smith,
and
Francesca
Marie Smith

Hey Arnold! is all about 9-year-old Arnold, who lives at the Sunset Arms boarding house in the inner city with his somewhat eccentric grandparents, Pookie and Phil, and an assortment of other entertaining characters. He has some good friends too, including Helga (who has a huge crush on him) and Gerald, a cool kid with street smarts and a vast knowledge of urban legends.

Arnold encounters a bunch of other kids in his day-to-day adventures in the fourth grade, including Rhonda, a popular fashion diva; Phoebe, the smartest girl in school; and Eugene, everyone's favorite geek. There are some kids that give Arnold trouble too, like bully Harold and his sidekicks, Stinky and Sid. In each episode, Arnold learns valuable lessons from his teachers, friends, or the other residents in the boarding house.

The city of Hillwood, where Arnold lives, is a mash-up of Seattle, Portland, and Brooklyn. With its nods to jazz and opera, and references to famous poets, such as Walt Whitman and William Carlos Williams, *Hey Arnold!* has expanded viewers' appreciation for the arts. The show has been praised for its portrayal of diversity and inner-city life, and quickly became a cult classic after its debut in 1994.

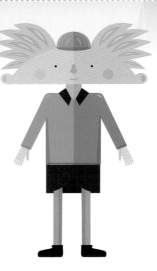

DID YOU KNOW?
Creator Craig Bartlett originally created Arnold as a Claymation character while working on *Pee-wee's Playhouse*.

Saw it! ☐   Rating: ☆☆☆☆☆
Date: ___/___/_____ With: _____
Notes: _____
_____

THE ROCKY & BULLWINKLE SHOW

81

Welcome to *The Rocky & Bullwinkle Show*, an entertaining mash up that's part variety show, part classic cartoon, and part satire. Over the seasons, this series was known by a few different names, including *Rocky and His Friends* and *The Bullwinkle Show*.

The main characters are Rocky, a flying squirrel, and Bullwinkle, a fairly dimwitted moose. Each episode features their run-ins with Boris and Natasha, two Russian spies that can't be trusted. Unlike other cartoons, there are weekly cliffhangers. The furry friends' first adventure spans 40 episodes, as Boris and Natasha plot to uncover the missing ingredient in their jet-fuel formula.

Episodes also include fractured fairy tales and poetry, all narrated by a moose. One delightful segment follows Mr. Peabody and Sherman, a genius dog and his boy. With satirical jokes aplenty and imaginative segments, *The Rocky & Bullwinkle Show* still shines today as a slyly sophisticated gem.

SPIN-OFFS

Boris and Natasha: The Movie
Dudley Do-Right
The Adventures of Rocky & Bullwinkle Movie
Mr. Peabody & Sherman
The Mr. Peabody & Sherman Show

DID YOU KNOW?

Boris and Natasha were inspired by the husband and wife in Charles Addams' *New Yorker* cartoons—the same characters that inspired Gomez and Morticia Addams of *The Addams Family!*

GENRE:
Animated Comedy

AGE:
8+

SEASONS:
5

STARRING:
June Foray, Bill Scott, and Paul Frees

Saw it! ☐ Rating: ☆☆☆☆☆
Date: ___ / ___ / _____ With: _____
Notes: _____
_____

82

THE JETSONS

GENRE:
Animated
Comedy

AGE:
5+

SEASONS:
3

MADE BY:
William Hanna
and Joseph
Barbera

"Jane! Stop this crazy thing!"
—George Jetson

Just like *The Flintstones*, *The Jetsons* is a 30-minute cartoon about a family and their day-to-day life. But this show is set far in the future. George Jetson, his wife Jane, daughter Judy, and son Elroy live in Orbit City, and just like *The Flintstones*, all the novel gizmos, architecture, and futuristic technology make the show memorable.

The buildings float high in the sky, and characters travel from structure to structure in glass aerocars. George's aerocar converts into his briefcase, which is just one of the many nifty visual wonders the show offers. Futuristic conveniences and time-saving devices, such as Rosie the Robot, who cleans the Jetsons' Skypad and brings a bit of sass to each episode, plus jet packs and dinners that appear at the push of a button, help create a utopian futurescape. Precursors to smart watches and video chatting are also part of this world. Episodes involve George getting lost on the moon or volunteering to test a new invention that shrinks him down to just six inches. In other episodes, Judy meets her teen idol, Jane enters a beauty pageant, and the family adopts their talking dog Astro.

It isn't the most accurate depiction of the future, but the show has inspired real-life fashion, movies, and more. Watching this show is the most fun way to travel to the past and the future all at once!

SPIN-OFFS

The Jetsons Meet the Flintstones
Rockin' with Judy Jetson

STARRING:
George O'Hanlon,
Penny Singleton,
Janet Waldo,
Daws Butler, and
Mel Blanc

NETWORK:
ABC

DID YOU KNOW?
The Jetsons was ABC's first show to be broadcast in color.

Saw it! ☐ Rating: ☆☆☆☆☆
Date: ___/___/_____ With: _____
Notes: _____
_____

83

UGLY BETTY

GENRE:
Comedy

AGE:
13+

SEASONS:
4

STARRING:
America Ferrera

Adapted from a Colombian soap opera, *Ugly Betty* follows a kind, smart 22-year-old girl from Queens who lands a job in Manhattan. But since she wears unflattering clothes and has frizzy bangs, bushy eyebrows, and braces, she doesn't quite fit in with everyone else who works at *Mode*, a high-fashion magazine.

The series shines with over-the-top, soap-opera-style drama that is both funny and absorbing. Early in the series, Betty makes all kinds of clumsy missteps and is often the butt of snide commentary from catty co-workers Mark and Amanda. Fortunately, Betty has a close-knit, supportive family at home, where the show's core values of love and inner beauty are shown. Betty eventually wins over some of the coldest hearts at work. While there are some adult themes, the drama never overshadows the comic hijinks, sarcastic one-liners, and quirky characters that make this series a winner.

DID YOU KNOW?

America Ferrera, the actress who played Betty, was also in the movie adaptation of *The Sisterhood of the Traveling Pants*. Producers gave a nod to her work by placing a copy of the book on Betty's nightstand.

Saw it! ☐   Rating: ☆☆☆☆☆
Date: ___/___/_____ With: _____
Notes: _____
_____

MR. BEAN

Mr. Bean is a British comedy that aired from 1992 to 1995. Created by Rowan Atkinson and Richard Curtis, the show stars Atkinson as a comically immature, socially awkward, clueless, all-around weirdo. Atkinson described his character as "a child in a grown man's body." He could also be described as selfish and annoying. Bean goes through his days making a mess of things, breaking things, and irritating people. He has zero sense of personal space. But in Atkinson's talented hands, Mr. Bean isn't just annoying, he's hilarious.

This 1990s show is a throwback to the simple slapstick comedy of *The Carol Burnett Show*, and even Charlie Chaplin. Most impressive is that the show is almost entirely wordless. While there is some dialogue, Atkinson keeps viewers entertained with an extraordinary range of facial expressions and physical antics. There are a few other characters for him to interact with, but they are mostly strangers who are inconvenienced and bothered by Mr. Bean's behavior. Bean can wreak havoc on himself in the simplest situations, including changing into a swimsuit, losing a shoe, or trying to make his TV work. But from the safe distance of your couch, Mr. Bean makes the world a happier, funnier place to be!

GENRE:
Comedy

AGE:
10+

SEASONS:
4

STARRING:
Rowan Atkinson

DID YOU KNOW?

The opening sequence shows Bean descending to Earth as a choir sings, "Ecce homo qui est faba" dramatically. But the translation isn't quite so dramatic. It means, "Behold the man who is a bean."

Saw it! ☐ Rating: ☆☆☆☆☆

Date: ___/___/_____ With: _____

Notes: _____

_____

85

MONTY PYTHON'S FLYING CIRCUS

GENRE:
Comedy

AGE:
14+

SEASONS:
4

MADE BY:
Graham
Chapman,
John Cleese,
Terry Gilliam,
Eric Idle,
Terry Jones, and
Michael Palin

"Nobody expects the Spanish Inquisition!"
—An absurd line from a Monty Python sketch that led to many more sketches and memes

DID YOU KNOW?

Anyone applying for British citizenship will want to spend hours watching *Monty Python*. The citizenship exam includes questions about Shakespeare, Stonehenge—and British classic *Monty Python*!

The creators considered naming the show everything from *Owl Stretching Time* to *Bunn, Wackett, Buzzard, Stubble and Boot*, which doesn't make any more sense than *Monty Python's Flying Circus*. And when it finally aired, the show was almost canceled after just one episode. But thankfully this classic comedy survived. The production values are humble, the camera work is a bit shoddy, and by today's standards, the program seems a tad amateurish, but for obsessed fans, sharing *Monty Python* with the next generation is a no-brainer. This British sketch comedy is recommended for anyone who has an outlandish, offbeat sense of humor and an appreciation for comedic anarchy.

With less structure and sillier jokes than Monty Python movies that came later, *The Flying Circus* is chaos. The highly educated writers and performers of the Monty Python troupe are as comfortable making jokes about deep thinkers like Marcel Proust and Karl Marx as they are dressing up as frumpy housewives. The comedy is absurd, sometimes surreal, and always ludicrous. Episodes are a mix of loopy skits, fanciful animation, cheeky humor, and songs. Nonsensical sketches often make use of stock footage, ridiculous accents, and a preposterous set up like a clinic where customers can pay for a 30-minute argument, a hospital for patients suffering from severe over-acting, a class for "self-defense against fresh fruit" and of course, a government agency called the Ministry of Silly Walks. When it comes to Monty Python, no one expects the Spanish Inquisition, but they can always expect to laugh.

STARRING:
Graham Chapman, John Cleese, Terry Gilliam, Eric Idle, Terry Jones, and Michael Palin

NETWORK:
BBC, PBS

SPIN-OFFS

And Now for Something Completely Different
Monty Python and the Holy Grail
Life of Brian
The Meaning of Life

Saw it! ☐ Rating: ☆☆☆☆☆

Date: ___ / ___ / _____ With: _____

Notes: _____

_____

86

PEE-WEE'S PLAYHOUSE

GENRE:
Comedy

AGE:
6+

SEASONS:
5

MADE BY:
Paul Reubens

"I know you are,
but what am I?"
—Pee-wee

Pee-wee's Playhouse, originally created for a stage act in 1980, features Paul Reubens' giddy, childlike character Pee-Wee Herman. He spends his day playing in a gorgeously conceived fantasy playhouse that would make any child happy. The set is bursting with color, toys, friends, and inanimate objects that surprise and dazzle. There's a talking window (Mr. Window) and a talking chair (Chairy), along with Globey, Clocky, and Conky the robot—the brain of the show. There are both human characters and puppets, as well as animated sequences. Friends also stop by all the time. Some of the show's regulars are Captain Carl and Cowboy Curtis, retro versions of a cowboy and a sea captain. Another recurring character is Jambi the Genie, a blue headed genie that grants wishes and lives in a jeweled box.

Throughout the show's run, Reubens had complete creative control. He also spent much of his own money to make the show a success. With a retro-vintage vibe inspired by Reubens' childhood favorite shows, *The Howdy Doody Show* and *Captain Kangaroo*, every episode is about having fun. With a diverse group of actors and its gender-neutral approach, this show is a big, loud, colorful celebration of individuality!

SPIN-OFFS
Pee-wee's Big Adventure
Big Top Pee-wee
Pee-wee's Playhouse: The Movie
The Pee-wee Herman Story
The Pee-wee Herman Show revival
Pee-wee's Big Holiday

STARRING:
Paul Reubens,
George McGrath,
and
Alison Mork

NETWORK:
CBS

DID YOU KNOW?
Paul Reubens auditioned to join the cast of *Saturday Night Live* but didn't make the cut. Thankfully that didn't stop him from sharing his delightful humor with the world!

Saw it! ☐ Rating: ☆☆☆☆☆
Date: ___ / ___ / _____ With: _____
Notes: _____
_____

87

THE MONKEES

GENRE:
Comedy

AGE:
7+

SEASONS:
2

STARRING:
Davy Jones,
Micky Dolenz,
Michael
Nesmith, and
Peter Tork

"Hey, hey, we're the Monkees!" This catchy line launched every episode of the popular 1960s show. Shortly after the Beatles made their big-screen, musical comedies *A Hard Day's Night* and *Help!*, The Monkees arrived. The band name alludes to another popular animal, and there's a dashing, shaggy-haired Brit to front the band, just like Paul McCartney in the Beatles. But in some ways the fictitious band is closer to *The Partridge Family,* with their real hit songs. The show charts the aspiring rock stars' madcap career and their fun-loving, freewheeling spirits. Their sound was a cross between The Beach Boys and—you guessed it—the Beatles.

While some of the episodes focus on their music and encounters with producers, publicists, and showbiz personnel, there are tons of zany stories too: The Monkees spend a night in a haunted house, The Monkees get stranded in a ghost town, and The Monkees have to hide a horse from their landlord. The show opens with the foursome fooling around, wearing crazy costumes, playing on the beach, and singing their famous song, "Hey, Hey, We're The Monkees." Other infectious hits include, "I'm a Believer" and "Last Train to Clarksville." Are you ready for a little Monkeemania?

SPIN-OFFS
New Monkees

Saw it! ☐   Rating: ☆☆☆☆☆
Date: ___/___/_____ With: _____
Notes: _____
_____

GIDGET

Surf's up, dudes! Gidget is a sassy teenage surfer girl who tends to find her way into trouble. She lives with her father, Russell Lawrence, a widower and professor, in sunny Southern California. She spends most of her time either with her best friend, Larue, or surfing at the beach.

When *Gidget* aired in 1965, the show featured a very different female lead than the other shows on television at the time. Gidget, an independent, smart, and lovable girl, isn't afraid to break the rules. And the adventures she goes on are as eccentric as she is—one episode revolves around a tiny frozen alligator! At the end of each episode, she turns to the camera and tells the audience what she learned, but by the next episode, she's ready to throw the rules out the window again!

Gidget may be a little boy-crazy. She's dating Jeff (also known as Moondoggie), but he's away at college, so she's free to flirt with other boys at the beach. Gidget's married older sister, Anne, often tries to offer advice, but it's usually the wise words of their father that reach Gidget the best. This fun, breezy summer show will have you wanting to hang ten at the beach and meet the Great Kahuna!

SPIN-OFFS
The New Gidget

GENRE:
Comedy

AGE:
7+

SEASONS:
1

STARRING:
Sally Field

DID YOU KNOW?

Sally Field, who plays Gidget, improvised saying, "Toodles!" at the end of an episode, and it became her catchphrase.

Saw it! ☐ Rating: ☆☆☆☆☆

Date: ___ / ____ / _____ With: _____

Notes: _____

_____

89

THE CAROL BURNETT SHOW

GENRE:
Comedy

AGE:
9+

SEASONS:
11

MADE BY:
Bob Banner
and
Joe Hamilton

"I'm so glad we had this time together Just to have a laugh or sing a song. Seems we just got started and before you know it Comes the time we have to say, 'So long.'"
—From the classic theme song

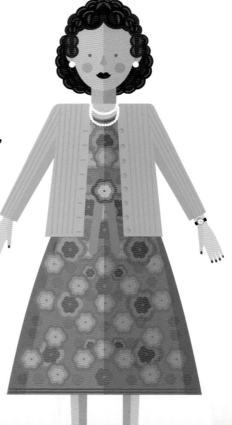

Like Lucille Ball, Carol Burnett is a timeless titan of cockamamie comedy. *The Carol Burnett Show*, which ran from the late 1960s to the late 1970s, is still hilarious 40 years later. It's a one-hour variety show with a huge range of stellar guests, from Ray Charles to Lily Tomlin. Steve Martin even joined the cast of regulars, which included Harvey Korman, Tim Conway, Vicki Lawrence, and Lyle Waggoner, in comic skits and musical numbers. The show featured regular characters, such as Mrs. Wiggins, a silly, incompetent secretary played by Burnett, and an incredibly old geezer played by Conway, who drives everyone crazy by moving so slowly. One of the funniest things about the show is watching the cast crack each other up. Conway would often go out of his way to make Korman laugh, and watching Korman try—and fail—to hold it together is highly entertaining. The show also featured plenty of movie parodies, and even if you don't know the films, the sketches are so wacky, you'll still find yourself laughing. One of the most memorable sketches was a parody of *Gone with the Wind*, in which Burnett as Scarlett O'Hara wears a dress made from window drapes. Sounds resourceful, not silly, right? Consider that she also wore the drape rod as shoulder pads. The result was perfectly preposterous and totally delirious!

SPIN-OFFS

Carol Burnett & Company
Eunice
Mama's Family

STARRING:
Carol Burnett,
Harvey Korman,
Vicki Lawrence,
Lyle Waggoner,
and
Tim Conway

NETWORK:
CBS

DID YOU KNOW?
The first variety show to be led by a woman, *The Carol Burnett Show* won 25 Emmys.

Saw it! ☐ Rating: ☆☆☆☆☆
Date: ___ / ___ / _____ With: _____
Notes: _____
_____

90

THE MICKEY MOUSE CLUB

GENRE:
Comedy

AGE:
2+

SEASONS:
4

MADE BY:
Walt Disney,
Bill Walsh,
and
Hal Adelquist

"Why? Because we like you!
—Jimmie at the end of each show, telling viewers there will be another episode tomorrow

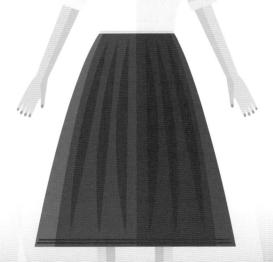

ANNETTE

Hey, there! Hi, there! Ho, there! "Who's the leader of the club that's made for you and me?" When you're talking about the *Mickey Mouse Club*, the answer is obvious. M-I-C-K-E-Y M-O-U-S-E!

First airing in 1955, this long-running variety show has entertained multiple generations. The original *Mickey Mouse Club* featured a line-up of teenage Mouseketeers, including Annette Funicello and Tommy Cole. Later the show was revived in full color for new audiences, with stars such as a young Britney Spears and Justin Timberlake.

Walt Disney himself designed the *Mickey Mouse Club* to include cartoons, singing, dancing, comedy, a touch of drama, and a news segment. Monday episodes are all about having fun with music. Tuesday shows feature guest stars. On Wednesdays, anything can happen. Thursdays are circus days. And Friday is a talent round up. At the beginning of each show, the Mouseketeers line up for roll call and introduce themselves. The teenagers are lead by Head Mouseketeer, Jimmie Dodd. He often offers bits of wisdom known as Doddisms and encourages kids to make good choices. Each episode ends with a slower version of the theme song and a promise to "See you real soon!"

Wholesome, precocious, and yet totally relatable, the teenagers feel like best friends. The cast often speaks directly to the camera, inviting viewers to join the jamboree and feel like one of the gang. Watch a few episodes, and soon you'll be longing for your own pair of mouse ears.

SPIN-OFFS
New Mickey Mouse Club
All New Mickey Mouse Club (MMC)

STARRING:
Annette Funicello,
Tommy Cole,
Jimmie Dodd,
and
Roy Williams

NETWORK:
Disney, ABC

DID YOU KNOW?
Walt Disney wanted to cast "regular" kids for the show, so he avoided hiring professional actors.

Saw it! ☐ Rating: ☆☆☆☆☆
Date: ___/___/_____ With: _____
Notes: _____
_____

91

THE WIGGLES

GENRE:
Comedy

AGE:
3+

SEASONS:
5

STARRING:
Murray Cook,
Jeff Fatt,
Anthony Field,
and
Greg Page

Did you learn to sing and dance with the Wiggles? If not, you're missing out! The Wiggles, a band from Australia, love to sing, dance, and hang out with their friends Wags the Dog, Dorothy the Dinosaur, Henry the Octopus, and of course, Captain Feathersword.

Since they first started playing together in 1991, The Wiggles have risen to international fame. They've earned many awards, their multi-platinum records are a hit, and they've toured the world. Originally there were just four Wiggles, but as of 2013, some new faces appeared, including the first female Wiggle.

Whether they are trying to wake Jeff up (Everyone yell: WAKE UP, JEFF!), teaching Captain Feathersword to spell, or just riding around in their Big Red Car, The Wiggles are always having fun. Friendship, imagination, and silly, goofy fun are what The Wiggles want to show you, and they have a catchy, colorful way of doing it. So come on, join the dance party and wiggle away!

DID YOU KNOW?
The Wiggles perform for over a million people every year—that's a lot of wiggling!

Saw it! ☐ Rating: ☆☆☆☆☆
Date: ___/___/_____ With: _____
Notes: _____
_____

YOU CAN'T DO THAT ON TELEVISION

92

You better not say "I don't know" on this show, or else you'll get a giant bucket of slime dumped on your head! You could also get soaked with water or get a pie in the face. There's never a dull moment on *You Can't Do That on Television!*

A variety sketch show featuring young actors, this show has it all: parodies of other TV shows and commercials, silly recurring gags and gimmicks, and a hilarious cast. Each episode is built around a theme, and all the skits go with it, down to the name of the production company listed in the end credits. (The divorce-themed episode was supposedly made by the "Split Down The Middle" production company.) Some sketches are recurring, such as the "opposites" sketch, where everything is opposite; locker jokes, where kids tell jokes from inside their lockers; and of course, the Barth's Burgers sketches where kids eat at a terrible restaurant.

You Can't Do That on Television is packed with slapstick comedy, a talented cast, and a whole lot of slime, which eventually became a hallmark of the Nickelodeon network!

GENRE:
Comedy

AGE:
12+

SEASONS:
10

STARRING:
Les Lye,
Abby Hagyard,
and
Christine
McGlade

DID YOU KNOW?
The green slime is made from a mixture of water, flour, and green gelatin!

Saw it! ☐ Rating: ☆☆☆☆☆

Date: ___ / ___ / _____ With: _____

Notes: _____

_____

93 LITTLE HOUSE ON THE PRAIRIE

GENRE:
Drama

AGE:
7+

SEASONS:
9

MADE BY:
Based on the books by Laura Ingalls Wilder

DID YOU KNOW?
Little House on the Prairie and *The Waltons* were marketed as family-friendly alternatives to edgier shows like *All In The Family*, *Sanford and Son*, and *Starsky and Hutch*.

"Home is the nicest word there is."
—Laura Ingalls Wilder

Based on Laura Ingalls Wilder's perennially popular autobiographical books about frontier life, *Little House on the Prairie* is set in the American frontier in the late 19th century. Although the stories were often simplistic and moralizing, the multidimensional acting set this show apart from other shows in the 1970s. (The show was nominated for 16 Emmys!)

Like the *Little House* novels, the series follows the life of the Ingalls family, told from the point of view of Laura, who is around 6 years old when the series begins. The Ingalls are homesteaders who settle in a quaint home in Walnut Grove, Minnesota. You don't have to be a Laura Ingalls Wilder reader to get hooked on this series. The show immerses viewers in an era of horse-drawn wagons, sleeping bonnets, and schoolhouses with writing tablets. And since the story runs until the Ingalls girls are grown and married, it also features soap-opera-style plotlines. Charles Ingalls, or "Pa," is a farmer and mill worker. Played by Michael Landon, Charles is a strong and compassionate family man. He's an attentive, adoring father and an ideal husband to his wife, Caroline. Their children are Mary, Laura, and Carrie. In later seasons, Grace is born, and three others are adopted. Hard working and self-sufficient, the family has little money, and when the girls start school, they become exposed to wealthier townspeople. One of the original love-to-hate-them characters, Nelly Oleson is a spoiled brat with a snobby mother. Nelly and her mother look down at the Ingalls, who can't afford a lot of things. But the Ingalls show they are truly the richer family. Watch this show and soon you'll agree; the Ingalls may live in a little house, but their hearts are as big as the prairie!

SPIN-OFFS
Little House: A New Beginning
Little House on the Prairie: A Look Back to Yesterday

STARRING:
Michael Landon,
Melissa Gilbert,
Karen Grassle,
and
Melissa Sue
Anderson

NETWORK:
NBC

Saw it! ☐ Rating: ☆☆☆☆☆
Date: ___ / ___ / _____ With: _____
Notes: _____
_____

DOOGIE HOWSER, M.D.

GENRE:
Drama

AGE:
12+

SEASONS:
4

STARRING:
Neil Patrick
Harris,
Max Casella,
Lisa Dean Ryan,
and
Lawrence
Pressman

Like many other kids, Doogie Howser feels a little out of place, whether he's with adults or other children. But unlike other kids, he's also the world's youngest doctor. *Doogie Howser, M.D.* is a drama about a prodigy who graduated from Princeton when he was 10. Played by a baby-faced Neil Patrick Harris, Doogie lives at home with his parents and follows their rules, but he practices medicine at a hospital where he makes life-saving decisions. The show's sweet mix of comedy and drama is appealing, and viewers can relate to Doogie being someone who doesn't quite fit in.

Doogie can often be found performing surgery, while also worrying about his first kiss or being liked by the popular kids. In one episode, he throws a party when his parents are away so the other kids won't think he's a "freak." Because of his grueling work schedule, Doogie often has to apologize for being late to his on-again/off-again girlfriend Wanda. Life lessons are introduced through medical story lines that touch on AIDS, teen pregnancy, race riots, and other weighty topics. But his goofy, girl-crazy best friend Vinnie Delpino makes sure Doogie never gets too serious.

DID YOU KNOW?
Neil Patrick Harris practiced making stitches on raw chickens.

Saw it! ☐ Rating: ☆☆☆☆☆
Date: ___/___/_____ With: _____
Notes: _____
_____

GILMORE GIRLS

This witty dramedy follows single mother Lorelai Gilmore and her 16-year-old daughter Rory. They are best friends who support each other through changes in jobs, schools, friends, and boyfriends.

The series effortlessly blends family drama with humor and social commentary, as mother and daughter navigate work, school, and dinner at Grandma's house. In the pilot episode, Lorelai asks her parents, Richard and Emily, to help pay for Rory's education at a prestigious private school. They agree to help only if Lorelai and Rory attend formal weekly dinners at their house. The story lines are set against the backdrop of the Gilmores' small hometown, Stars Hollow, Connecticut, where they are surrounded by eccentric characters, such as Lorelei's klutzy best friend, Sookie St. James, and the owner of Luke's Diner, who adds casual humor to the show.

For many fans, the characters' clever dialogue makes the show addictive. Lorelei and Rory are famous for their snarky, rapid-fire banter full of pop-culture references. The series was widely embraced for its feminist role models and quirky depiction of a sisterly mother/daughter relationship.

GENRE:
Drama

AGE:
14+

SEASONS:
7

STARRING:
Lauren Graham, Alexis Bledel, Scott Patterson, Kelly Bishop, and Edward Herrmann

DID YOU KNOW?

The exterior shot of the Dragonfly Inn, where Lorelai works, is the same family home from *The Waltons*.

Saw it! ☐ Rating: ☆☆☆☆☆

Date: ___/___/_____ With: _____

Notes: _____

_____

96

DEGRASSI: THE NEXT GENERATION

GENRE:
Drama

AGE:
14+

SEASONS:
14

MADE BY:
Kit Hood
and
Linda Schuyler

"It's just been one disaster after another after another. That school is cursed." —Ashley

Taking place 14 years after the original show *Degrassi Junior High*, *Degrassi: The Next Generation* brings the drama! From tragedy to scandal, the kids at Degrassi Community School experience it all. While there are definitely moments of lighthearted fun, *Degrassi* features the more serious issues of teenage life, including divorce, teen pregnancy, bullying, eating disorders, and even a school shooting. (Of course, they're also dealing with cliques, crushes, homework, frenemies, team tryouts, and prom.) These very real issues are handled with honesty, care, and empathy. The characters are believable and sympathetic, and it's easy to become invested in their story lines and relationships. Alli struggles to balance her conservative Muslim heritage with her boy-crazy impulses. Jenna learns to find her way as a young mother. And viewers' hearts melt as Adam navigates being a transgender teen. While the cast changes throughout the years as the kids grow up and graduate, *Degrassi* consistently keeps viewers captivated with compelling story lines, insightful dialogue, and talented young actors.

The show launched the careers of several young stars, most notably Aubrey Graham, aka mega recording star Drake, who played Jimmy Brooks. *Degrassi* has won more than 50 awards for writing, directing, and acting. Legions of fans will be pleased to know a new series is in the works on Netflix. Let the *Degrassi* drama continue...

SPIN-OFFS
Degrassi: Next Class

STARRING:
Melinda Shankar, Aislinn Paul, A.J. Saudin, Miriam McDonald, Shane Kippel, Stefan Brogren and Drake

NETWORK:
CTV, TeenNick

DID YOU KNOW?
Each episode is named after a song from the 1980s. Totally rad!

Saw it! ☐ Rating: ☆☆☆☆☆

Date: ___ / ___ / _____ With: _____

Notes: _____

_____

97

FREAKS AND GEEKS

GENRE:
Drama

AGE:
14+

SEASONS:
1

MADE BY:
Judd Apatow
and Paul Feig

*"Wait a minute.
If I think I'm cool then people will
think I'm cool too? But I already
think I'm cool. But nobody else does."*
—Neil Schweiber

Freaks and Geeks is critically acclaimed and beloved by audiences. Set in the 1980s, each episode features an authentic story line and a stellar cast of young actors who went on to become big stars. As the title suggests, the series follows two groups of high-school students: the freshman "geeks" and the junior and senior "freaks" who are more interested in partying than studying.

The show focuses on Lindsay and Sam Weir. Sam is a ninth-grader who's frequently bullied. His older sister Lindsay is a well-behaved rule follower and an "A" student who starts hanging out with the "freaks." Lindsay must balance her allegiance to school and family with her emerging independence and desire to hang out with the "cool kids." The cool kids include a fresh-faced Seth Rogen as Ken and a young Jason Segel as Nick. Like his older sister, Sam is trying to navigate growing up. He and his friends are socially awkward, obsessed with Steve Martin, devoted to playing Dungeons and Dragons, and determined to figure out where girls fit into their lives.

Unlike their new friends, Lindsay and Sam come from a loving and concerned family, with a nurturing but worried mom and an alarmed dad with a deadpan sense of humor. The show is quirky and a little edgy, but at its core, it's about growing pains and figuring out how to make good choices. The series was inexplicably canceled after one season, which was a true television tragedy for its devoted fans.

STARRING:
Linda Cardellini,
John Francis Daley,
James Franco,
Samm Levine,
Seth Rogen,
Jason Segel,
Martin Starr,
Becky Ann Baker,
Joe Flaherty,
and
Busy Philipps

NETWORK:
NBC

DID YOU KNOW?
Every plot point in *Freaks and Geeks* was based on a real event that happened in the lives of the show's writers.

Saw it! ☐ Rating: ☆☆☆☆☆

Date: ___/___/_____ With: _____

Notes: _____

_____

98

LASSIE

GENRE:
Drama

AGE:
5+

SEASONS:
19

STARRING:
Jon Provost,
June Lockhart,
and
Hugh Reilly

If your dog is your best friend, you know how smart and clever canine pals can be. Over 19 seasons, Lassie and her human family have all types of adventures on their farm. Whether Lassie is tending to motherless baby birds or helping Timmy out of a jam, she's always the hero.

Lassie is an extraordinarily smart, brave, and sensitive collie; it's almost as if she can communicate with her human companions just by barking. In the first few seasons of the show, Lassie is part of the Miller family. Later she is part of the Martin family, and eventually she joins the US Forest Service. In every episode, Lassie either goes to get help when people are in trouble, or jumps in to save them herself if needed.

The show was based on a series of popular movies in the 1940s and early 1950s. Originally, the show was in black and white, but it made the transition to color in 1965. As one of the longest running shows in television history, *Lassie* is not only famous for portraying a really smart dog, but also for telling the story of a farm family with strong values. Of course, this heartwarming classic is worth a watch just to see how Lassie always manages to save the day.

DID YOU KNOW?

In the pilot, Lassie was played by a dog named Pal, but for the rest of the show, Pal's pups, Lassie Junior, Spook, and Baby played Lassie.

Saw it! ☐　Rating: ☆☆☆☆☆☆

Date: ___/ ___/ _____　With: _____

Notes: _____

_____

THE WALTONS

Told from the viewpoint of adult John-Boy, the oldest of seven siblings, *The Waltons* follows a family living in rural Virginia during the Great Depression and World War II. The Walton family includes Olivia and John (or Ma and Pa), their children, and the grandparents.

In each episode, the family works together to do the right thing, whether they open their home to a stranded traveler, help an orphaned kid learn what a loving and trusting family looks like, or lend a hand in their community. Traditional, wholesome values and lessons are woven throughout every storyline. Money is tight in the Walton home, and the family must come together to support each other and make ends meet. As the seasons roll on, the family experiences a lot together: college, courtships, marriages, career changes, new babies, and even illness and death.

Each episode ends with everyone in the house going to sleep. As the lights go out, everyone says goodnight to each other. Watching *The Waltons* will make you feel like you are a part of their big family, and you'll soon be saying "Goodnight, John-Boy" too!

DID YOU KNOW?

The cast of *The Waltons* consider themselves family and have stayed friends for over 50 years.

GENRE:
Drama

AGE:
7+

SEASONS:
9

STARRING:
Jon Walmsley,
Mary Beth,
McDonough,
Eric Scott,
Judy Norton,
David W. Harper,
Kami Cotler,
and
Richard Thomas

Saw it! ☐ Rating: ☆☆☆☆☆

Date: ___/___/_____ With: _____

Notes: _____

_____

100

SHELLEY DUVALL'S FAERIE TALE THEATRE

GENRE:
Drama

AGE:
7+

SEASONS:
6

MADE BY:
Shelley Duvall

Gretel: Why would you want to eat him? Witch: I am going to eat him, because that is what witches like to do!

Some of the most beloved stories have been told over and over for hundreds of years. *Faerie Tale Theatre*, which first aired in 1982, retells some of these classic stories. Shelley Duvall, the actress who has given a variety of quirky performances, including the odd-ball Olive Oyl in the movie version of *Popeye*, created and produced this enchanting anthology of fables.

Duvall enlists renowned directors like Tim Burton and Francis Ford Coppola to contribute to the series. Stars such as Pee-wee Herman and Robin Williams play classic characters like Pinocchio, the frog prince, the princess in *The Princess and the Pea*, witches, sorcerers, and more. While the tales are timeless, this show updates the stories to include more modern, humorous dialogue. For example, the snobbish princess in *The Tale of the Frog Prince* complains about the prince by calling him a "miserable creep" who has the "brains of a shrimp." The cast is also more racially diverse than many of those found on television.

The episodes are clearly staged as a play, and the action takes place on sets with far less razzle dazzle than you may be used to, but the emphasis is on the language and the excellent performances. More than 30 years later, this show still deserves a standing ovation.

SPIN-OFFS
Shelley Duvall's Tall Tales & Legends

STARRING:
Shelley Duvall

NETWORK:
Showtime

DID YOU KNOW?
The series was inspired by *Shirley Temple's Storybook*, a TV series that was popular in the late 1950s and early 1960s.

Saw it! ☐ Rating: ☆☆☆☆☆

Date: ___/___/_____ With: _____

Notes: _____

_____

101

MY SO-CALLED LIFE

GENRE:
Drama

AGE:
14+

SEASONS:
1

STARRING:
Claire Danes,
Jared Leto,
Wilson Cruz,
Devon
Gummersall,
and
A.J. Langer

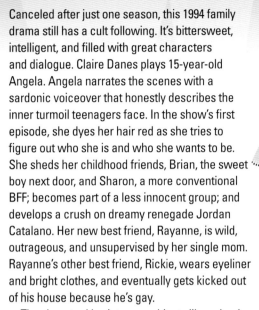

Canceled after just one season, this 1994 family drama still has a cult following. It's bittersweet, intelligent, and filled with great characters and dialogue. Claire Danes plays 15-year-old Angela. Angela narrates the scenes with a sardonic voiceover that honestly describes the inner turmoil teenagers face. In the show's first episode, she dyes her hair red as she tries to figure out who she is and who she wants to be. She sheds her childhood friends, Brian, the sweet boy next door, and Sharon, a more conventional BFF; becomes part of a less innocent group; and develops a crush on dreamy renegade Jordan Catalano. Her new best friend, Rayanne, is wild, outrageous, and unsupervised by her single mom. Rayanne's other best friend, Rickie, wears eyeliner and bright clothes, and eventually gets kicked out of his house because he's gay.

The show tackles intense subjects like school violence, censorship, homelessness, and more. The show could have been very dark, but with witty, clever writing and authentic, likable characters, instead it's an absolute treasure.

DID YOU KNOW?

The school scenes were filmed at University High School in Los Angeles, where other popular shows such as *Lizzie McGuire*, *7th Heaven,* and *Parenthood* were also filmed.

Saw it! ☐ Rating: ☆☆☆☆☆
Date: ___/___/_____ With: _____
Notes: _____
_____

101

Books to Read
Before You Grow Up

A Note
From the Author

There are so many amazing books to be discovered and read—
and far too many to list in one fun book. The 101 awesome books contained
in these pages have one collective message:

Be kind, be brave, and make good choices. Remember the struggles
of those that came before you. Always dream of the fantastical future ahead of
you and those who will come after you. Be true to yourself, and with every
page you turn, live your life like an epic adventure.

Written by Bianca Schulze
Illustrated by Shaw Nielsen

T ble of Cont nts

The stories in this book
are organized by age level, but we think they are
timeless and enjoyable no matter how old you are.
Are you in the mood for something silly or mysterious?
Something fantastical or adventurous? Take a look
at page 142, where each book
is listed by genre.

Where the Wild Things Are

Written and Illustrated by Maurice Sendak

AGES:
4+

GENRE:
FANTASY

PUBLISHER:
HARPERCOLLINS

PUBLICATION DATE:
1963

PAGE COUNT:
48

Have you ever felt wild? Wild with anger? Wild with excitement? Wild with your imagination? On the night that Max puts on his wolf suit and makes mischief, his mother sends him to bed without any supper. Alone in his room, Max sees a forest grow, and an ocean and boat appear. He sails off to where the wild things are, and he becomes the king of all the wild things. But when all becomes quiet and the wild rumpus is over, Max feels lonely and returns home to find his supper waiting for him. It's even still hot!

It's both strange and exciting to see how brave and fearless Max is while encountering the monstrous wild things. With few words and illustrations that fill up each page, this is a captivating book you will want to read night and day, for weeks on end. We all feel wild at times, and it's totally acceptable to be wild about this book!

Did you know?

An elementary school in North Hollywood, California, is named in Maurice Sendak's honor.

What to read next?

- *In the Night Kitchen* by Maurice Sendak
- *Nutshell Library* by Maurice Sendak
- *Alexander and the Terrible, Horrible, No Good, Very Bad Day* by Judith Viorst
- *Mr. Tiger Goes Wild* by Peter Brown

Did you know?

Where the Wild Things Are actually began as a story called *Where the Wild Horses Are*. But Sendak had trouble drawing horses, so he knew he needed to come up with something different. That's when the term "wild things" came to him.

"'AND NOW,' CRIED MAX, 'LET THE WILD RUMPUS START!'"

Read it! ☐   Rating: ☆☆☆☆☆

Favorite Character: _____

Notes: _____

_____

2 Oh, the Places You'll Go
Written and Illustrated by Dr. Seuss

AGES:
4+

GENRE:
POETRY & RHYME

PUBLISHER:
RANDOM HOUSE

PUBLICATION DATE:
1960

PAGE COUNT:
56

Have you read this book? As Dr. Seuss says in *One Fish Two Fish Red Fish Blue Fish*, "If you never did you should. These things are fun and fun is good." From soaring to high heights and seeing great sights, to being left in a lurch on a prickly perch, *Oh, the Places You'll Go* has to be one of the most inspiring and encouraging books ever.

Yes. E. V. E. R. There are so many reasons to love this tale, including the sheer absurdity of Dr. Seuss's zany characters. From the words of wisdom to the iconic illustrations, this is a favorite for many people. It's perfect for all ages—adults, kids graduating from one grade to another, or anyone just learning to read. Thanks to Dr. Seuss's clever rhyming, this book sounds great when it is read aloud, so find a friend or a dog (*Go, Dog! Go!*) and host your own read-aloud session, or pretend you're standing on a podium giving an inspiring speech to your graduating class. *Oh, the Places You'll Go* is so entertaining, and the words will have you (and your friends) reaching for the stars, dreaming big, and moving mountains. Oh, the places you will go after reading this book!

Did you know?
Dr. Seuss's real name is Theodor Seuss Geisel.

What to read next?
- *I Wish That I Had Duck Feet* by Dr. Seuss
- *The Lorax* by Dr. Seuss
- *Green Eggs and Ham* by Dr. Seuss
- *Are You My Mother?* by P. D. Eastman
- *The Giving Tree* by Shel Silverstein

Did you know?
Publishers rejected his first book, *And to Think That I Saw It on Mulberry Street*, numerous times.

Did you know?
Hundreds of millions of Dr. Seuss books have been published around the world in many different languages.

"YOU'RE OFF TO GREAT PLACES! TODAY IS YOUR DAY! YOUR MOUNTAIN IS WAITING, SO...GET ON YOUR WAY!"

Read it! ☐   Rating: ☆☆☆☆☆

Favorite Character: _____

Notes: _____

_____

3 The Giving Tree

Written and Illustrated by Shel Silverstein

AGES:
4+

GENRE:
POETRY & RHYME

PUBLISHER:
HARPERCOLLINS

PUBLICATION DATE:
1964

PAGE COUNT:
64

"Once there was a tree…and she loved a little boy." Every day, in *The Giving Tree*, a boy visits his favorite tree. He makes crowns from her leaves, climbs her trunk, swings from her branches, and eats her apples; and the tree is very happy because she loves him unconditionally. The boy loves her back, but as he grows up, they spend less time together. Nevertheless, when the boy does return, the tree keeps on giving. The boy never seems to give back, only wanting more from her. Alas, she loves the boy, and so she stays true to her roots and continues giving until she is reduced to a mere stump.

Do you think the tree is happy or sad? As the reader, you'll get to decide the meaning of this story for yourself. Is it about love, growing up, or being thankful? Is it about friendship, or is it about something entirely different? One thing is for sure: If you're reading *The Giving Tree* with a grown-up, you'll probably have to pass them a tissue to wipe away their tears. There aren't too many words on each page, and the pictures are splendidly simple. You could try drawing your own Giving Tree in the artist's special style! Do you have a big heart like the tree? Can you be as kind and generous? Read and decide for yourself.

What to read next?

- *Where the Sidewalk Ends* by Shel Silverstein
- *A Light in the Attic* by Shel Silverstein
- *Runny Babbit: A Billy Sook* by Shel Silverstein
- *Love You Forever* by Robert Munsch

Did you know?

Shel Silverstein was a Grammy-winning, Oscar-nominated songwriter. He was also a cartoonist, playwright, poet, and performer.

Read it! ☐   Rating: ☆☆☆☆☆

Favorite Character: _____

Notes: _____
_____

4 Whoever You Are

Written by Mem Fox • Illustrated by Leslie Staub

Did you know that whoever you are and wherever you are, there are people just like you somewhere in the world? Well, there are, and this sprightly, soulful picture book celebrates this fact. Even though we may look different, sound different, and live in different homes, we are all truly the same beneath our skin. We all feel many things on any given day, like being happy, sad, or loved.

Whoever You Are is filled with colorful pictures that depict many different people and places around our wonderful world. If you are ready to read a book that makes you feel warm and fuzzy, then this book is the one you will want to pick up next. It is filled with love for the world and everyone in it. What more can a reader ask for?

What to read next?
- *It's Okay to Be Different*
  by Todd Parr
- *The Colors of Us* by Karen Katz
- *Time for Bed* by Mem Fox
- *Possum Magic* by Mem Fox

Did you know?
Mem Fox is an Australian author and expert on how people learn to read. She loves it when parents and children read books aloud together, because it can change their lives forever.

The author's full name is Merrion Frances Fox, but since she was thirteen, people have been calling her Mem.

AGES:
4+

GENRE:
POETRY & RHYME

PUBLISHER:
HMH BOOKS
FOR YOUNG
READERS

**PUBLICATION
DATE:**
1997

PAGE COUNT:
32

Read it! ☐   Rating: ☆☆☆☆☆

Favorite Character: _____

Notes: _____

_____

5

The Seven Silly Eaters

Written by Mary Ann Hoberman • Illustrated by Marla Frazee

AGES:
4+

GENRE:
POETRY & RHYME

PUBLISHER:
HMH BOOKS
FOR YOUNG
READERS

**PUBLICATION
DATE:**
1997

PAGE COUNT:
40

You may want to bring a snack with you when you sit down to read this book, because it is stuffed with plenty of mouth-watering fun! Mrs. Peters is every kid's dream mom. All seven of her kids are picky eaters. But even though they each want something different, she always makes her kids their favorite food. Peter only ever wants milk, Lucy will only drink homemade lemonade, Jack only eats applesauce, and so it goes. With seven kids in the family, Mrs. Peters begins to feel worn out. It's tough whipping up seven different menus every mealtime! On her birthday, the kids come up with a plan to surprise Mrs. Peters with a meal of her own. And guess what? It's a meal that just might please everyone in the family.

The Seven Silly Eaters is written in rhyme, and every page is sweetened with delicious pictures to feast your eyes on. It's definitely one drool-worthy picture book.

What to read next?
• *I Will Never Not Ever Eat a Tomato* by Lauren Child
• *Bread and Jam for Frances* by Russell Hoban
• *Blueberries for Sal* by Robert McCloskey
• *Jamberry* by Bruce Degen

Did you know?

Mary Ann Hoberman decided she wanted to be a writer before she even knew how to write!

"THEY ALL TAKE TURNS IN MIXING IT.
THEY ALL TAKE TURNS IN FIXING IT.
IT'S THICK TO BEAT AND QUICK TO BAKE—
IT'S FINE TO EAT AND FUN TO MAKE—
IT'S MRS. PETERS' BIRTHDAY CAKE!"

Read it! ☐   Rating: ☆☆☆☆☆

Favorite Character: _____

Notes: _____

_____

6

The Story of Ferdinand

Written by Munro Leaf • Illustrated by Robert Lawson

AGES:
4+

GENRE:
ANIMALS

PUBLISHER:
GROSSET &
DUNLAP

**PUBLICATION
DATE:**
1936

PAGE COUNT:
32

This is a book that everyone wants a "peace" of (pun intended)! Most people would assume that all bulls enjoy bullfights, but not little Ferdinand. Ferdinand much prefers to lie around and smell the flowers than butt heads with the other calves. Even when Ferdinand grows into the largest and strongest bull—and all the other bulls are dreaming of fighting in Madrid—he still prefers his flowers. When five men come to the pasture to choose a bull for a fight, Ferdinand accidentally sits on a bee and sets off running furiously through the field. The men mistake him for a ferocious bull, calling him "Ferdinand the Fierce," and they take him to Madrid to go up against a famous matador. Will Ferdinand live up to his new name? Or will he stay true to himself and remain a peaceful bull? Hint: This is a book full of wonderful goodness. Ferdinand will always choose peace over war. Olé!

What to read next?
- *How to Speak Politely and Why* by Munro Leaf
- *The Lion and the Mouse* by Jerry Pinkney
- *The Peace Book* by Todd Parr
- *Zen Shorts* by Jon J. Muth

Did you know?
The Story of Ferdinand was published right before the start of the Spanish Civil War. Many countries that did not support its peaceful message banned the book, and in Nazi Germany, Adolf Hitler went as far as ordering the book to be burned. It was believed to be one of Indian leader Mahatma Gandhi's favorite books.

Read it! ☐   Rating: ☆☆☆☆☆

Favorite Character: _____

Notes: _____

_____

7 The Little House

Written and Illustrated by Virginia Lee Burton

The Little House, well-built and strong, is perched on a hill surrounded by the beautiful countryside. She happily watches the days, seasons, and years go by—daisies bloom, apple trees blossom, snow falls, and the moon grows fuller and rounder before transforming back into a thin sliver in the sky. As the years go by, the house notices the city lights getting closer. The quiet country soon becomes a bustling city of its own, and the house is eventually surrounded by tall, city buildings that block her view of the sun, stars, and moon.

Virginia Lee Burton's illustrations in *The Little House* are captivating and clever. While we all know that houses do not actually have faces, this little house has features that allow her to display powerful emotions. As she becomes sad with her city life, missing the countryside that's slowly disappearing, readers will notice the slight changes in the shape of the house's front step, which represent a smile or a frown. But never fear, there is a happy ending, complete with a smiling stoop!

What to read next?

- *Mike Mulligan and His Steam Shovel* by Virginia Lee Burton
- *City Dog, Country Frog* by Mo Willems
- *Miss Rumphius* by Barbara Cooney
- *The Story of Ferdinand* by Munro Leaf

Did you know?

Virginia Lee Burton cut and added text for *The Little House* to better fit the illustrations. She's one of the first authors to do so, saying that "primitive man thought in pictures, not in words."

AGES:
4+

GENRE:
ADVENTURE

PUBLISHER:
HMH BOOKS FOR YOUNG READERS

1942

PUBLICATION DATE:
1942

PAGE COUNT:
44

Read it! ☐   Rating: ☆☆☆☆☆

Favorite Character: _____

Notes: _____

_____

8   The Polar Express

Written and Illustrated by Chris Van Allsburg

AGES:
4+

GENRE:
ADVENTURE

PUBLISHER:
HMH BOOKS
FOR YOUNG
READERS

**PUBLICATION
DATE:**
1985

PAGE COUNT:
32

Have you ever lay awake on Christmas Eve, waiting to catch a glimpse of Santa Claus and his reindeer? So many of us have, but I've never met a person who has managed to stay awake! Besides, Santa will only come once we have fallen asleep, and even then, only if we believe in the magic of Christmas. In *The Polar Express*, one of the greatest books ever written about Santa, a young boy lays awake hoping to hear the sounds of Santa's sleigh bells. And, do you know what? He does hear something! Only it's not sleigh bells, it's the sound of steam hissing and metal squeaking as a grand, old train stops right outside his house. Dressed in his pajamas, the boy boards the train and has an amazing, adventurous ride to the North Pole. Once there, he is granted a wish that will help him believe in the magic of Christmas forever.

The illustrations in this book are so enchanting—you'll wish you could jump inside the pages and go to the North Pole too! Santa Claus may just be the most magical guy around, so a book about him must surely be marvelous if it is to become a holiday-favorite. And *The Polar Express* is a favorite for many families! Hey, did you hear that? *Jingle, jingle, jingle.*

Did you know?

Chris Van Allsburg includes an illustration of a little white dog in all his books. Be sure to look for it when you read *The Polar Express*.

What to read next?
- *How the Grinch Stole Christmas!* by Dr. Seuss
- *Jumanji* by Chris Van Allsburg
- *The Night Before Christmas* by Clement C. Moore
- *The Garden of Abdul Gasazi* by Chris Van Allsburg

Did you know?

The Polar Express has been made into a very popular holiday movie, narrated by Tom Hanks.

"THOUGH I'VE GROWN OLD, THE BELL STILL RINGS FOR ME, AS IT DOES FOR ALL WHO TRULY BELIEVE."

Read it! ☐   Rating: ☆☆☆☆☆

Favorite Character: _____

Notes: _____

_____

Cloudy with a Chance of Meatballs

Written by Judi Barrett • Illustrated by Ronald Barrett

AGES:
4+

GENRE:
HUMOR

PUBLISHER:
SIMON &
SCHUSTER

PUBLICATION DATE:
1978

PAGE COUNT:
32

You know a story has to be entertaining when it's set in a town called Chewandswallow. As told by a grandfather to his grandchildren, Chewandswallow appears to be like any other town. What makes it unique is that the weather comes three times a day: once for breakfast, once for lunch, and once for dinner. What's so special about that, you ask? Well, for starters, it doesn't rain rain or snow snow in Chewandswallow. No, among other appetizing items, it rains juice and snows mashed potatoes, and a giant Jell-O sets in the sky after dinner. The people of the town are all very happy and well-fed, without a worry in the world…until things get messy and the food portions become larger-than-life, causing some serious damage. Nobody wants to be squashed by a tomato tornado or flattened by a pancake. How will the people survive? What will they do? This bedtime story is completely silly, and that's why you'll love it. The illustrations are as full as a banquet dinner, and you can pore over them, relishing in all the details and extra laughs they provide.

What to read next?

- *Pickles to Pittsburgh* by Judi Barrett
- *Animals Should Definitely Not Wear Clothing* by Judi Barrett
- *Bread and Jam for Frances* by Russell Hoban

Did you know?

Judi Barrett teaches art to kindergarten students.

In 2009, Sony released a *Cloudy with a Chance of Meatballs* movie. It's based on the book, but it's quite a bit different.

Read it! ☐   Rating: ☆☆☆☆☆

Favorite Character: _____

Notes: _____

_____

10 | Last Stop on Market Street

Written by Matt de la Peña • Illustrated by Christian Robinson

It's time to jump on board this bus with CJ and ride it all the way to the last stop on Market Street, because this is a story that will certainly get your wheels spinning! Every Sunday after church, CJ and his grandmother wait for the bus. On this particular day, CJ wonders why they don't have a car and why the part of town they live in is so run-down. He feels envious of other kids who have more than he does. On the lively bus trip through the humming city, his thoughtful and loving grandmother helps him see how beautiful it is that people come in all different shapes, sizes, and colors, with different ages and personalities. "Sometimes when you're surrounded by dirt, CJ," his grandmother tells him, "you're a better witness for what's beautiful."

The brightly colored pictures are great to look at, and they really bring CJ's journey to life. *Last Stop on Market Street* is filled with so much love, friendship, and happiness that reading it will surely make you smile.

What to read next?
- *Whistle for Willie* by Ezra Jack Keats
- *Nana in the City* by Lauren Castillo
- *Sidewalk Flowers* by JonArno Lawson
- *Trombone Shorty* by Troy Andrews

Did you know?

Matt de la Peña is the first Hispanic author to have won the Newbery Award.

Growing up with less than others shaped de la Peña and is something he proudly writes about in his book.

AGES:
4+

GENRE:
FAMILY

PUBLISHER:
G.P. PUTNAM'S SONS BOOKS FOR YOUNG READERS

PUBLICATION DATE:
2015

PAGE COUNT:
32

Read it! ☐   Rating: ☆☆☆☆☆

Favorite Character: _____

Notes: _____

_____

11

Tikki Tikki Tembo

Written by Arlene Mosel • Illustrated by Blair Lent

AGES:
4+

GENRE:
FAIRY TALES,
FOLK TALES,
AND MYTHS

PUBLISHER:
SQUARE FISH

PUBLICATION
DATE:
1968

PAGE COUNT:
48

Who doesn't love a good tongue twister? Here's one for you: "Tikki tikki tembo-no sa rembo-chari bari ruchi-pip peri pembo!" This tongue twister is the amazing and most honorable name given to a young boy who's his mother's first-born child.

In this retelling of a Chinese folktale, we learn that "first and honored" sons are given great long names, and second sons are given very short names. Tikki Tikki Tembo, which means "The Most Wonderful Thing in the Whole Wide World," is very close to his brother Chang, whose name means "Little or Nothing." The two brothers love to play near a well and sometimes even *on* it. However, playing on the well leads to some serious trouble for the boys. When they need help from the Old Man with the Ladder, readers learn that it may not be so great to have such a grand long name, and according to this folktale, that's why Chinese people started giving their children short names. Only a few colors make up the illustrations, reminding us that this story takes place a long time ago. *Tikki Tikki Tembo* is a playful tale best read out loud. "Tikki tikki tembo-no sa rembo-chari bari ruchi-pip peri pembo" is repeated throughout the book, and it's just so much fun to say. You'll read this book and say Tikki's name so many times that you will still be able to chant it when you're all grown up!

What to read next?
• *The Funny Little Woman* by Arlene Mosel
• *Stone Soup* by Marcia Brown
• *Strega Nona* by Tomie dePaola
• *The Five Chinese Brothers*
  by Claire Huchet Bishop

Did you know?

Tikki Tikki Tembo is Arlene Mosel's retelling of a folktale she heard as a child.

"TIKKI TIKKI TEMBO-NO SA REMBO-CHARI BARI RUCHI-PIP PERI PEMBO, WHICH MEANT, 'THE MOST WONDERFUL THING IN THE WHOLE WIDE WORLD!'"

Read it! ☐   Rating: ☆☆☆☆☆

Favorite Character: _____

Notes: _____

_____

12

The Snail and the Whale

Written by Julia Donaldson • Illustrated by Axel Scheffler

AGES:
4+

GENRE:
ANIMALS

PUBLISHER:
PUFFIN BOOKS

PUBLICATION DATE:
2003

PAGE COUNT:
32

In this rhyming picture book, a tiny snail who has never strayed from his black-as-soot rock decides to hitch a ride to far-off lands on the back of a humpback whale. These unlikely new friends travel together past underwater caves, fiery mountains, golden sands, and towering icebergs. "And she gazed at the sky, the sea, the land, The waves and the caves and the golden sand. She gazed and gazed, amazed by it all, And she said to the whale, 'I feel so small.'" All is well as the snail and the whale continue their adventure, until the day the whale swims too close to the shore, and the snail must find a way to come to the rescue. But how can a tiny snail save a giant humpback whale?

The Snail and the Whale is so much fun to read aloud. The illustrations are bright and colorful, and it soon becomes pretty clear that even the smallest being can make a difference.

What to read next?

- *Room on the Broom* by Julia Donaldson
- *Stickman* by Julia Donaldson
- *The Gruffalo* by Julia Donaldson
- *Giraffes Can't Dance* by Giles Andreae

Did you know?

Before becoming a children's book author, Julia Donaldson was a singer-songwriter for children's television. One of her songs, *A Squash and a Squeeze*, was adapted into her first book.

Read it! ☐   Rating: ☆☆☆☆☆

Favorite Character: _____

Notes: _____

_____

13 Journey

Written and Illustrated by Aaron Becker

Sometimes there are no words to describe a book. And sometimes there are no words *in* the actual book itself. This is one of those books—it's both wordless and wondrous (which I guess means there *are* actually words to describe it!). When a young girl draws a magic door on her bedroom wall with her red marker, she walks through it, leaving a drab world and entering a magical one filled with color and adventure. Using her marker, she creates ways to navigate this unknown place, drawing a boat, a balloon, a flying carpet, and a tandem bike. Amidst the beauty of the world, there is also danger. An evil emperor captures the girl. How will she escape? How will she return home? No spoilers here, but an unexpected friendship comes out of this incredibly gorgeous tale told only through the artwork on each page. The little girl is adventurous, courageous, kind, and she knows how to have fun. She is sure to inspire you to take your own imaginative journey…if you can tear yourself away from this book.

Did you know?

Aaron Becker has worked for several film studios, including Lucasfilm, Disney, and Pixar.

What to read next?

- *Quest* by Aaron Becker
- *Return* by Aaron Becker
- *Harold and the Purple Crayon* by Crockett Johnson
- *The Red Book* by Barbara Lehman

AGES:
5+

GENRE:
ADVENTURE

PUBLISHER:
CANDLEWICK

PUBLICATION DATE:
2013

PAGE COUNT:
40

Read it! ☐   Rating: ☆☆☆☆☆

Favorite Character: _____

Notes: _____

_____

14 Bread and Jam for Frances

Written by Russell Hoban • Illustrated by Lillian Hoban

AGES:
5+

GENRE:
ANIMALS

PUBLISHER:
HARPERCOLLINS

PUBLICATION DATE:
1964

PAGE COUNT:
48

I know. I know. Grown-ups don't always prepare the yummiest of foods, but let's be honest, Frances the badger is a pretty picky eater. She refuses to eat anything other than bread and jam. She's pretty lucky, too, because her mother keeps giving her just what she likes: bread and jam for breakfast, lunch, and dinner. But maybe, just maybe, Frances's mother has a plan that will have her eating a well-balanced meal in no time. You can gobble up this story yourself or have it read aloud to you—either way it's deliciously fun. The illustrations that appear on every page are an enjoyable feast for the eyes. Just like your favorite food, this will be a book you'll want to devour morning, noon, and night. Just for fun: say "pretty picky eater" five times really fast!

What to read next?

- *Bedtime for Frances* by Russell Hoban
- *A Bargain for Frances* by Russell Hoban
- *A Baby Sister for Frances* by Russell Hoban
- *Best Friends for Frances* by Russell Hoban
- *A Birthday for Frances* by Russell Hoban

Read it! ☐   Rating: ☆☆☆☆☆

Favorite Character: _____

Notes: _____

_____

Rosie Revere, Engineer

Written by Andrea Beaty • Illustrated by David Roberts

It's time for a little lesson in following our dreams, and flying high. With Rosie, "We can do it!"

AGES:
5+

In *Rosie Revere, Engineer*, Rosie learns to listen to her heart and never give up. She is so talented. She loves making gizmos out of the stuff lying around her home—even trash! She makes a hot dog dispenser *(yummy!)*, helium pants, and a hat that shoots cheese at snakes to keep them away from her uncle, a zookeeper. Feeling inspired to create a flying machine for her great aunt, Rosie quickly gets to work, with her imagination and know-how to back her up. But every so often, Rosie's creations don't work out, and after her uncle laughs at her cheese hat and her flying machine fails, Rosie is ready to give up on her engineering dreams. However, Rosie soon learns that failing is an important stop on the road to success, and she is, quite possibly, on the road to creating a flying machine that *actually* works. *Rosie Revere, Engineer* rhymes all the way through, and the pictures are filled with details that will have you smiling. This book is funny, fun, and very well done!

GENRE:
POETRY & RHYME

PUBLISHER:
HARRY N.
ABRAMS

PUBLICATION DATE:
2013

Did you know?

Andrea Beaty was raised in southern Illinois in a town so small she knew everybody and their pets...and they all knew her.

What to read next?

- *Iggy Peck, Architect* by Andrea Beaty
- *Ada Twist, Scientist* by Andrea Beaty
- *What Do You Do with an Idea?* by Kobi Yamada
- *Interstellar Cinderella* by Deborah Underwood

PAGE COUNT:
32

Read it! ☐   Rating: ☆☆☆☆☆

Favorite Character: _____

Notes: _____

_____

16 Mango, Abuela, and Me

Written by Meg Medina • Illustrated by Angela Dominguez

AGES:
5+

GENRE:
FAMILY

PUBLISHER:
CANDLEWICK

PUBLICATION DATE:
2015

PAGE COUNT:
32

Have you ever had to learn something new? Learning new things can be hard, especially learning a new language or learning to read a book. Mia's *abuela* (Spanish for *grandmother*) has come to stay. Abuela has left her own house to move in with Mia and her parents in the city. When Mia decides to share her favorite book with Abuela, she discovers that Abuela cannot read the words. Mia sets about teaching Abuela to speak English, and along the way, Mia also learns some Spanish. When Mia spots a parrot through the window of a pet shop, she buys it to keep Abuela company. The parrot learns both English and Spanish, and Mia and Abuela's bond grows, speaking louder than words. *Mango, Abuela, and Me*'s illustrations are bright and beautiful, just like the story itself. When it's time to try something new, like Abuela does, give this book a read.

What to read next?

- *Tía Isa Wants a Car* by Meg Medina
- *The Cazuela That the Farm Maiden Stirred* by Samantha R. Vamos
- *Green Is a Chile Pepper: A Book of Colors* by Roseanne Greenfield Thong
- *Nana in the City* by Lauren Castillo

Did you know?

Both of Meg Medina's parents emigrated from Cuba before she was born. Her Latin heritage is a great inspiration for her storytelling.

Read it! ☐   Rating: ☆☆☆☆☆

Favorite Character: _____

Notes: _____

_____

Written by A. A. Milne • Illustrated by Ernest H. Shepard

The Complete Tales of Winnie-the-Pooh is a collection of stories and poems about a wonderfully muddled, honey-loving bear named Winnie-the-Pooh who speaks right to readers' hearts with his simple words of wisdom. Together with his trusted friends Christopher Robin, bouncing Tigger, little Piglet, gloomy Eeyore, clever Rabbit, mama and son Kanga and Roo, and know-it-all Owl, there are many precious adventures to be had in the Hundred Acre Wood. Some are silly and some are clever, and all of them are decorated with pretty little pictures.

Read by yourself or enjoy the story with a grown-up before bed. If you happen to drift off to dreamland before Pooh's adventure has come to an end, never mind, "because the Forest will always be there...and anybody who is Friendly with Bears can find it."

Did you know?

Winnie-the-Pooh was named after a real-life baby bear that veterinarian Harry Colebourn found on his way to serve in World War I. He named the bear "Winnie," after his home in Winnipeg, Canada.

What to read next?

- *Finding Winnie: The True Story of the World's Most Famous Bear* by Lindsay Mattick
- *The Paddington Treasury* by Michael Bond
- *Beatrix Potter: The Complete Tales* by Beatrix Potter
- *The Complete Adventures of Curious George* by H. A. Rey

AGES:
5+

GENRE:
ANIMALS

PUBLISHER:
DUTTON BOOKS FOR YOUNG READERS

1926

PUBLICATION DATE:
1926

PAGE COUNT:
368

Read it! ☐   Rating: ☆☆☆☆☆

Favorite Character: _____

Notes: _____

_____

18 The Paper Bag Princess

Written by Robert Munsch • Illustrated by Michael Martchenko

AGES:
5+

GENRE:
FANTASY

PUBLISHER:
ANNICK PRESS

PUBLICATION DATE:
1980

PAGE COUNT:
32

If ever there were a book with the most perfect plot twist, this could be it. In most princess books, an evil force kidnaps the princess, and a prince rescues her, then the two marry and ride off into the sunset. Well, no siree, not in this book! In *The Paper Bag Princess*, a dragon smashes Princess Elizabeth's castle and burns all her expensive clothes with his fiery breath. Afterward, the very smart, spirited, and beautiful princess leaves home to rescue Prince Ronald, her betrothed, from the dragon. Ever so bravely, she dresses herself in the only thing she can find, a brown paper bag, and with the use of outstanding trickery, she sets about saving the day.

Then it happens—the most unexpected and perfect ending to a story. But don't expect me to spoil the biggest plot twist of all. I want you to have the satisfaction of reading it yourself! *The Paper Bag Princess* is a short, sweet, and funny book that you can bet you weren't expecting.

What to read next?
- *Rosie Revere, Engineer* by Andrea Beaty
- *Princess Smartypants* by Babette Cole
- *Interstellar Cinderella* by Deborah Underwood
- *Ada Twist, Scientist* by Andrea Beaty

Did you know?
Robert Munsch's book, *Love You Forever*, is possibly his most popular, but the story started out as a song.

Read it! ☐   Rating: ☆☆☆☆☆

Favorite Character: _____

Notes: _____

_____

19 Lon Po Po

Written and Illustrated by Ed Young

This is not your sweet old grandmother's version of the classic tale, Little Red Riding Hood. This version is wickedly entertaining, as three daughters are tricked by a sneaky wolf, Lon, pretending to be their grandmother, Po Po. When clever Shang, the oldest of the sisters, becomes suspicious of his cunning character and wolf-like features, she keeps her sisters safe by luring Lon Po Po into a dangerous trap that will keep him from ever returning.

The artwork in *Lon Po Po* is filled with stunning shadows that draw readers deep into this Chinese Red-Riding Hood tale. Are you feeling brave today?

What to read next?
- *The True Story of the Three Little Pigs* by Jon Scieszka
- *Tikki Tikki Tembo* by Arlene Mosel
- *The Paper Bag Princess* by Robert Munsch
- *Strega Nona* by Tomie dePaola

AGES:
5+

GENRE:
FAIRY TALES,
FOLK TALES,
AND MYTHS

PUBLISHER:
PUFFIN BOOKS

PUBLICATION
DATE:
1989

PAGE COUNT:
32

Read it! ☐   Rating: ☆☆☆☆☆

Favorite Character: _____

Notes: _____

_____

20 The Hundred Dresses

Written by Eleanor Estes • Illustrated by Louis Slobodkin

AGES:
6+

GENRE:
HISTORICAL
FICTION

PUBLISHER:
HMH BOOKS
FOR YOUNG
READERS

1944

PUBLICATION
DATE:
1944

PAGE COUNT:
96

People can be mean sometimes. They can say hurtful things, and they can be bullies. So it's up to us to stand up for what's right! Wanda Petronski is Polish, her family is poor, and she does not have any friends. The fact that she talks with an accent immediately makes her different from all the other girls at her Connecticut school. Can you imagine going to class and feeling as though you don't fit in? The other kids see Wanda in the same faded blue dress every day, and they begin to tease her, so Wanda tells them she has a hundred beautiful dresses at home that she wears for special occasions. Of course, it's not true, none of the girls believe her, and Wanda's fib only makes them taunt her more.

Maddie, Wanda's classmate, knows teasing Wanda is not right, but she does not say anything because she is afraid the others will turn against her. When Wanda's parents remove her from school, the girls feel real remorse. Maddie may never get the chance to apologize, but she decides to never be afraid of speaking up again. *The Hundred Dresses* reminds us to be compassionate, kind, and to stand up for one another. This is a book that will keep you thinking long after you've put it back on the shelf.

What to read next?

- *Pinky Pye* by Eleanor Estes
- *The Middle Moffat* by Eleanor Estes
- *Rufus M.* by Eleanor Estes
- *The Invisible Boy* by Trudy Ludwig

Read it! ☐   Rating: ☆☆☆☆☆

Favorite Character: _____

Notes: _____

_____

Alexander and the Terrible, Horrible, No Good, Very Bad Day

Written by Judith Viorst • Illustrated by Ray Cruz

Some days are better than others. But Alexander is having one of the worst days ever. It's so bad, in fact, that he just wants to move to Australia. Who can blame him? Australia is a beautiful country, after all. Alexander starts his day by waking up with gum in his hair, and from there, things only get worse. He doesn't get a window seat in the carpool to school, there is no dessert in his lunch box, he goes to the dentist and learns he has a cavity, and then, worst of all, there is kissing on TV! Alexander sure is cranky, but get ready to smile because the tale of his terrible day is a fun one. It's easier to see the sunny side of a not-so-sunny situation when you're on the outside looking in. In *Alexander and the Terrible, Horrible, No Good, Very Bad Day*, you'll learn that everyone has bad days…even in Australia.

What to read next?

- *Alexander, Who Used to be Rich Last Sunday* by Judith Viorst
- *Alexander, Who's Not (Do You Hear Me? I Mean It!) Going to Move* by Judith Viorst
- *Cloudy with a Chance of Meatballs* by Judi Barrett

AGES:
6+

GENRE:
HUMOR

PUBLISHER:
SIMON &
SCHUSTER

PUBLICATION DATE:
1972

PAGE COUNT:
32

Did you know?

The Alexander of Viorst's book is based on her own son, Alexander, who had been having a series of bad days before his mother decided to write down his story.

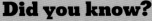

Read it! ☐   Rating: ☆☆☆☆☆

Favorite Character: _____

Notes: _____

AGES:
6+

GENRE:
HISTORICAL
FICTION

PUBLISHER:
SCHOLASTIC

2007

**PUBLICATION
DATE:**
2007

PAGE COUNT:
40

Henry's Freedom Box is a retelling of a true story about Henry "Box" Brown, who courageously escaped slavery to find freedom. Henry, born a slave on a plantation, dreams about freedom, but it never seems to be quite within his grasp. He is taken from his family and put to work in a factory where he is treated very poorly. When he is older, Henry marries another slave, and together, they have three children. But soon his wife and children are taken from him too, and sold at a slave market. As he watches them disappear, he realizes that his only chance at finding freedom is to mail himself inside a crate to a place where there is no slavery.

The illustrations are incredibly real and beautifully depict Henry's feelings. It's hard to imagine this story is based on real events, but by reading it, we can learn much about the past and how we can be better people in the future—fearless and determined defenders of freedom, just like Henry Brown. If you still have questions after reading the story, the author provides some great answers at the end of the book.

What to read next?

- *Heart and Soul: The Story of America and African Americans* by Kadir Nelson
- *Crossing Bok Chitto: A Choctaw Tale of Friendship & Freedom* by Tim Tingle
- *The Story of Ruby Bridges* by Robert Coles

Read it! ☐   Rating: ☆☆☆☆☆

Favorite Character: _____

Notes: _____

_____

The Invisible Boy

Written by Trudy Ludwig • Illustrated by Patrice Barton

Being invisible sounds like an awesome superpower! But what if you didn't choose to be invisible? Brian is a quiet boy, and he feels invisible all of the time. He constantly feels left out. He isn't included in games or invited to birthday parties. But when a new boy, Justin, comes to school, Brian is the first kid to welcome him, and the pair end up working together on a class project. Once Brian feels included, he begins to blossom.

The top-notch illustrations beautifully demonstrate Brian's experience and feelings throughout every step of his transformation. Have you ever felt like Brian, or do you know anyone like him? Reading this book is a great reminder of how easy it is to make another person feel special. A simple act of kindness can be all that is needed to help someone feel included.

What to read next?

- *My Secret Bully* by Trudy Ludwig
- *One* by Kathryn Otoshi
- *Do Unto Otters: A Book About Manners* by Laurie Keller
- *Bully* by Patricia Polacco

AGES:
6+

GENRE:
REALISTIC

PUBLISHER:
ALFRED A. KNOPF

PUBLICATION DATE:
2013

PAGE COUNT:
40

Did you know?

Some of Trudy Ludwig's favorite children's books are *Charlie and the Chocolate Factory* by Roald Dahl and *The Story of Ferdinand* by Munro Leaf (one of which we couldn't quite squeeze into this book, and one that just happens to be #6 on our list!)

Read it! ☐   Rating: ☆☆☆☆☆

Favorite Character: _____

Notes: _____

_____

24 Matilda

Written by Roald Dahl • Illustrated by Quentin Blake

AGES:
6+

GENRE:
FANTASY

PUBLISHER:
PUFFIN BOOKS

PUBLICATION DATE:
1988

PAGE COUNT:
256

Matilda is a kind, gifted, intelligent, book-loving five-year-old who taught herself to read. She has read every children's book in the library, as well as a few for adults. She can even do advanced math in her head. Her father, a rotten car salesman, and her mother, who is obsessed with playing bingo, are completely clueless and treat her terribly—almost as terribly as the child-hating, ex-Olympic hammer-throwing headmistress at school, Miss Trunchbull. When Matilda meets Miss Honey, a warm-hearted and sweet teacher, she finds her inner-strength and uses her newly discovered talent, the ability to control things with her mind, to fight back and set more than a few things right in her world.

Matilda's character is empowering and brave, and the entire story is freckled with funny bits and peppered with plenty of practical jokes. You'll be snickering all the way from start to finish.

What to read next?
- *Esio Trot* by Roald Dahl
- *James and the Giant Peach* by Roald Dahl
- *Pippi Longstocking* by Astrid Lindgren
- *Mrs. Piggle-Wiggle* by Betty MacDonald

Did you know?
Matilda is a very kind-hearted character, but when Dahl first wrote the book, she was very different. At first, she was a wicked child who used her powers to help her teacher fix a horse race.

Read it! ☐ Rating: ☆☆☆☆☆

Favorite Character: _____

Notes: _____

_____

25 Fantastic Mr. Fox

Written by Roald Dahl • Illustrated by Quentin Blake

This story is both wickedly clever *and* funny. It involves three nasty farmers, one ambitious fox and his family, a community of animals with oddball characteristics, and a wonderful world of tunnels beneath the ground. When the farmers, Boggis, Bunce, and Bean, discover that Mr. Fox has been stealing food from them (a fox has got to eat), they join forces to capture the chicken thief. Mr. Fox, intent on outsmarting the farmers, devises the most fantastic plan. Nobody outfoxes Fantastic Mr. Fox! Or *do* they?

Hold onto your tail as Mr. Fox, his family, and the band of animals in the community fight for their lives in an escapade filled with twists and turns to boot. *Fantastic Mr. Fox* is a fun and quick read. There is also a good splattering of eccentric illustrations by the famous illustrator Quentin Blake. It's so very enjoyable—you'll really dig it!

What to read next?
- *The BFG* by Roald Dahl
- *James and the Giant Peach* by Roald Dahl
- *The Twits* by Roald Dahl
- *The Wind in the Willows* by Kenneth Grahame

AGES:
6+

GENRE:
ANIMALS

PUBLISHER:
PUFFIN BOOKS

PUBLICATION DATE:
1970

PAGE COUNT:
112

Did you know?

Roald Dahl is known by many as the world's best children's storyteller. But he was also a spy, top-notch fighter pilot, chocolate historian, and medical inventor.

Read it! ☐   Rating: ☆☆☆☆☆

Favorite Character: _____

Notes: _____

_____

26 Anna Hibiscus

Written by Atinuke • Illustrated by Lauren Tobia

AGES:
6+

GENRE:
FAMILY

PUBLISHER:
KANE MILLER

PUBLICATION DATE:
2010

PAGE COUNT:
109

If you have ever wondered what it is like to live inside another person's home or in an entirely different country, *Anna Hibiscus* will give you the opportunity to find out. Anna lives in Africa surrounded by lots of family—her Canadian mom, African dad, twin baby brothers, grandparents, aunts, uncles, and cousins—all in one home. Her life is busy!

Readers join Anna on adventures as she climbs the mango tree in her backyard, sells oranges, splashes in the sea, and dreams of seeing snow. *Anna Hibiscus* has four chapters that are each like little, individual stories perfect for slipping a bookmark into each night. The pictures are wonderful, and if you don't already have a large family, you will wish you had one as big as Anna's living under the same roof. This is one very happy book!

What to read next?
- *Hooray for Anna Hibiscus!* by Atinuke
- *Love From Anna Hibiscus* by Atinuke
- *Ling & Ting: Not Exactly the Same!* by Grace Lin

Did you know?

Atinuke is a Nigerian storyteller. As a child, Atinuke attended boarding school in England. She was inspired to write *Anna Hibiscus* after realizing how little the kids she went to school with knew about Africa, especially her Africa.

Read it! ☐   Rating: ☆☆☆☆☆

Favorite Character: _____

Notes: _____

_____

27 | The 13-Story Treehouse

Written by Andy Griffiths • Illustrated by Terry Denton

Nothing but absurdity and crazy fun to find here! Andy and Terry live in an amazing thirteen-story treehouse. It has a game room, a bowling alley, a vegetable vaporizer, a see-through swimming pool, and a machine that shoots marshmallows into your mouth whenever you are hungry, just to name a few glorious features. Andy is an author, and Terry is an illustrator. The pair make books together, and they are currently behind on the deadline for their latest book. Their lives are lively, and things like a burp-filled bubblegum bubble, a bunch of monkeys, and flying cats keep them distracted from their work. How will Andy and Terry come up with a story in time for their deadline?

The black and white comic-style illustrations play a large role in the storytelling, and they are loaded with wisecracks. This is a book that will certainly unleash your creativity, and after you're done, you'll want to design your own outrageous tree house!

What to read next?
- *The 26-Story Treehouse* by Andy Griffiths
- *The 39-Story Treehouse* by Andy Griffiths
- *The Day My Butt Went Psycho* by Andy Griffiths
- *Big Nate: In a Class By Himself* by Lincoln Peirce

Did you know?

Andy Griffiths is an Australian author who began his career by selling photocopies of his stories at shops and markets in Melbourne, Australia. During this time, he was also sending his work to publishers. After many rejections and years, a publisher said yes.

AGES:
7+

GENRE:
HUMOR

PUBLISHER:
SQUARE FISH

PUBLICATION DATE:
2011

PAGE COUNT:
272

Read it! ☐   Rating: ☆☆☆☆☆

Favorite Character: _____

Notes: _____

_____

28 Charlotte's Web

Written by E.B. White • Illustrated by Garth Williams

AGES:
7+

GENRE:
ANIMALS

PUBLISHER:
HARPERCOLLINS

PUBLICATION DATE:
1952

PAGE COUNT:
192

Charlotte's Web is about an energetic barnyard pig named Wilbur who can talk, a barn spider named Charlotte who can write, and a young girl named Fern who stands up for her beliefs. The runt of his litter, Wilbur finds his life is in the hands of the farmer, Mr. Zuckerman. Charlotte comes up with an amazing plan to save Wilbur's life: She uses her web to write powerful messages to help convince Mr. Zuckerman that Wilbur should live. Readers will learn what it means to be a true friend in this beautiful and powerful story about friendship and love, life and death, and new beginnings.

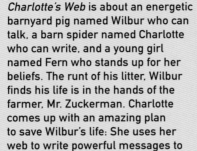

Did you know?
Garth Williams also illustrated E.B. White's *Stuart Little* and Laura Ingalls Wilder's *Little House* series.

What to read next?
- *Stuart Little* by E.B White
- *The Trumpet of the Swan* by E.B. White
- *Mr. Poppers Penguins* by Richard Atwater
- *Winnie-the-Pooh* by A. A. Milne
- *The Wind in the Willows* by Kenneth Grahame

Did you know?
Charlotte's Web is one of the best-selling children's books of all time. It has sold more than 45 million copies and has been translated into 23 languages.

Did you know?
Charlotte's Web has been adapted into both an animated and live-action film. There has also been a musical stage production and a video game.

"'YOU HAVE BEEN MY FRIEND,' REPLIED CHARLOTTE, 'THAT IN ITSELF IS A TREMENDOUS THING.'"

Read it! ☐   Rating: ☆☆☆☆☆

Favorite Character: _____

Notes: _____

_____

29

The Boxcar Children

Written by Gertrude Chandler Warner

AGES:
7+

GENRE:
ADVENTURE

PUBLISHER:
ALBERT WHITMAN
& COMPANY

PUBLICATION DATE:
1942

PAGE COUNT:
154

Henry, Jessie, Violet, and Benny Alden are orphans. The only person left to take care of them is their grandfather, who they believe to be a very unkind man. The kids hide from him by taking shelter in a bakery, where they overhear the baker's plans to keep all the kids except for Benny, the youngest, who will be sent to a children's home. The kids run away from the bakery and discover an abandoned boxcar in the forest, where they make their home. Henry, the oldest, finds work and earns enough money to buy food and other essentials. The kids do quite well with no grown-ups to help—that is until Violet falls ill, and they must take her to see a doctor. The doctor recognizes the kids' last name and connects it to a notice he read in the newspaper: James Henry Alden is offering $5,000 to the person who finds his four missing grandchildren. Will the doctor give the kids over to their grandfather? Are the children's lives about to be derailed? *The Boxcar Children* is an adventure from start to finish, and you'll want to ride the pages all the way to the end. All aboard!

Did you know?

In Connecticut, there is a museum inside a real 1920s boxcar in honor of Gertrude and this special book series.

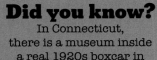

What to read next?
- *The Boxcar Children: Surprise Island* by Gertrude Chandler Warner
- *Pippi Longstocking* by Astrid Lindgren
- *Encyclopedia Brown: Boy Detective* by Donald J. Sobol
- *The Indian in the Cupboard* by Lynne Reid Banks

Did you know?

Gertrude Chandler Warner wrote 19 books in the *Boxcar Children* series. Other authors have continued the series, and there are now well over 100.

Did you know?

There is an animated movie based on *The Boxcar Children*.

"ONE WARM NIGHT FOUR CHILDREN STOOD IN FRONT OF A BAKERY. NO ONE KNEW THEM. NO ONE KNEW WHERE THEY HAD COME FROM."

Read it! ☐   Rating: ☆☆☆☆☆

Favorite Character: _____

Notes: _____

_____

30

Beezus and Ramona

Written by Beverly Cleary • Illustrated by Jacqueline Rogers

AGES:
7+

GENRE:
FAMILY

PUBLISHER:
HARPERCOLLINS

PUBLICATION DATE:
1955

PAGE COUNT:
176

Raise your hand if you have a sister. Raise your hand if you find her annoying. Sister or no sister, *Beezus and Ramona* is a very funny book about a nine-year-old girl named Beezus Quimby, short for Beatrice, and her relationship with her younger sister, Ramona. Ramona is four years old and has a big imagination. She is always testing Beezus's patience and creating embarrassing situations—the kind of situations that cause the girls to fight. Ramona likes to wear handmade rabbit ears and pretend to be the Easter bunny. She takes one bite out of every apple in a box. She enjoys walking her pretend lizard Ralph. She invites 15 kids to her house without permission, and she ruins two cakes made for Beezus's 10th birthday. The cakes are the last straw for Beezus, but when she learns of her mom and Aunt Beatrice's own childhood experiences, Beezus begins to realize that all sibling relationships have their challenges.

While it's definitely not easy to have a sister like Ramona, it's hard not to love family. Thanks to Beezus and Ramona, we learn that it's our family that helps shape a big part of who we become when we grow up. This book is so good—it's a riot!

Did you know?
The movie *Ramona and Beezus* is based off several books in the eight-book *Ramona* series.

What to read next?
- *Ramona the Pest* by Beverly Cleary
- *Ramona the Brave* by Beverly Cleary
- *Ramona and Her Father* by Beverly Cleary
- *Ramona and Her Mother* by Beverly Cleary
- *Ramona Quimby, Age 8* by Beverly Cleary
- *Ramona Forever* by Beverly Cleary
- *Ramona's World* by Beverly Cleary
- *The Mouse and the Motorcycle* by Beverly Cleary

Did you know?
As a child, Beverly Cleary struggled as a reader and writer, but she grew up to be a librarian and an award-winning author.

"I WANTED TO READ ABOUT THE SORT OF BOYS AND GIRLS THAT I KNEW IN MY NEIGHBORHOOD AND IN MY SCHOOL… I THINK CHILDREN LIKE TO FIND THEMSELVES IN BOOKS."
–BEVERLY CLEARY

Read it! ☐   Rating: ☆☆☆☆☆

Favorite Character: _____

Notes: _____

_____

31 The Borrowers

Written by Mary Norton • Illustrated by Beth and Joe Krush

AGES:
7+

GENRE:
FANTASY

PUBLISHER:
HMH BOOKS
FOR YOUNG
READERS

PUBLICATION DATE:
1952

PAGE COUNT:
192

When something goes missing in your home, where do you think it goes? According to *The Borrowers*, hidden away safely in houses are tiny people known as Borrowers. They survive by "borrowing" whatever they can from "human beans," and it's so fun to discover how they repurpose these items. Arrietty is the teenage daughter of Pod and Homily Clock, Borrowers who want nothing more than to keep their daughter out of harm's way, unseen by the human beans. Together, they live under the floorboards of a quiet country house where the very curious Arrietty feels bored and lonely. One day, Pod returns from borrowing a toy teacup, shaken because he has been seen by a human bean, a sick boy who has been sent to live with his great aunt. Homily and Pod agree that Arrietty should go with Pod on the next borrowing trip. When she does, her curiosity gets the best of her, and she too is seen by the boy. The pair become good friends, until the mean housekeeper, Mrs. Driver, realizes there are Borrowers in the house and calls the rat-catcher. Will Arrietty and her family be captured? The thrill and suspense will suck you in!

Be prepared! After reading this charming story, you will be keeping your eyes and ears open for the family of Borrowers that may be living in your own house. How else do you explain all those missing socks?

Did you know?

Mary Norton is also the author of a book titled *Bed-Knob and Broomstick*. This book was used as the basis for the Disney movie *Bedknobs and Broomsticks*.

What to read next?
- *The Borrowers Afield* by Mary Norton
- *The Borrowers Afloat* by Mary Norton
- *The Borrowers Aloft* by Mary Norton
- *The Borrowers Avenged* by Mary Norton

Did you know?

The Borrowers has also been made into multiple films, perhaps the most recognizable being the beautiful animated, *Arrietty*.

"SHE HAD LEARNED A LOT AND SOME OF THE THINGS SHE LEARNED WERE HARD TO ACCEPT."

Read it! ☐   Rating: ☆☆☆☆☆

Favorite Character: _____

Notes: _____

_____

Crossing Bok Chitto: A Choctaw Tale of Friendship & Freedom

Written by Tim Tingle • Illustrated by Jeanne Rorex Bridges

AGES:
7+

GENRE:
HISTORICAL
FICTION

PUBLISHER:
CINCO PUNTOS
PRESS

2006

**PUBLICATION
DATE:**
2006

PAGE COUNT:
40

Tim Tingle isn't just an author—he is a Choctaw storyteller. In this beautiful Choctaw tale, we learn about the friendships made between Native and African Americans in the 1800s. A river, the Bok Chitto, separates Choctaw land from a slave plantation. While picking blackberries, a young Choctaw, Martha Tom, breaks the rules when she crosses to the other side of the river and befriends a slave boy named little Mo. Breaking the boundaries of both the river and their cultures, their friendship strengthens. When Martha learns that little Mo's mother will be sold, she helps his family escape to freedom. The illustrations, created by Cherokee artist Jeanne Rorex Bridges, are beautiful paintings rich in dark color. Many readers say it looks as though the people in the pages are looking directly at them. Friendship and kindness are powerful things, as is this story. It's special when we can learn a little history by immersing ourselves in wonderful storytelling.

What to read next?

- *How I Became a Ghost: A Choctaw Trail of Tears Story* by Tim Tingle
- *Esperanza Rising* by Pam Muñoz Ryan
- *Inside Out and Back Again* by Thanhha Lai
- *Giving Thanks: A Native American Good Morning Message* by Chief Jake Swamp
- *Buffalo Bird Girl: A Hidasta Story* by S. D. Nelson

Read it! ☐   Rating: ☆☆☆☆☆

Favorite Character: _____

Notes: _____

_____

33 Rickshaw Girl

Written by Mitali Perkins • Illustrated by Jamie Hogan

Books are amazing. They can take you anywhere you want to go, both real and imagined. In *Rickshaw Girl*, readers are treated to the sights, sounds, and smells of Bangladesh. Ten-year-old Naima is a talented alpana painter who lives in a village in Bangladesh. Her family struggles to make ends meet, and she wants to help. However, in Bangladesh, girls are not allowed to work. Naima considers dressing as a boy and driving the rickshaw that her father borrowed money to buy. When the rickshaw accidentally breaks on her test drive, she decides the only way to fix the problem and help her family is to dress up as a boy and use her artistic talents to paint rickshaws. The chapters in this brilliant story are short and sweet, filled with unexpected surprises as Naima works to make amends for her mistake.

What to read next?

- *Tiger Boy* by Mitali Perkins
- *Anna Hibiscus* by Atinuke
- *Hooray for Anna Hibiscus!* by Atinuke
- *Ling and Ting: Not Exactly the Same!* by Grace Lin

AGES:
7+

GENRE:
FAMILY

PUBLISHER:
CHARLESBRIDGE

PUBLICATION DATE:
2007

PAGE COUNT:
96

Did you know?

The author's first name, Mitali, means "friendly" in the Bangla language.

Read it! ☐   Rating: ☆☆☆☆☆

Favorite Character: _____

Notes: _____

_____

Pippi Longstocking

Written by Astrid Lindgren • Illustrated by Michael Chesworth

AGES:
7+

GENRE:
ADVENTURE

PUBLISHER:
PUFFIN BOOKS

1950

PUBLICATION DATE:
1950

PAGE COUNT:
160

Hold onto your stockings (or socks)! This is quite possibly the most entertaining and preposterous tale that exists. Pippi Longstocking is a clever orphan girl with superhuman strength. Her hair is the color of a carrot, and she wears it in two braids that stick out on both sides of her head. Her mother passed away when she was a baby, and her father, a sea captain, is lost at sea. With a suitcase filled with gold coins, she lives alone in a garden home called "Villa Villekulla," along with a monkey and a horse that stays on her porch. She has no parents to tell her what to do or when to go to bed. She's outrageously fun but can't seem to avoid trouble. She plays tag with police officers, dances with burglars, and tries going to school—which lasts for a day.

Simply put, Pippi is like no other child you have met. She's unique, free spirited, and a character that you will have to read about to believe. *Pippi Longstocking* is nothing but fun, fun, fun!

What to read next?
- *Mrs. Piggle-Wiggle* by Betty MacDonald
- *Mr. Popper's Penguins* by Richard Atwater
- *Beezus and Ramona* by Beverly Cleary
- *Ivy and Bean* by Annie Barrows

Did you know?

Astrid Lindgren originally created the character Pippi to entertain her daughter, Karin, who was seven at the time and sick with pneumonia. It is said that Karin came up with the name Pippi.

Read it! ☐   Rating: ☆☆☆☆☆

Favorite Character: _____

Notes: _____

_____

35 The Phantom Tollbooth

Written by Norton Juster • Illustrated by Jules Feiffer

Do your days sometimes feel boring, like there is just nothing at all to do? Even your room full of toys seems to have nothing to offer. 10-year-old Milo, the main character in *The Phantom Tollbooth*, can totally relate to that feeling, until the day a magic tollbooth randomly and most curiously appears in his room. Ready for some adventure, Milo decides to drive through the tollbooth in his toy car. He meets the most fascinating array of characters—a ticking watchdog named Tock, Humbug the Mathemagician, the Whether Man from Dictionopolis—and ends up on a rescue mission to return Princesses Rhyme and Reason back to the Kingdom of Wisdom.

There are drawings throughout, as well as a marvelous map of all the places Milo visits on his journey through the tollbooth. This story will inspire you to dust off your toys and see where they'll take you. Many readers consider this the BEST BOOK EVER! Will you?

What to read next?

- *The Dot and the Line: A Romance in Lower Mathematics* by Norton Juster
- *Alice's Adventures in Wonderland* by Lewis Carroll
- *The Wonderful Wizard of Oz* by L. Frank Baum
- *A Wrinkle in Time* by Madeleine L'Engle

AGES:
8+

GENRE:
ADVENTURE

PUBLISHER:
RANDOM HOUSE

1961

PUBLICATION DATE:
1961

PAGE COUNT:
272

Did you know?

The Phantom Tollbooth has been made into an animated feature film, which Norton Juster does not like, calling it "drivel." It's possible that Warner Brothers will remake the movie in live-action.

Read it! ☐   Rating: ☆☆☆☆☆

Favorite Character: _____

Notes: _____

_____

36 The Invention of Hugo Cabret

Written and Illustrated by Brian Selznick

AGES:
8+

GENRE:
HISTORICAL
FICTION

PUBLISHER:
SCHOLASTIC
PRESS

PUBLICATION DATE:
2007

PAGE COUNT:
533

The Invention of Hugo Cabret begins like a movie. The black-and-white illustrations set the scene with a dark night and a full moon. As the reader turns the pages, the scene transforms into morning in Paris, France. The story is about a 12-year-old boy, Hugo, who is an orphan secretly living inside the walls of a Paris train station. Before Hugo's father, a clockmaker, passed away in a fire, he had been fixing an adult-sized windup figure. Now Hugo is determined to fix the figure himself, even if that means stealing. Hugo believes that, once reassembled, the figure will reveal a message left for him by his father. After he's caught stealing mechanical parts from a toy shop in the station, Hugo develops relationships with the shop's owner, George (a character based on a famous filmmaker, Georges Méliès, who collected windup figures) and his book-smart goddaughter. Little does Hugo know, cranky George and his goddaughter may be able to help him reach his goal.

The Invention of Hugo Cabret is a gorgeous book. It's massive at 533 pages, so it *can* look a bit intimidating. However, more than half of the book's pages are illustrated, and it is a very easy read. The illustrations are so very cool. The drawings are a vital component of the story and provide important clues to the ever-evolving mystery.

What to read next?
- *Wonder Struck* by Brian Selznick
- *The Marvels* by Brian Selznick

Did you know?

Georges Méliès sold toys from a booth in the Montparnasse railway station in Paris. Brian Selznick drew Méliès' real door and other details from the station in his illustrations.

"MACHINES NEVER HAVE ANY EXTRA PARTS. THEY HAVE THE EXACT NUMBER AND TYPE OF PARTS THEY NEED. SO I FIGURE IF THE ENTIRE WORLD IS A BIG MACHINE, I HAVE TO BE HERE FOR SOME REASON. AND THAT MEANS YOU HAVE TO BE HERE FOR SOME REASON, TOO."

Read it! ☐   Rating: ☆☆☆☆☆

Favorite Character: _____

Notes: _____

_____

37 The One and Only Ivan

Written by Katherine Applegate • Illustrated by Patricia Castelao

AGES:
8+

GENRE:
ANIMALS

PUBLISHER:
HARPERCOLLINS

PUBLICATION DATE:
2012

PAGE COUNT:
336

A bestselling novel, *The One and Only Ivan*, is a beautiful story of hope and friendship inspired by a real silverback gorilla named Ivan who was held captive for 27 years. Narrated by Ivan himself, the story is about Ivan's friendship with an elephant named Stella and a stray dog named Bob. Ivan is comfortable in his shopping mall domain, where he watches TV and creates artwork that is sold to the spectators who watch him through glass windows far from the jungle. Stella, on the other hand, has a longer memory than Ivan, and she longs to live in a zoo where larger habitats are provided. Ruby, a baby elephant who has been plucked from the wild, is introduced to the Big Top Mall to learn circus tricks from Stella. But soon after, Stella becomes sick. Before she passes away, she puts Ruby in Ivan's care. Over time, Ivan begins to recall his life in the jungle. His desire for freedom and drive to help Ruby grows.

The One and Only Ivan will make you feel all kinds of emotions. The author's note at the end of the book is a wonderful addition; Katherine Applegate discusses the differences between the true events in Ivan's life and her story.

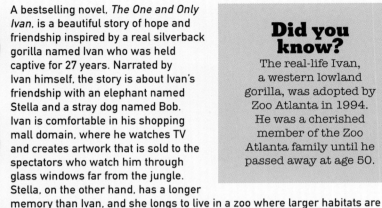

Did you know?

The real-life Ivan, a western lowland gorilla, was adopted by Zoo Atlanta in 1994. He was a cherished member of the Zoo Atlanta family until he passed away at age 50.

What to read next?
- *Crenshaw* by Katherine Applegate
- *Charlotte's Web* by E.B. White

Did you know?
Disney announced in 2014 that they might make an adaption of the book. Fingers crossed!

"HUMANS WASTE WORDS. THEY TOSS THEM LIKE BANANA PEELS AND LEAVE THEM TO ROT. EVERYONE KNOWS THE PEELS ARE THE BEST PART."

Read it! ☐   Rating: ☆☆☆☆☆

Favorite Character: _____

Notes: _____

_____

38 The Wonderful Wizard of Oz

Written by L. Frank Baum • Illustrated by W. W. Denslow

AGES:
8+

GENRE:
FANTASY

PUBLISHER:
PENGUIN

PUBLICATION DATE:
1900

PAGE COUNT:
389

A cyclone, good and bad witches, a powerful wizard, wolves, winged monkeys, and a pair of magical shoes. Do I have your attention yet?

During a terrible storm, Dorothy and her little dog, Toto, are still inside their farmhouse when they are whisked away by a cyclone. When the house lands in a magical land—right on top of The Wicked Witch of the East—Dorothy and Toto discover they are not in Kansas anymore. The Good Witch of the North arrives and tells Dorothy to follow the yellow brick road to the Emerald City of Oz and seek out a wizard who can help her return home. On the way, Dorothy befriends a scarecrow, a tin woodman, and a cowardly lion. The three of them help her along on her journey to Oz. And she could use the help, because the Wicked Witch of the West, sister to the fallen Witch of the East, will stop at nothing to make sure Dorothy and her new companions never make it to the Emerald City.

The Wonderful Wizard of Oz has everything you could possibly want, including pictures! There is so much incredible action and whimsical adventure. But you're probably wondering if Dorothy ever makes it to meet the wizard, and if he's truly wonderful? Will Dorothy and her friends ever defeat the wicked witch and make it home? You'll need to read the book to find out the answers, just as Dorothy must learn for herself that "there is no place like home."

What to read next?
- *Alice's Adventures in Wonderland* by Lewis Carroll
- *Peter Pan* by J.M. Barrie
- *Charlie and the Chocolate Factory* by Roald Dahl
- *The Phantom Tollbooth* by Norton Juster

"THERE IS NO LIVING THING THAT IS NOT AFRAID WHEN IT FACES DANGER. THE TRUE COURAGE IS IN FACING DANGER WHEN YOU ARE AFRAID, AND THAT KIND OF COURAGE YOU HAVE IN PLENTY."

Read it! ☐   Rating: ☆☆☆☆☆

Favorite Character: _____

Notes: _____

_____

39

El Deafo

Written and Illustrated by Cece Bell

AGES:
8+

GENRE:
GRAPHIC NOVEL

PUBLISHER:
HARRY N. ABRAMS

2014

PUBLICATION DATE:
2014

PAGE COUNT:
248

This is not your typical superhero book, but it's the superhero book you've been waiting for! *El Deafo* shows us that "our differences are our superpowers."

What if you couldn't hear and couldn't make friends? These are two things that Cece Bell, a very sweet rabbit, thinks about every day. It can be hard to make friends, but it's extra hard for a hearing impaired rabbit. At age four, Cece lost her hearing due to an infection known as "spinal meningitis." At her old school, everyone was deaf, but at her new school, the Phonic Ear she must strap to her chest so she can hear sets her apart from the other kids in her class. However, when it turns out that she is able to hear things others cannot, she realizes she has a newfound superpower, and she gives herself the secret superhero name "El Deafo."

El Deafo is written and illustrated in a colorful graphic-novel format, and the pictures show Cece coming to terms with her disability and herself. Will she manage to find true friendship without hiding behind her superhero counterpart? Either way, Cece and her story can only be loved!

What to read next?
- *Smile* by Raina Telgemeier
- *Roller Girl* by Victoria Jamieson
- *Sunny Side Up* by Jennifer L. Holm
- *Zita the Spacegirl* by Ben Hatke

Did you know?

El Deafo is based loosely on the author's childhood and growing up hearing impaired. She depicted the characters as bunnies because they are known for having big ears and excellent hearing.

Read it! ☐   Rating: ☆☆☆☆☆

Favorite Character: _____

Notes: _____

_____

40 The Year of the Dog

Written by Grace Lin

This is your year to read *The Year of the Dog*. Friendship and family are the key to exploring one year in the life of Pacy, the only Taiwanese-American girl at her school. It's the Chinese Year of the Dog, and it's the year that Pacy is supposed to "find herself." When she meets Melody, another Asian girl, luck comes her way. The girls work together on a science-fair project, enter a book contest, and discuss everything from Halloween costumes to boys. Thanks to this new friendship and the support of her parents, Pacy begins to blossom into her true self.

This is a book for everyone, no matter who you are or where you come from. Readers will see how Pacy navigates the typical challenges of growing up, while also trying to find a balance between two cultures. Be sure to read *The Year of the Dog* when you're in the mood for something deliciously sweet, and "like the last dumpling on a plate," don't leave it on the shelf too long.

What to read next?

- *The Year of the Rat* by Grace Lin
- *Where the Mountain Meets the Moon* by Grace Lin
- *Starry River of the Sky* by Grace Lin
- *Dumpling Days* by Grace Lin

Did you know?

Grace Lin wrote *The Year of the Dog* because it was the book she wished she had when she was growing up, a book with someone like her in it.

AGES:
8+

GENRE:
REALISTIC

PUBLISHER:
LITTLE, BROWN
BOOKS FOR
YOUNG READERS

PUBLICATION DATE:
2005

PAGE COUNT:
160

Read it! ☐   Rating: ☆☆☆☆☆

Favorite Character: _____

Notes: _____

41

All-of-a-Kind Family

Written by Sydney Taylor

AGES:
8+

GENRE:
HISTORICAL
FICTION

PUBLISHER:
RANDOM HOUSE
CHILDREN'S
BOOKS

**PUBLICATION
DATE:**
1951

PAGE COUNT:
192

It's the early 1900s, and five mischievous sisters—Ella, Henny, Sarah, Charlotte, and Gertie—live with their parents in a poor area of New York City. *All-of-a-Kind Family* follows the lives of these sisters and the fun experiences they have growing up as a Jewish immigrant family. The sisters share a bedroom, and they love to do everything together: visit the library, go to the Rivington Street Market with Mama, swim at Coney Island, celebrate holidays, and even do chores. The girls embody kindness and happiness. They find pleasure in the little things, like discovering a button while dusting.

Wonderful descriptions of Jewish life and traditions are shared within the pages of Taylor's book, as readers learn about Judaism and the beautiful holidays celebrated by Jewish people. Based on the author's own childhood, *All-of-a-Kind Family* is a warm and funny story that reminds us that it's not what we have that makes us rich; it's the size of our heart that counts. You'll love this book, and when you're finished reading, you'll want to be a member of this family too.

What to read next?
- *More All-Of-A-Kind Family* by Sydney Taylor
- *All-of-a-Kind Family Uptown* by Sydney Taylor
- *Little House in the Big Woods* by Laura Ingalls Wilder
- *A Tree Grows in Brooklyn* by Betty Smith

"IT MEANS WE'RE ALL CLOSE AND LOVING AND LOYAL—AND OUR FAMILY WILL ALWAYS BE THAT."

Did you know?

Sydney Taylor has an award named after her—the Sydney Taylor Book Award, which honors excellent new books that portray the Jewish experience for children and teens.

Read it! ☐   Rating: ☆☆☆☆☆

Favorite Character: _____

Notes: _____

_____

42 Harry Potter and the Sorcerer's Stone

Written by J.K. Rowling

AGES:
8+

GENRE:
FANTASY

PUBLISHER:
SCHOLASTIC

PUBLICATION
DATE:
1997

PAGE COUNT:
310

Get your tickets ready. The grand, shiny red Hogwarts Express is ready to depart from platform 9¾, and you won't want to miss the enchanting ride into the spellbinding wizarding world of Harry Potter.

Harry is an orphan who has been living with Aunt Petunia, Uncle Vernon, and cousin Dudley Dursley since he was a baby. The Dursleys are plain despicable and make Harry sleep in a cupboard under the stairs. On Harry's eleventh birthday, mysterious letters addressed to Harry Potter begin arriving at the house, and his aunt and uncle try everything they can to keep them from Harry. That's when a very large man, Hagrid, shows up to deliver the letter in person, along with a very important message: "You're a wizard, Harry!" Unknown to Harry, he isn't just any wizard. He is a very famous wizard with a destiny waiting to be fulfilled—a destiny that explains the peculiar lightning bolt scar on his forehead.

Harry's whole world changes as he embarks on an exciting journey to Hogwarts School of Witchcraft and Wizardry, located in a remote location in a majestic castle nestled against the Forbidden Forest. Amid a flurry of new magical activities (like flying broomsticks and playing the wizard sport of choice, Quidditch) and classes (like Care of Magical Creatures and Defense Against the Dark Arts), it becomes apparent that a dark power is growing stronger...the kind of power that could only come from the most feared wizard, He Who Shall Not Be Named. Could Harry and his lightning bolt scar be connected to this dark wizard? There is only one way to find out. Grab your invisibility cloak, and jump headfirst into this adventurous, mysterious, perilous, and highly entertaining book about muggles and magical folk.

What to read next?
- *Harry Potter and the Chamber of Secrets* by J.K. Rowling
- *Harry Potter and the Prisoner of Azkaban* by J.K. Rowling
- *The Lightning Thief* by Rick Riordan
- *The Graveyard Book* by Neil Gaiman

Did you know?

J.K. Rowling received twelve rejection letters from publishers before Bloomsbury UK accepted the book for publication. One of the rejection letters even told her not to give up her day job!

"IT TAKES A GREAT DEAL OF BRAVERY TO STAND UP TO OUR ENEMIES, BUT JUST AS MUCH TO STAND UP TO OUR FRIENDS."

Did you know?

In most countries outside the United States, *Harry Potter and the Sorcerer's Stone* is actually titled *Harry Potter and the Philosopher's Stone.*

Read it! ☐   Rating: ☆☆☆☆☆

Favorite Character: _____

Notes: _____

_____

The Lion, the Witch and the Wardrobe

Written by C. S. Lewis

AGES:
8+

GENRE:
FANTASY

PUBLISHER:
HARPERCOLLINS

PUBLICATION DATE:
1950

PAGE COUNT:
208

The Lion, the Witch and the Wardrobe is a book in an enchanting series, *The Chronicles of Narnia*, in which good conquers evil.

Four children, Peter, Edmund, Lucy, and Susan, discover that a wardrobe in a professor's old country house contains a gateway into the magical land of Narnia. The children travel through it and find a country frozen in eternal winter, waiting to be set free from the powers of the horrible White Witch. Ready for adventure, the children encounter far more fearsome action than they could have ever imagined, and just as things appear to be hopeless, the gentle yet powerful lion, Aslan, returns to Narnia. Tension and suspense build as the White Witch requests a meeting with Aslan and declares that Edmund is a traitor who must die. What will Aslan and the children do? Will Edmund survive, or will this be the last time anyone ventures in and out of Narnia? Get ready to read this story over and over again because once you're a Narnia lover, you'll always be a Narnia lover.

What to read next?
- *Prince Caspian* by C. S. Lewis
- *The Voyage of the Dawn Treader* by C. S. Lewis
- *The Tale of Despereaux* by Kate DiCamillo
- *The Indian in the Cupboard* by Lynne Reid Banks

Did you know?

During World War II, three girls briefly came to live with C. S. Lewis for safekeeping in his countryside house. A similar event takes place in *The Lion, the Witch and the Wardrobe* when Peter, Edmund, Lucy, and Susan are sent to live with the old Professor in his country home.

"WRONG WILL BE RIGHT, WHEN ASLAN COMES IN SIGHT, AT THE SOUND OF HIS ROAR, SORROWS WILL BE NO MORE, WHEN HE BARES HIS TEETH, WINTER MEETS ITS DEATH, AND WHEN HE SHAKES HIS MANE, WE SHALL SPRING AGAIN."

Read it! ☐   Rating: ☆☆☆☆☆

Favorite Character: _____

Notes: _____

_____

44 D'Aulaire's Book of Greek Myths

Written by Ingri d'Aulaire and Edgar Parin d'Aulaire

AGES:
8+

GENRE:
FAIRY TALES,
FOLK TALES,
AND MYTHS

PUBLISHER:
DELACORTE BOOKS
FOR YOUNG
READERS

1962

PUBLICATION DATE:
1962

PAGE COUNT:
192

This is a treasure of a book filled with commotion, emotion, and humor! From Zeus, the lord of the universe, to Gaea, Mother Earth; Athena, goddess of wisdom, to Poseidon, ruler of the sea; it's time to get acquainted with the gods and goddesses, kings and heroes of ancient Greece in this wonderfully illustrated book. Discover everything about them, including their different personalities, good deeds, and feisty interactions. And don't forget about the minor gods such as nymphs, satyrs, and centaurs. Draw yourself a lightning bolt bookmark, find a throne to rest upon, and enjoy *D'Aulaire's Book of Greek Myths* chapter by chapter—or choose to be vanquished.

What to read next?
- *The Lightning Thief* by Rick Riordan
- *Percy Jackson's Greek Gods* by Rick Riordan
- *Percy Jackson's Greek Heroes* by Rick Riordan
- *Treasury of Greek Mythology* by Donna Jo Napoli

Did you know?
Greek mythology is a collection of myths originating from the ancient Greeks. The myths are about their gods, goddesses, heroes, and the nature of the world.

Read it! ☐   Rating: ☆☆☆☆☆

Favorite Character: _____

Notes: _____

_____

45 A Wrinkle in Time

Written by Madeleine L'Engle

So mysterious and unusual…Meg Murry's father, a scientist who works for the government, has disappeared while working on the secretive tesseract issue. (A tesseract is a space warp or a wrinkle in time, naturally.) Many people don't believe Meg's father is missing at all; they believe the troublesome 13-year-old Meg and her genius 5-year-old brother Charles aren't too bright and that their father has actually left the family. With their new friend Calvin, a popular high school junior, Meg and Charles set out to find their father. With the help of Mrs. Whatsit, Mrs. Who, and Mrs. Which, the kids are transported into space by way of the tesseract and embark on an adventure full of danger. As they travel through the cosmos, which loom with an evil power that threatens to take over their minds, they must find their inner strength and work together to discover the truth. *A Wrinkle in Time*'s pages are filled with mystery, time travel, a little love, and battles between good and evil—all excellent elements for an exhilarating and imaginative excursion.

If you can make your own wrinkle in time and transport yourself through space, be sure to take this book with you and enjoy it from a galaxy of your choice. And for full effect, begin reading it on "a dark and stormy night."

What to read next?

- *A Wrinkle in Time: The Graphic Novel* by Madeleine L'Engle and Hope Larson
- *A Wind in the Door* by Madeleine L'Engle
- *A Swiftly Tilting Planet* by Madeleine L'Engle
- *Many Waters* by Madeleine L'Engle
- *An Acceptable Time* by Madeleine L'Engle

AGES:
9+

GENRE:
ADVENTURE

PUBLISHER:
SQUARE FISH

PUBLICATION DATE:
1962

PAGE COUNT:
256

Read it! ☐   Rating: ☆☆☆☆☆

Favorite Character: _____

Notes: _____

_____

46 The Watsons Go to Birmingham–1963

Written by Christopher Paul Curtis

AGES:
9+

GENRE:
HISTORICAL
FICTION

PUBLISHER:
LAUREL LEAF

PUBLICATION DATE:
1995

PAGE COUNT:
224

It's time for a road trip. Will you go to Birmingham with Kenny Watson and his family? Here is what you will find in this hard-to-put down novel: adventure, hardship, heartache, wit, and a family, all in a story based on real-life events.

Nine-year-old Kenny tells the story of his middle-class African-American family, known as the "Weird Watsons," and the events that took place during the summer of 1963. Kenny's 13-year-old brother, Byron, is constantly in trouble, so the Watsons decide to take a road trip from Flint, Michigan, to Birmingham, Alabama, to see if Grandma can put him in line. While in Birmingham, a tragedy takes place when Grandma's church is blown up. Through Kenny's remarkable eyes, readers of *The Watsons Go to Birmingham—1963* will learn about racism, civil rights, and the strength of family. While the events in the book are serious, the author weaves humor throughout the pages, telling a mesmerizing story that will have you on a roller coaster of emotions.

What to read next?

- *Bud, Not Buddy*
  by Christopher Paul Curtis
- *One Crazy Summer*
  by Rita Williams-Garcia
- *Roll of Thunder, Hear My Cry*
  by Mildred D. Taylor

Did you know?

Christopher Paul Curtis was born and raised in Flint, Michigan, which is the same town the Watson's live in.

Read it! ☐   Rating: ☆☆☆☆☆

Favorite Character: _____

Notes: _____

_____

47 Harriet the Spy

Written by Louise Fitzhugh

Harriet M. Welsch is an extraordinarily real character. She is a precocious and incredibly curious 11-year-old who aspires to be a writer. Encouraged by her nanny, Ole Golly, to master her writing skills by observing people and writing about what she sees, Harriet follows an afternoon "spy-route" and writes down everything she notices about her friends, neighbors, and classmates in a secret notebook. When Harriet learns that Ole Golly will no longer be her nanny, her life begins to turn upside down—especially after she loses her notebook at school during a game of tag. Her classmates find the notebook and discover all of the honest, matter-of-fact, and awful things she has written about them. Harriet finds herself an outcast. Could the only way to make amends and find happiness be through her writing?

Harriet the Spy is an incredibly witty and funny book. Anyone who has ever felt like an outsider will relate to Harriet; and everyone, even grown-ups, can learn from her mistakes and plain ol' bad manners.

What to read next?
• *The Long Secret* by Louise Fitzhugh

Did you know?

Harriet the Spy was adapted into a live-action film of the same name. It was the first film ever to be produced by Nickelodeon Movies.

In two of her later books, *The Long Secret* and *Sport*, Fitzhugh featured two characters from *Harriet the Spy*, Beth Ellen and Sport.

AGES:

9+

GENRE:
REALISTIC

PUBLISHER:
YEARLING

PUBLICATION DATE:
1964

PAGE COUNT:
320

Read it! ☐   Rating: ☆☆☆☆☆

Favorite Character: _____

Notes: _____

_____

48 George

Written by Alex Gino

AGES:
9+

GENRE:
REALISTIC

PUBLISHER:
SCHOLASTIC
PRESS

2015

PUBLICATION DATE:
2015

PAGE COUNT:
240

If there were ever a novel to encourage you to be who you are, to be true to yourself, this is it. If you were to look at George, you would assume you were looking at a boy. George, however, knows she is a girl and believes that this will be a secret she must keep forever. But when her teacher shares the news that the class play will be *Charlotte's Web*, George wants to play the role of Charlotte more than anything. Unfortunately, her teacher turns her down for the role because she says she's a boy, and there are already too many girls who want the part. Her best friend, Kelly, comes to the rescue and helps George devise a plan that will help her come out to the world, including her own family, as she sees herself—a girl.

Will George find her moment to shine and be the person she knows she is? One thing is for sure: George will inspire you to be courageous, no matter where your dreams lead you.

What to read next?
- *Lily and Dunkin* by Donna Gephart
- *Gracefully Grayson* by Ami Polonsky
- *Wandering Son* by Shimura Takako
- *The Misadventures of the Family Fletcher* by Dana Alison Levy

Did you know?
Alex Gino is a proud member of the wonderful organization, We Need Diverse Books, which is dedicated to creating a world in which all children can see themselves in the pages of books.

Read it! ☐   Rating: ☆☆☆☆☆

Favorite Character: _____

Notes: _____

_____

49 Number the Stars

Written by Lois Lowry

It's 1943 in Copenhagen, Denmark. During World War II, German troops took Jewish people from their homes and sent them to concentration camps—now they are after the Jews in Denmark. Ten-year-old Annemarie Johansen and her family take in her Jewish best friend, Ellen Rosen, and pretend she is part of the family to keep her safe. But the German soldiers are suspicious of Ellen because of her dark hair.

As told by Annemarie, *Number the Stars* is the story of how the Danish Resistance heroically relocated almost all of the Danish-Jewish population—approximately 7,000 people—across the sea to Sweden and how she and her family courageously helped smuggle Ellen's family to safety. This is a historical-fiction book, meaning it's a fictionalized story of real events. There is a lot of danger and plenty of bravery. It's incredible what people can do when they stand together.

What to read next?
- *The Giver* by Lois Lowry
- *Hatchet* by Gary Paulsen
- *A Long Walk to Water* by Linda Sue Park
- *The Watsons Go to Birmingham—1963* by Christopher Paul Curtis

AGES:
9+

GENRE:
HISTORICAL
FICTION

PUBLISHER:
HMH BOOKS
FOR YOUNG
READERS

**PUBLICATION
DATE:**
1989

PAGE COUNT:
156

Did you know?
Lois Lowry is also an accomplished photographer. Her photos have been used on the covers of *The Giver* and *Number the Stars*.

Read it! ☐   Rating: ☆☆☆☆☆

Favorite Character: _____

Notes: _____

_____

Sadako and the Thousand Paper Cranes

Written by Eleanor Coerr • Illustrated by Ronald Himler

AGES:
9+

GENRE:
HISTORICAL
FICTION

PUBLISHER:
PUFFIN BOOKS

PUBLICATION
DATE:
1977

PAGE COUNT:
80

Talk about unforgettable! *Sadako and the Thousand Paper Cranes* is an extraordinary story based on real events that have inspired many people to seek peace in the world.

Sadako Sasaki lives in Hiroshima, Japan, during World War II. When she is just two years old, an atomic bomb is dropped near her home. She survives and even becomes the star of the school running team. But after she turns 12, Sadako begins to get dizzy spells, and her neck swells. A year later, she has purple spots on her legs. The doctors discover that Sadako has developed leukemia, which her mother calls the "atom bomb disease," and she only has one year, at most, to live. Inspired by a Japanese legend that says those who make one thousand origami cranes will be granted a wish by the gods, Sadako begins a race against time to fold enough paper cranes for her one wish: to live. Sadako's sad yet hopeful story is one that will reach your heart and stay there always.

Did you know?

The Sasaki family has donated some of Sadako's cranes to many meaningful places around the world, including the 9/11 memorial in New York City and a war memorial at Pearl Harbor, Hawaii.

What to read next?
- *Mieko and the Fifth Treasure* by Eleanor Coerr
- *Number the Stars* by Lois Lowry
- *Lily's Crossing* by Patricia Reilly Giff
- *The War that Saved My Life* by Kimberly Brubaker Bradley

Did you know?

Many students read this book to learn about the horrible effects of war and the importance of peace. At the Hiroshima Peace Park, there is a statue of Sadako holding a gold crane. On the statue, there is a plaque with these words: "This is our cry. This is our prayer. Peace on Earth." Many children come to the statue and leave paper cranes to honor Sadako's spirit.

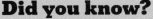

"I WILL WRITE PEACE ON YOUR WINGS AND YOU WILL FLY ALL OVER THE WORLD."

Read it! ☐   Rating: ☆☆☆☆☆

Favorite Character: _____

Notes: _____

_____

51 The Crossover

Written by Kwame Alexander

AGES:
9+

GENRE:
REALISTIC

PUBLISHER:
HMH BOOKS
FOR YOUNG
READERS

**PUBLICATION
DATE:**
2014

PAGE COUNT:
240

Talk about a slam-dunk! *The Crossover* is filled with play-by-play action as Josh and Jordan Bell, 12-year-old twins, navigate life as junior-high basketball stars. The boys learned their love of the sport from their dad, Chuck "Da Man" Bell, a retired basketball superstar. The championship playoffs are coming up, and Josh and Jordan, who are normally inseparable, are beginning to grow apart. Jordon falls for the new girl in the pink Reeboks, which means he is spending less time with Josh. At the same time, their mom tries to convince their dad to see a doctor about some health issues he's having. Ultimately, there is a huge game-changing moment for the family. The question is: will Josh and Jordan be able to come back together?

This story is filled with sibling rivalry, humor, drama, sports, and music. Josh is such a cool guy, likable and funny, and the story is told from his perspective. It's important to know that this book is also told in verse, but wait! Before you freak out and say you don't read poetry, know that Kwame Alexander's powerful writing is like no other. *The Crossover* is like a cool hip-hop track, and you can feel the strength of the Bell family throughout each beat.

"Basketball Rule #4: If you miss enough of life's free throws you will pay in the end." And reading this book is like being given one of life's free throws. Will you take the shot? *Swish!*

What to read next?
- *Booked* by Kwame Alexander
- *Full Cicada Moon* by Marilyn Hilton
- *Lost in the Sun* by Lisa Graff
- *The Way Home Looks Now* by Wendy Wan-Long Shang

Did you know?

Kwame Alexander is multi-talented.
He is a poet, children's book author, playwright,
producer, public speaker, and performer.

"WITH A BOLT OF LIGHTNING ON MY KICKS...THE COURT IS SIZZLING. MY SWEAT IS DRIZZLING. STOP ALL THAT QUIVERING. CUZ TONIGHT I'M DELIVERING."

Read it! ☐   Rating: ☆☆☆☆☆

Favorite Character: _____

Notes: _____

_____

Written by Carolyn Keene

AGES:
9+

GENRE:
MYSTERY

PUBLISHER:
GROSSET & DUNLAP

PUBLICATION DATE:
1930

PAGE COUNT:
192

Problem solvers and super-sleuths, get ready to kick off the ultimate mystery series as 18-year-old Nancy Drew investigates crime in the first book of 64 in the original *Nancy Drew Mystery Stories*. Nancy is the daughter of the well-known lawyer, Carson Drew, who often discusses puzzling aspects of his cases with her. Nancy uses her intuition to help.

After delivering some legal papers for her father, Nancy witnesses a young girl dash in front of a moving van that barely misses her before she topples off the side of a bridge. Thankfully, the young girl is okay, and when Nancy safely returns the girl to her two aunts, Nancy gets her hands on a mystery worth solving.

Nancy has such a good heart and is always ready to help those in need. Her determination and clever instincts for gathering clues and piecing them together add up to a very rewarding ending. For added fun, try reading this book by flashlight—the ultimate Nancy Drew tool!

What to read next?
- *The Hidden Staircase* by Carolyn Keene
- *The Tower Treasure* by Franklin W. Dixon
- *Harriet the Spy* by Louise Fitzhugh
- *Encyclopedia Brown* by Donald J. Sobol

Did you know?
Carolyn Keene is the pen name used by the dozens of ghostwriters who have written *Nancy Drew* stories. The first Carolyn Keene, whose real name was Mildred Wirt Benson, wrote 23 of the first 30 books in the series.

Read it! ☐   Rating: ☆☆☆☆☆

Favorite Character: _____

Notes: _____

_____

53 The True Confessions of Charlotte Doyle

Written by Avi

Yarr! What a treasure of a tale this beauty is!

"Not every thirteen-year-old girl is accused of murder, brought to trial, and found guilty." The year is 1832, and Charlotte Doyle is aboard a ship, returning from her school in England to her family in Rhode Island. The ship is manned by a captain on the brink of losing his mind and a band of mutinous sailors. As the only female passenger, Charlotte tells the story of her voyage across the Atlantic.

At the beginning of *The True Confessions of Charlotte Doyle*, Charlotte herself offers the following warning: "If strong ideas and action offend you, read no more. Find another companion to share your idle hours. For my part I intend to tell the truth as I lived it." If that doesn't tempt you to read this book, I don't know what will. Charlotte challenges us to dig deep and dream big. Filled with exhilarating non-stop adventure, this is one swashbuckling novel. Read it, or walk the plank!

What to read next?

- *Sophia's War: A Tale of the Revolution* by Avi
- *Treasure Island* by Robert Louis Stevenson
- *Island of the Blue Dolphins* by Scott O'Dell
- *Esperanza Rising* by Pam Muñoz Ryan

Did you know?

The True Confessions of Charlotte Doyle was set to be adapted into a film directed by Danny DeVito. Dakota Fanning was originally cast as Charlotte, but as production kept halting, she grew too old for the role.

AGES:
9+

GENRE:
HISTORICAL
FICTION

PUBLISHER:
SCHOLASTIC

1990

**PUBLICATION
DATE:**
1990

PAGE COUNT:
240

Read it! ☐   Rating: ☆☆☆☆☆

Favorite Character: _____

Notes: _____

_____

The Stinky Cheese Man And Other Fairly Stupid Tales

Written by Jon Scieszka • Illustrated by Lane Smith

AGES:
9+

GENRE:
FAIRY TALES,
FOLK TALES
AND MYTHS

PUBLISHER:
VIKING BOOKS
FOR YOUNG
READERS

1992

**PUBLICATION
DATE:**
1992

PAGE COUNT:
56

Get ready to laugh because *The Stinky Cheese Man And Other Fairly Stupid Tales* is downright hilarious! In this book, Jon Scieszka (whose last name rhymes with Fresca) has turned well-known fairy tales upside down, twisted them a couple of times, and created a very clever book in the process. You might recognize the tales of *Jack and the Beanstalk* (Jack is actually the star of this book), *Little Red Riding Hood*, *The Ugly Duckling*, *The Gingerbread Man*, *The Tortoise and the Hare*, and more. However, don't be fooled. These are not the same fairy tales you heard as a youngster. The illustrations are chaotic (in a cool way) and an essential part of making you laugh. This is a book that demands you have fun from cover to cover!

Hey! Who cut the cheese? It wasn't me. The Stinky Cheese Man must be close by. "Run, run, run...as fast as you can. You can't catch me, I'm the stinky cheese man!"

What to read next?

- *The True Story of the 3 Little Pigs* by Jon Scieszka
- *Math Curse* by Jon Scieszka
- *Revolting Rhymes* by Roald Dahl
- *Mind Your Manners, B.B. Wolf* by Judy Sierra

Did you know?

Jon Scieszka is the second oldest of six boys. He claims to be the nicest.

Jon Scieszka has many pets, including two zebra finches, two owl finches, two cordon bleu finches, and 75 western harvester ants—all of which have a name!

Read it! ☐   Rating: ☆☆☆☆☆

Favorite Character: _____

Notes: _____

_____

55 Tales of a Fourth Grade Nothing

Written by Judy Blume

On those sneaky nights you stay up late reading with a flashlight, be warned that *Tales of a Fourth Grade Nothing* is so fun it might make you laugh out loud...you might even wake your little brother! It's the first of five books in a super entertaining series about Peter Warren Hatcher and his younger brother, Farley Drexel Hatcher, also known as "Fudge." Everyone loves little Fudge, and fourth grader Peter can't understand why. Fudge is always in Peter's way. He messes up everything he sees, throws temper tantrums in public, and does the unthinkable with Peter's pet turtle. Why can't Peter's parents see how annoying Fudge is? He's embarrassing and always causes trouble. Doesn't anybody care about Peter, or is he just a fourth grade nothing? What can Peter do to make his parents see what a terror Fudge really is? Yes, having siblings can be simply annoying at times, but because of them, we have this fabulously funny story to read.

What to read next?

- *Superfudge* by Judy Blume
- *Fudge-a-Mania* by Judy Blume
- *Double Fudge* by Judy Blume
- *Otherwise Known as Sheila the Great* by Judy Blume

AGES:
9+

GENRE:
FAMILY

PUBLISHER:
PUFFIN BOOKS

PUBLICATION DATE:
1972

PAGE COUNT:
144

Did you know?

The babysitter who watched Judy Blume's children gave her an article about a toddler who swallowed a tiny pet turtle. The article inspired this story, and several publishers turned it down (one out of concern it might encourage children to swallow turtles).

Read it! ☐   Rating: ☆☆☆☆☆

Favorite Character: _____

Notes: _____
_____

Mrs. Frisby and the Rats of NIMH

Written by Robert C. O'Brien

AGES:
9+

GENRE:
ANIMALS

PUBLISHER:
ALADDIN

1971

PUBLICATION DATE:
1971

PAGE COUNT:
240

Are you ready to be captivated by the action that takes place in this story about a mouse family (the Frisbys) and a mischief of rats that escape from a laboratory? I hope so, because this book is near purrr-fect—though, out of respect for Mrs. Frisby, we should probably save the cat jokes for another time.

Mrs. Frisby is a widowed mouse with four children. Her son, Timothy, is in serious danger. Mr. Fitzgibbon, a farmer, is getting ready to plow the garden where the Frisby family lives, and Timothy has fallen ill and cannot be moved to safety. With nowhere else to turn, Mrs. Frisby seeks help from the rats of NIMH, an extraordinary and intelligent bunch who were once experimented on in the NIMH laboratory. The rats of NIMH devise a plan to save Mrs. Frisby's son. Involving sleeping pills and a cat, the plan is very dangerous, but Mrs. Frisby will stop at nothing to keep her family safe. There is so much to enjoy in this perilous adventure—this is a book that you will be squeaking about for a long time.

What to read next?

- *The Borrowers* by Mary Norton
- *The Tale of Despereaux* by Kate DiCamillo
- *The Mouse and the Motorcycle* by Beverly Cleary
- *The Silver Crown* by Robert C. O'Brien

Did you know?

This book was inspired by real research done on mice and rats by Dr. John B. Calhoun at the National Institute of Mental Health from the 1940s to the 1960s.

Mrs. Frisby and the Rats of NIMH was adapted into an animated film named *The Secret of NIMH*.

Read it! ☐ Rating: ☆☆☆☆☆

Favorite Character: _____

Notes: _____

_____

57

From the Mixed-Up Files of Mrs. Basil E. Frankweiler

Written by E. L. Konigsburg

Spending a night in a museum is one thing, but how amazing would it be to live inside a museum for an entire week, doing things like bathing in a fancy fountain and sleeping in antique canopied beds? Twelve-year-old Claudia Kincaid, a straight-A student, feels unappreciated by her parents, so she decides to run away to some place elegant for just long enough to be missed. She takes her younger brother, Jamie, with her, along with all of the money he has saved up, and the pair set themselves up inside the Metropolitan Museum of Art in New York City, where they become enraptured by a marble statue of an angel. The statue was purchased from an auction for a mere $225, but it's possible it was created by Michelangelo, a famous Renaissance artist, making it worth millions! Working to solve the mystery of the statue, Claudia and Jamie meet Mrs. Basil E. Frankweiler, the elderly woman who sold the statue to the museum. Could she have the answer Claudia and Jamie have been looking for? As the mystery of the statue unfolds, Claudia may just learn some important things about herself as well.

AGES:
9+

GENRE:
MYSTERY

PUBLISHER:
ATHENEUM BOOKS
FOR YOUNG
READERS

**PUBLICATION
DATE:**
1967

What to read next?

- *The Phantom Tollbooth* by Norton Juster
- *A Wrinkle in Time* by Madeleine L'Engle
- *The Mysterious Benedict Society* by Trenton Lee Stewart
- *Escape from Mr. Lemoncello's Library* by Chris Grabenstein

PAGE COUNT:
176

Did you know?

The novel was inspired by a 1965 *New York Times* article about the Metropolitan Museum purchasing a statue called *The Lady with Primroses* for $225.

Read it! ☐   Rating: ☆☆☆☆☆

Favorite Character: _____

Notes: _____

_____

58 Bridge to Terabithia

Written by Katherine Paterson

AGES:
9+

GENRE:
FRIENDSHIP

PUBLISHER:
HARPERCOLLINS

PUBLICATION
DATE:
1977

PAGE COUNT:
320

Bridge to Terabithia is an amazing story about an unlikely friendship between Leslie Burke, the new girl at school, and a fifth-grade boy named Jess Aarons, who wants to be the fastest runner in his grade. Jess has been practicing all summer long, running through the fields that surround his family's farmhouse, and he would have been the fastest if, on the first day of school, Leslie hadn't shown up and outrun everyone. After a rocky start, the pair end up being the best of friends. They play together in the woods behind Leslie's house and use their imaginations to create a magical kingdom, Terabithia. There they reign as king and queen. The only way to enter is by an enchanted rope that swings over a creek. When Jess and Leslie are not fighting off giants and the walking dead, the friends have deep talks about the school kids who tease them.

Everything is perfect until the day Leslie decides to visit Terabithia alone, and the enchanted rope breaks as she crosses. You might just need a box of tissues at this point of the story, because something terrible, something real, something big, and something immensely sad happens to her. It's at this point that you must soldier on to discover how Jess deals with the deepest sorrow he has ever experienced. I can't go on because I might cry, but please do me a favor and read this book. I assure you that, while there is great sadness contained with in its pages, you will smile too.

What to read next?
- *The Great Gilly Hopkins* by Katherine Paterson
- *Jacob Have I Loved* by Katherine Paterson
- *The Lion, the Witch and the Wardrobe* by C. S. Lewis

Did you know?
The book has been made into two movies, a feature film and a TV adaptation.

"LESLIE WAS ONE OF THOSE PEOPLE WHO SAT QUIETLY AT HER DESK, NEVER WHISPERING OR DAYDREAMING OR CHEWING GUM, DOING BEAUTIFUL SCHOOLWORK, AND YET HER BRAIN WAS SO FULL OF MISCHIEF THAT IF THE TEACHER COULD HAVE ONCE SEEN THROUGH THAT MASK OF PERFECTION, SHE WOULD HAVE THROWN HER OUT IN HORROR."

Did you know?

Bridge to Terabithia was inspired by a real tragedy that happened in 1976. When Katherine Paterson's son David was 8 years old, his friend Lisa Hill was struck by lightning and passed away.

Read it! ☐   Rating: ☆☆☆☆☆

Favorite Character: _____

Notes: _____

_____

59 Because of Winn-Dixie

Written by Kate DiCamillo

AGES:
9+

GENRE:
REALISTIC

PUBLISHER:
CANDLEWICK

PUBLICATION DATE:
2000

PAGE COUNT:
208

Hot-diggity-dog! Here's a book with a lot of bark. Opal is new to a small town in Florida, and she is having trouble making friends. Her mother is gone, and she thinks about her all of the time. One day, while in the Winn-Dixie supermarket, Opal encounters a big, stinky stray dog causing loads of trouble in the produce department. When the dog gives her a real smile, Opal knows she needs to protect him. She claims him as her own, naming him Winn-Dixie. Because of the funny and friendly Winn-Dixie, Opal begins to make connections with a quirky but soulful group of characters, young and old, including the local librarian, Miss Franny Block, who knows how to tell a story (Opal loves stories); Miss Gloria Dump, a nearly blind lady who listens to Opal with an open heart; and Otis, an ex-con who lets the animals in his pet store roam free while he plays his guitar for them. Thanks to her new friends, Opal begins to see that she's not alone and learns that all people suffer from a little sadness in their lives. Not only this, she realizes that life isn't all candy and ice cream, but good friends and a little forgiveness can go a long way. You don't have to be Sherlock Bones to figure out that this is a great story!

What to read next?
- *Raymie Nightingale* by Kate DiCamillo
- *The Tale of Despereaux* by Kate DiCamillo
- *The Magician's Elephant* by Kate DiCamillo
- *The Miraculous Journey of Edward Tulane* by Kate DiCamillo

Did you know?

Kate DiCamillo wrote *Because of Winn-Dixie* during a very cold winter in Minnesota. All she wanted to do was go to Florida, but she couldn't afford the trip. So she wrote a book that could take her there. It took her about six months to write. She once said, if you made her pick her favorite character, it would probably be Gloria Dump. She'd like to sit in Gloria's backyard and tell her all of her problems.

"YOU CAN'T ALWAYS JUDGE PEOPLE BY THE THINGS THEY DONE. YOU GOT TO JUDGE THEM BY WHAT THEY ARE DOING NOW."

Read it! ☐   Rating: ☆☆☆☆☆

Favorite Character: _____

Notes: _____

_____

Tuck Everlasting

Written by Natalie Babbitt

AGES:

9+

GENRE:
FANTASY

PUBLISHER:
SQUARE FISH

1975

PUBLICATION DATE:
1975

PAGE COUNT:
160

What if you could live forever? Would you want to? After drinking from a spring near their home in the woods, the Tuck family discovers they've been given the gift of eternal life. The family keeps the secret of the spring and their immortality for 87 years, but their quiet life begins to unravel when 10-year-old Winnie, runs away from her overprotective family and encounters the Tuck family and their enchanted spring. Concerned that Winnie will spill their secret, the Tucks whisk her away to their humble home hidden in the woods and try to explain to her that living forever is not all it's cracked up to be. There are people who would abuse the power of immortality, including one strange man in a yellow suit who keeps following Winnie.

Tuck Everlasting has just a teensy tiny bit of romance, but mostly, it's a book full of exciting adventure—even murder and a jail break! But most importantly, this is a sensitive story about the meaning of life and death (*whoa!*). It's deep, powerful, and believable. You will remember reading this book forever. *Forever? What if you could live forever?* Then you could read it a million times over!

What to read next?
- *Kneeknock Rise* by Natalie Babbitt
- *The Search for Delicious* by Natalie Babbitt
- *Bridge to Terabithia* by Katherine Paterson

Did you know?

Tuck Everlasting has been made into two feature films, the latest of which was made by Disney in 2002. The book has also been adapted into a Broadway stage musical.

Read it! ☐   Rating: ☆☆☆☆☆

Favorite Character: _____

Notes: _____

_____

A Little Princess

Written by Frances Hodgson Burnett

How remarkable is it that this wonderful book was written in 1905, and people are still reading it today? That's so old it's almost timeless! In most princess stories, the main character goes from rags to riches. But in this one, the well-mannered and intelligent Sara Crewe goes from riches to rags when her loving father takes her away from her life of luxury in India to attend a boarding school, Miss Minchin's Select Seminary for Young Ladies, in London. When Sara's father leaves her an orphan, Miss Minchin, the awful headmistress, banishes Sara to the attic and forces her to work as a servant. Through every obstacle life throws at her, Sara manages to remain kind, using her imagination to get her through each day.

While reading *A Little Princess*, your eyes might just water from both laughter *and* sadness, but you'll definitely be totally absorbed in this exciting story all the way to its own fairy-tale ending.

What to read next?
- *The Secret Garden* by Frances Hodgson Burnett
- *Matilda* by Roald Dahl
- *Anne of Green Gables* by L.M. Montgomery
- *Heidi* by Johanna Spyri

AGES:
9+

GENRE:
FRIENDSHIP

PUBLISHER:
PENGUIN
CLASSICS

PUBLICATION
DATE:
1905

PAGE COUNT:
242

Did you know?

At 19, Frances Hodgson Burnett needed to help with the family finances, so she began publishing stories in magazines. Although she is mostly known these days for her children's books, Burnett also wrote mushy romance books for grown-ups.

Read it! ☐   Rating: ☆☆☆☆☆

Favorite Character: _____

Notes: _____

_____

62 Where the Red Fern Grows

Written by Wilson Rawls

AGES:
9+

GENRE:
ANIMALS

PUBLISHER:
YEARLING

PUBLICATION DATE:
1961

PAGE COUNT:
304

Get ready to be seriously moved by this story about a boy and his two dogs. Billy desperately wants a dog, specifically two redbone coonhounds. When his parents tell him they can't afford this breed, Billy, with his strong sense of right and wrong, works hard for two years to earn his own money. When he can finally afford to buy his puppies, he hikes 60 miles through Cherokee country with no shoes to retrieve them and bring them home. He names them Old Dan and Little Ann, and he trains them to be champion hunting dogs. The three explore the woods and mountains freely, having all kinds of amazing adventures, until one day a tragic and heartbreaking battle with a mountain lion takes place.

Billy is a brave character, and his bond with his loyal dogs is incredible to experience. Although you may cry a little while reading this book, the tears are worth it, my friend—a thousand times over!

What to read next?
- *Shiloh* by Phyllis Reynolds Naylor
- *Because of Winn-Dixie* by Kate DiCamillo
- *Old Yeller* by Fred Gipson
- *Summer of the Monkeys* by Wilson Rawls

Did you know?

Wilson Rawls grew up on a small farm in Oklahoma where there were no schools, so his mother taught him to write and read. The first time he realized that he wanted to be a writer was after reading *The Call of the Wild*. The book changed his life, and his father told him, "Son, a man can do anything he sets out to do, if he doesn't give up."

"YOU WERE WORTH IT, OLD FRIEND, AND A THOUSAND TIMES OVER."

Read it! ☐   Rating: ☆☆☆☆☆

Favorite Character: _____

Notes: _____

_____

63 The Bad Beginning

Written by Lemony Snicket • Illustrated by Brett Helquist

AGES:
9+

GENRE:
FANTASY

PUBLISHER:
HARPERCOLLINS

PUBLICATION DATE:
1999

PAGE COUNT:
176

Danger! Danger! Danger! This book has a very bad beginning, but it's the first book in a 13-volume series called *A Series of Unfortunate Events*, so you know the entire book must be awesome or the publisher wouldn't have published 12 more.

After the Baudelaire' parents die in a fire, Violet (age 14), Klaus (age 12), and Sunny (just a baby) are sent to live with their evil relative Count Olaf, who's not to be confused with the adorable snowman from Disney's movie *Frozen*. Count Olaf can't wait to get his hands on the children's family fortune. From this moment on, a series of very unfortunate events take place, and everything about this book is dark, twisted, and grim—and also wickedly exciting all the way to the to-be-continued end!

Now remember, this book only has a bad beginning, and anyway, as Lemony Snicket writes, "I don't know if you've ever noticed this, but first impressions are often entirely wrong." What's your impression? Are you brave enough to take on this energetic and hilarious adventure?

What to read next?
- *The Reptile Room* by Lemony Snicket
- *The Sisters Grimm: The Fairy Tale Detectives* by Michael Buckley
- *Coraline* by Neil Gaiman
- *The Mysterious Benedict Society* by Trenton Lee Stewart

Did you know?

Lemony Snicket is actually the pen name of author Daniel Handler. While doing research for his first book, *The Basic Eight*, Handler decided he didn't want to use his real name so he came up with Lemony Snicket.

"THERE ARE MANY, MANY TYPES OF BOOKS IN THE WORLD, WHICH MAKES GOOD SENSE, BECAUSE THERE ARE MANY, MANY TYPES OF PEOPLE, AND EVERYBODY WANTS TO READ SOMETHING DIFFERENT."

Read it! ☐   Rating: ☆☆☆☆☆

Favorite Character: _____

Notes: _____

_____

The Lightning Thief
Written by Rick Riordan

AGES:
9+

GENRE:
FANTASY

PUBLISHER:
DISNEY-HYPERION

2005

PUBLICATION DATE:
2005

PAGE COUNT:
416

Exciting, gritty, and fun are just a few words that describe this fantastical novel that combines the world as we know it with Greek mythology. Twelve-year-old Percy Jackson, who has dyslexia and ADHD, has been kicked out of six schools in six years, but now he is about to get pulled into a dangerous and exhilarating scene where the action never subsides. On a field trip to the Metropolitan Museum of Art, Percy stands up for a friend who is being bullied, changing his life forever. He is taken on a perilous mission across the United States to prevent a major war between the gods—Zeus, Poseidon, and Hades—by catching a thief who has stolen Zeus's thunderbolt. With the help of a demigod and a satyr, Percy must defeat mythological monsters that will stop at nothing to keep him from his task. The entire story, from start to end, will have your heart racing, leaving you desperate for the next book in the *Percy Jackson and the Olympians* series.

What to read next?
- *The Sea of Monsters* by Rick Riordan
- *D'Aulaires' Book of Greek Myths* by Ingri d'Aulaire and Edgar Parin d'Aulaire
- *Harry Potter and the Sorcerer's Stone* by J.K. Rowling
- *The City of Ember* by Jeanne DuPrau

Did you know?
Rick Riordan's inspiration for *The Lightning Thief* began from stories he created for his son, who was diagnosed with ADHD and dyslexia. When he ran out, his son asked him to make up new stories using the same characters, and soon Percy Jackson was born.

Read it! ☐   Rating: ☆☆☆☆☆

Favorite Character: _____

Notes: _____

_____

65 | Diary of a Wimpy Kid

Written and Illustrated by Jeff Kinney

Greg Heffley is a kid who really wants to do the right thing but often makes the wrong choice. His mother forces him to keep a diary, but don't worry. It's not a boring "Dear Diary" type of journal. In his diary he writes about all of the crazy shenanigans he gets up to during his first year in middle school, complete with hilarious illustrations drawn in comic-book style. Many kids strive to be popular, and Greg is no different. So when his best buddy, Rowley, begins to move up in the school's popularity ranks, Greg takes things into his own hands and sets about finding his own claim to fame.

AGES:

9+

GENRE:
GRAPHIC NOVEL

PUBLISHER:
AMULET BOOKS

2007

PUBLICATION DATE:
2007

PAGE COUNT:
224

Did you know?

Diary of a Wimpy Kid started out as daily entries on a website. It became extremely popular and many people requested a printed version, which spurred the launch of the book series.

We all know we should never read someone else's personal diary, and Greg's diary entries seem so real it's hard not to feel guilty! But this is a chance to see life through someone else's eyes. And Greg's life can be really hard. He makes some of the mistakes for you, so just maybe you don't have to do the same things! *Diary of a Wimpy Kid* is just the book if you're in the mood for something that's easy to read and incredibly fun.

What to read next?

- *The Strange Case of Origami Yoda* by Tom Angleberger
- *The Adventures of Captain Underpants* by Dav Pilkey
- *Lunch Lady and the Cyborg Substitute* by Jarrett J. Krosoczka
- *Knucklehead: Tall Tales and Almost True Stories of Growing Up Scieszka* by Jon Scieszka

Read it! ☐   Rating: ☆☆☆☆☆

Favorite Character: _____

Notes: _____

Frindle

Written by Andrew Clements • Illustrated by Brian Selznick

AGES:
9+

GENRE:
HUMOR

PUBLISHER:
ATHENEUM BOOKS
FOR YOUNG
READERS

PUBLICATION DATE:
1996

PAGE COUNT:
112

Do you love making up words? Have you ever created a secret language that only you and your friends understand? If you answered yes to either of these questions, then Andrew Clements' hilarious story will definitely make you laugh and smile.

Fifth-grader Nick Allen is not so much a troublemaker as a boy who likes to have a slightly disruptive, yet creative, good time. In an attempt to annoy Mrs. Granger, his teacher, Nick creates the word *frindle* in exchange for the word *pen*. This creates a teacher-student war that results in after-school punishment and a visit from the principal. The use of *frindle* spirals out of control as Nick's friends, the community, and people around the country begin picking it up. It eventually ends up in the dictionary. Will the power of words be enough to resolve the challenges between Mrs. Granger and Nick?

Complete with funny black-and-white illustrations, *Frindle* is a book that you will be telling all of your friends they have to read. Better yet, ask your teacher to read it aloud to the entire class, and see what fun new words you can come up with!

What to read next?
- *No Talking* by Andrew Clements
- *The Lemonade War* by Jacqueline Davies
- *Tales of a Fourth Grade Nothing* by Judy Blume
- *The Invention of Hugo Cabret* by Brian Selznick

Did you know?
The story of *Frindle* came about when Andrew Clements wondered what would happen if a kid made up a word that his teacher didn't like but all of the kids at school did.

Read it! ☐   Rating: ☆☆☆☆☆

Favorite Character: _____

Notes: _____

_____

67 The Magic Pudding

Written and Illustrated by Norman Lindsay

Get ready for some "Rumpus Bumpus!" Imagine an endless supply of your favorite food—that's exactly what the Magic Pudding is. Well, to be exact, he is actually a cantankerous, walking, talking pudding named Albert. To be even more exact, he is a pudding that changes flavors on demand. The best part? The Magic Pudding never runs out, no matter how much you eat. Now that's magical! And if you are a member of the Noble Society of Pudding Owners, you "are required to wander along the roads, indulgin' in conversation, song and story, and eatin' at regular intervals from the Pudding."

So join the zany characters—the polite koala Bunyip Bluegum, the kooky sailor Bill Barnacle, and the wacky penguin Sam Sawnoff—and slice your way through this tale as they break into ridiculous rhymes and verses while working hard to keep Albert safe from the thieving scoundrels, Possum and Wombat. You'll be in for one of the most far-out, absurd, and deliciously humorous illustrated reads you've ever had. Some people say this is the funniest book ever written! What will you think?

What to read next?

- *The Muddle-headed Wombat* by Ruth Park
- *The Complete Adventures of Blinky Bill* by Dorothy Wall
- *Alice's Adventures in Wonderland* by Lewis Carroll
- *The Wonderful Wizard of Oz* by L. Frank Baum

Did you know?

In Melbourne, Australia, you can find a sculpture of the four main characters in *The Magic Pudding* in the Children's Garden at the Royal Botanic Gardens.

AGES:
9+

GENRE:
HUMOR

PUBLISHER:
NEW YORK REVIEW CHILDREN'S COLLECTION

PUBLICATION DATE:
1918

PAGE COUNT:
184

Read it! ☐   Rating: ☆☆☆☆☆

Favorite Character: _____

Notes: _____

_____

The Graveyard Book

Written by Neil Gaiman

AGES:
9+

GENRE:
FANTASY

PUBLISHER:
HARPERCOLLINS

2008

PUBLICATION DATE:
2008

PAGE COUNT:
336

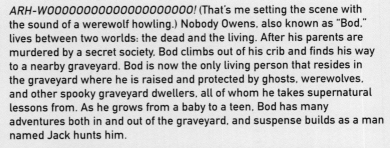

ARH-WOOOOOOOOOOOOOOOOOOOO! (That's me setting the scene with the sound of a werewolf howling.) Nobody Owens, also known as "Bod," lives between two worlds: the dead and the living. After his parents are murdered by a secret society, Bod climbs out of his crib and finds his way to a nearby graveyard. Bod is now the only living person that resides in the graveyard where he is raised and protected by ghosts, werewolves, and other spooky graveyard dwellers, all of whom he takes supernatural lessons from. As he grows from a baby to a teen, Bod has many adventures both in and out of the graveyard, and suspense builds as a man named Jack hunts him.

Once readers get past the frightful opening chapter, in which Bod loses his parents, this is nothing but an exceptionally exciting, sometimes funny, warmhearted, and deliciously spooky book that you can choose to read with all of the lights on or with a flashlight in the dark.

What to read next?
- *Coraline* by Neil Gaiman
- *The Wolves in the Walls* by Neil Gaiman
- *The Jungle Book* by Rudyard Kipling
- *Harry Potter and the Sorcerer's Stone* by J.K. Rowling

Did you know?

Neil Gaiman's inspiration for *The Graveyard Book* came to him while watching his son, who was two at the time, ride his bike around a graveyard. His son looked so comfortable that Neil thought he could write a story like *The Jungle Book*, but set in a graveyard. This happened in 1985, many years before he actually completed the story.

"FACE YOUR LIFE, ITS PAIN, ITS PLEASURE, LEAVE NO PATH UNTAKEN."

Read it! ☐   Rating: ☆☆☆☆☆

Favorite Character: _____

Notes: _____

_____

69

The Hobbit
Written by J. R. R. Tolkien

AGES:
9+

GENRE:
FANTASY

PUBLISHER:
HOUGHTON
MIFFLIN

PUBLICATION DATE:
1937

PAGE COUNT:
300

"There is nothing like looking, if you want to find something," says Thorin Oakenshield. "You certainly usually find something, if you look, but it is not always quite the something you were after." Thanks to pages filled with dwarves, elves, trolls, goblins, spiders, eagles, wizards, and, of course, hobbits, *The Hobbit* is almost certainly the adventure you have been looking for.

Hobbits, as a rule, do not like adventure, but when 13 dwarves and Gandalf the wizard show up for tea at the home of the hairy-footed hobbit Bilbo Baggins, adventure is exactly what this hobbit gets. Gandalf and the dwarves hire Bilbo as a thief to reclaim their treasure. Smaug the Magnificent, a hoarding fiery dragon, guards the treasure, and the only way to get to it is to travel "far over the misty mountains cold, to dungeons deep and caverns old." Bilbo much prefers the safety and comfort of his hobbit-hole, but he reluctantly agrees to go on the dangerous quest. Bilbo's life is never the same again, especially once he finds a powerful ring and encounters the ghastly creature Gollum.

Danger lurks at every twist and turn as Bilbo and the dwarves are captured, almost cooked by trolls, and forced to fight deadly battles. Bilbo's journey through Middle-earth is one of the most unforgettable adventures that has ever taken place in a book. There are even maps included so you don't get lost in this wild world. Bilbo's bravery and loyalty is outstanding. May you enjoy this book immensely, and may the hair never fall out of your toes!

What to read next?
- *Eragon* by Christopher Paolini
- *The Ruins of Gorlan* by John Flanagan
- *The Golden Compass* by Philip Pullman
- *Magyk* by Angie Sage

Did you know?
A 10-year-old boy is the reason *The Hobbit* became a book. The publisher Stanley Unwin gave the manuscript to his son to write a report about whether or not it should be published. His son had plenty of positive things to say, and soon it was published. Now it is even a popular movie trilogy!

"FAR OVER THE MISTY MOUNTAINS COLD
TO DUNGEONS DEEP AND CAVERNS OLD
WE MUST AWAY, ERE BREAK OF DAY,
TO CLAIM OUR
LONG-FORGOTTEN GOLD."

Read it! ☐   Rating: ☆☆☆☆☆

Favorite Character: _____

Notes: _____

_____

70 Alice's Adventures in Wonderland

Written by Lewis Carroll

AGES:
9+

GENRE:
FANTASY

PUBLISHER:
PUFFIN BOOKS

1865

PUBLICATION
DATE:
1865

PAGE COUNT:
192

You would be completely mad not to read this book! If ever there were a tall tale, this might be the tallest. Alice, who is feeling bored and sleepy while listening to her sister read a book with no pictures, falls down a rabbit hole and finds herself in a fantastical world known as Wonderland. She takes a journey through Wonderland, and you'll be happy to go along with her as she encounters curious characters and loads of peculiar nonsense. There is the clothed White Rabbit rushing about with his pocket watch, the Cheshire Cat who becomes invisible except for his big grin, the Hatter who is completely mad, and The Queen of Hearts who is very difficult to please. There are riddles to solve, quirky poems, and a tea party Alice can't wait to leave.

I can't tell you what The Queen of Hearts would have to say if you decide not to read this book, but I recommend that you just go ahead and start now. As sure as ferrets are ferrets, you'll be charmed by the words and fascinated by the illustrations. *Alice's Adventures in Wonderland* is dreamy!

Did you know?

Lewis Carroll is the pen name for Charles Lutwidge Dodgson.

What to read next?

- *Through the Looking-Glass* by Lewis Carroll
- *The Looking Glass Wars* by Frank Beddor
- *The Wonderful Wizard of Oz* by L. Frank Baum
- *Peter Pan* by J. M. Barrie

Did you know?

Queen Victoria was one of the first well-known fans of *Alice's Adventures in Wonderland*. With even royalty loving the book, it's no wonder that the story has been adapted into multiple movies, live performances, and comic books.

"IT'S NO USE GOING BACK TO YESTERDAY, BECAUSE I WAS A DIFFERENT PERSON THEN."

Read it! ☐   Rating: ☆☆☆☆☆

Favorite Character: _____

Notes: _____

_____

71 Ballet Shoes

Written by Noel Streatfeild • Illustrated by Diane Goode

AGES:
9+

GENRE:
FAMILY

PUBLISHER:
YEARLING

PUBLICATION DATE:
1937

PAGE COUNT:
256

With a title like *Ballet Shoes*, you may think you have to enjoy ballet to enjoy this book. Not true! This is a book for anyone who has ever dreamed. And, yes, any kind of dreamer will do.

Ballet Shoes is an energetic read about three orphan girls and the many adventures they have when their caretaker, Great Uncle Max (a paleontologist), is gone for many years on an expedition, leaving the household with an ever-decreasing bank account. Propelled by a great group of offbeat characters, Pauline, Petrova, and Posie begin attending the Children's Academy of Dancing and Stage Training so they can use their experiences as performers to give back to their adopted family. Each of the girls discovers her own special talents, learning that with hard work and plenty of practice, their dreams of making history will come true. But it's also possible that performing arts isn't the right choice for one of the sisters, who prefers automobiles over arabesques any day. From their birth to their teens, we see the girls grow up, staying together even while paving out their own individual paths through life. We experience their highs and lows in all of this story's fascinating glory. *Ballet Shoes* is warm, inspiring, and funny.

What to read next?
- *Theater Shoes* by Noel Streatfeild
- *Skating Shoes* by Noel Streatfeild
- *The Four-Story Mistake* by Elizabeth Enright
- *A Little Princess* by Frances Hodgson Burnett

Did you know?
Noel Streatfeild was born in 1895, and she worked as an actress for 10 years before turning her artistic talents to writing books for children. Her experiences came in handy while writing the *Shoe Book* series, of which *Ballet Shoes* was the first.

Read it! ☐   Rating: ☆☆☆☆☆

Favorite Character: _____

Notes: _____

_____

72 Peter Pan

Written by J. M. Barrie • Illustrated by Michael Hague

Peter Pan is the magical story of Wendy, Michael, and John Darling and the gripping adventures that take place when they meet the mischievous Peter Pan, a boy who can fly and never wants to grow up. Peter lives on the small island of Neverland, where he is the leader of the The Lost Boys gang. On the night that Peter flies into the bedroom of the Darling children with his feisty fairy companion, Tinker Bell, the Darling children return to Neverland with him, and readers are treated to action galore. There are mermaids, Native Americans, pirates, a tick-tocking crocodile, and exciting battles with great escapes.

And just as Peter teaches the Darling children to fly, this book will lift you up into the air. Take the second star to the right, and go straight on till morning, all the way to Neverland!

What to read next?

- *Peter and the Starcatchers* by Dave Barry and Ridley Pearson
- *The Wizard of Oz* by L. Frank Baum
- *Treasure Island* by Robert Louis Stevenson
- *Alice's Adventures in Wonderland* by Lewis Carroll

AGES:
9+

GENRE:
FANTASY

PUBLISHER:
HENRY HOLT
AND CO.

1911

PUBLICATION
DATE:
1911

PAGE COUNT:
176

Did you know?

Peter Pan was a play before it was made into a book. It has been said that when the story was first created, Peter and the Lost Boys could fly without the use of fairy dust, but after a few reports of children hurting themselves as they attempted to fly off their beds, J. M. Barrie added the necessary step of sprinkling oneself with fairy dust.

Read it! ☐   Rating: ☆☆☆☆☆

Favorite Character: _____

Notes: _____

_____

73

Anne of Green Gables

Written by L. M. Montgomery

AGES:
9+

GENRE:
FRIENDSHIP

PUBLISHER:
PUFFIN BOOKS

PUBLICATION DATE:
1908

PAGE COUNT:
320

Anne of Green Gables has been making hearts sing for more than 100 years. 11-year-old redheaded-orphan Anne Shirley has been in and out of homes and orphanages for most of her life. When she is sent to live with Marilla and Matthew Cuthbert, she falls in love with the picturesque home and farm known as Green Gables. When Anne discovers that Marilla and Matthew had actually requested a boy to help with the farm work, and they have no use for a girl, she does her best to win them over. Anne is impulsive, intelligent, and incredibly chatty, and she has the greatest imagination. The combination often leads her into trouble, like falling off of a roof and dyeing her hair green!

From busybody Rachel Lynde to bosom buddy Diana Barry and fellow student Gilbert Blythe, who teases Anne about the color of her hair by calling her "Carrots," the characters in this book make it easy to get swept up in Anne's antics. You may be wondering if Anne wins Marilla and Matthew Cuthbert over, or if she gets to stay at Green Gables? Here's the only thing I'll tell you: Anne Shirley could possibly be your literary kindred spirit. "It's been my experience," says Anne, "that you can nearly always enjoy things if you make up your mind firmly that you will." Is your mind made up yet?

Did you know?

The L. M. in L. M. Montgomery stands for Lucy Maud.

What to read next?
- *Anne of Avonlea* by L. M. Montgomery
- *The Water and the Wild* by K. E. Ormsbee
- *Little Women* by Louisa May Alcott
- *A Little Princess* by Frances Hodgson Burnett

Did you know?

Anne of Green Gables is the beginning of a wonderful series inspired by L. M. Montgomery's childhood experiences on Prince Edward Island and notes that she took as a young girl about a couple who were indeed sent an orphan girl instead of a boy.

"LIFE IS WORTH LIVING AS LONG AS THERE'S A LAUGH IN IT."

Read it! ☐   Rating: ☆☆☆☆☆

Favorite Character: _____

Notes: _____

_____

74

The Birchbark House
Written by Louise Erdrich

AGES:
9+

GENRE:
HISTORICAL
FICTION

PUBLISHER:
DISNEY-HYPERION

1999

PUBLICATION DATE:
1999

PAGE COUNT:
256

Learn about the everyday life of a Native-American family during 1847—America's pioneer times. This book tells the story of a full year of 7-year-old Ojibwa, Omakayas', or "Little Frog" (because her first step was a hop) life, taking readers through all four seasons. Sadly, she is the only survivor of smallpox on Spirit Island. She is rescued and adopted as a baby by an Ojibwa family who lives on Madeline Island. The family lives in a birchbark house, and their daily life often involves harvesting, frightful encounters with bears, and ghost stories around the fire. When smallpox spreads through the island, Omakayas once again survives the disease, but not everyone in her family is so lucky. Many emotions are felt throughout this mystical book, and there is a lot for readers to take in and enjoy. The characters are so likable, the Ojibwa words used throughout the story are fun to learn, the pencil drawings are beautiful to look at, and there is even a map of the Ojibwa community. This is a wonderful read! What are you waiting for?

What to read next?
- *The Game of Silence* by Louise Erdrich
- *The Porcupine Year* by Louise Erdrich
- *Crossing Bok Chitto: A Choctaw Tale of Friendship & Freedom* by Tim Tingle
- *Where the Mountain Meets the Moon* by Grace Lin

Did you know?
Louise Erdrich is a member of the Turtle Mountain Band of Chippewa. Her own ancestry inspired the *Birchbark* series. She spent time with her children on Madeline Island and spoke to Ojibwa elders about its spirit and significance.

Read it! ☐   Rating: ☆☆☆☆☆
Favorite Character: _____
Notes: _____
_____

75 Stargirl

Written by Jerry Spinelli

Magic can be as simple and powerful as a character or person who stays true to him or herself. Stargirl Caraway is new at Mica High School, and she is magical. She makes quite an impression on the other students—especially Leo, the narrator of the book—with her unique sense of fashion, ukulele playing, incredible kindness, and the fact that she dances even when there is no music playing. Some might say she marches to the beat of her own drum. Stargirl is completely different than anyone else at the school, and the students are enamored by her...until they are not. When Stargirl's popularity status goes from hero to zero, her new crush Leo encourages her to be "normal." Will Stargirl remain loyal to herself, or will she choose to follow the crowd and be the same as everyone else? To fit in or not to fit in—that is the question! *Stargirl* is a quick read, so dive in to this positively heartfelt tale and find out for yourself.

What to read next?
- *Rules* by Cynthia Lord
- *Loser* by Jerry Spinelli
- *Maniac Magee* by Jerry Spinelli
- *Smile* by Raina Telgemeier

Did you know?

Jerry Spinelli became a children's book author by accident. Over 12 years, he wrote four books for adults, none of which were accepted by publishers. His fifth book was rejected too. But luckily for us, a children's publisher loved it, and Spinelli found his sweet spot writing for kids.

AGES:
10+

GENRE:
FRIENDSHIP

PUBLISHER:
ALFRED A. KNOPF

PUBLICATION
DATE:
2000

PAGE COUNT:
208

Read it! ☐   Rating: ☆☆☆☆☆

Favorite Character: _____

Notes: _____

76 Out of My Mind

Written by Sharon M. Draper

AGES:
10+

GENRE:
REALISTIC

PUBLISHER:
ATHENEUM BOOKS
FOR YOUNG
READERS

**PUBLICATION
DATE:**
2010

PAGE COUNT:
320

Melody Brooks, a lively girl with cerebral palsy, often finds life frustrating because she can't speak, write, feed herself, or go to the bathroom without help. Melody has a photographic memory, which means she can recall everything she experiences in detail. When her mom becomes pregnant, she hears her parents discussing fears that this baby will also have special needs. Baby Penny is born healthy and "normal." At times, Melody's relieved, but sometimes she gets jealous as she watches Penny learn to do things she will never be able to.

Her parents try everything they can to help her live a normal life. They enroll her in a public school that allows special-needs students to participate. Melody is given a device that helps her communicate with people. The kids in class think she is simpleminded, until she passes a test with a perfect score. Soon Melody takes another test to join the trivia team. While things may be looking up for Melody, it's not all sun-shiny days and smooth sailing. When a family catastrophe takes place and her sister is injured, Melody blames herself. Will she make it onto the team? Will her sister be okay? *Out of My Mind* teaches and challenges us to be accepting, thoughtful, and kind to all people, including those who are different from us. Understanding what Melody goes through every day is powerful. Her efforts to show her intelligence to the world make her a brave and inspiring shining star.

What to read next?
- *Stella by Starlight* by Sharon M. Draper
- *Wonder* by R. J. Palacio
- *Paperboy* by Vince Vawter
- *Fish in a Tree* by Lynda Mullaly Hunt

Did you know?

As a child, Sharon M. Draper was a voracious reader. Her mother took her to the library every Saturday to check out 10 books.

"MAYBE I'M NOT SO DIFFERENT FROM EVERYONE ELSE AFTER ALL. IT'S LIKE SOMEBODY GAVE ME A PUZZLE, BUT I DON'T HAVE THE BOX WITH THE PICTURE ON IT. SO I DON'T KNOW WHAT THE FINAL THING IS SUPPOSED TO LOOK LIKE. I'M NOT EVEN SURE IF I HAVE ALL THE PIECES."

Read it! ☐   Rating: ☆☆☆☆☆

Favorite Character: _____

Notes: _____

_____

Better Nate than Never

Written by Tim Federle

AGES:
10+

GENRE:
REALISTIC

PUBLISHER:
SIMON &
SCHUSTER

PUBLICATION DATE:
2013

PAGE COUNT:
304

Turn out the lights and open those stage curtains, Nate Foster is ready to dance his way into your heart. Five, six, seven, eight...

Nate is a funny boy with big dreams. He wants to be a star on Broadway, but in Jankburg, Pennsylvania, his best friend, Libby, is the only one who appreciates a good show tune. With help from Libby, Nate plans a secret overnight trip to New York. When he gets there, his plan is to audition for *E.T.: The Musical*, land the role, and make his dreams come true.

From start to finish, Nate takes us on a fantastic journey through New York, filled with humor and a brilliant assortment of characters. Of course, the road to being a Broadway star, or even just Nate, is not always easy, so this story is also an exploration of bullying, family relationships, and self-identity. *Better Nate than Ever* is definitely a book to phone home about. What are you waiting for? I bet you can't wait to find out if Nate gets a part in the musical! Put down those jazz hands, read this book, and get inspired to make your own dreams come true. *Bravo!*

What to read next?

- *Five, Six, Seven, Nate!* by Tim Federle
- *Drama* by Raina Telgemeier
- *Two Weeks with the Queen* by Morris Gleitzman
- *The Boy in the Dress* by David Walliams

Did you know?

The author, Tim Federle, danced in several Broadway musicals and, in 2010, he was an associate choreographer for the musical *Billy Elliot*.

Read it! ☐   Rating: ☆☆☆☆☆

Favorite Character: _____

Notes: _____

_____

78 | Mockingbird

Written by Kathryn Erskine

Did you know?

Kathryn Erskine spent a lot of time growing up overseas. She attended eight different schools, including her favorite, a Hogwarts-style castle in Scotland.

Erskine has a daughter with Asperger syndrome. When her daughter read *Mockingbird*, she said that she thought it was a very accurate depiction of the way a child with Asperger's sees the world.

Do you like to read books that feel real? *Mockingbird* is a book that certainly offers that. Caitlin Smith is a fifth grader with Asperger syndrome; everything in her world is either black or white, and the rest is just plain confusing. Devon, her older brother, has always been there to help her navigate through life. But after a devastating middle-school shooting, Caitlin is left without him, and now she and the community must learn to cope with loss. But how? Caitlin spends a lot of time drawing and looking through dictionaries, where she comes across the word closure and decides it could be just what she needs to help herself and everyone else affected by the shooting. Searching for closure becomes her focus. Will she be able to find it?

Getting to know Caitlin, who is strong and funny, is a gift in itself, and her voice will carry you through this powerful story. Caitlin likes to read some books over and over, and you may just find yourself doing the same with *Mockingbird*. For real!

What to read next?
• *Out of My Mind* by Sharon M. Draper
• *Counting by 7s* by Holly Goldberg Sloan
• *Wonder* by R. J. Palacio
• *Fish in a Tree* by Lynda Mullaly Hunt

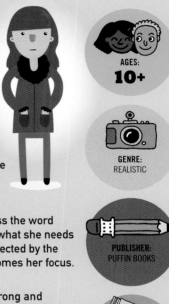

AGES:
10+

GENRE:
REALISTIC

PUBLISHER:
PUFFIN BOOKS

PUBLICATION DATE:
2010

PAGE COUNT:
256

Read it! ☐   Rating: ☆☆☆☆☆

Favorite Character: _____

Notes: _____

_____

Hating Alison Ashley

Written by Robin Klein

AGES:
10+

GENRE:
FRIENDSHIP

PUBLISHER:
PUFFIN BOOKS

PUBLICATION DATE:
1984

PAGE COUNT:
192

Now here's an ace Australian novel that will make you laugh out loud. Erica Yurken, also known as Erk, Yuk, and Gherkin, thinks she is far better than everyone else. She thinks she should be living somewhere far more posh than Barringa East, especially because she believes she is destined to be a famous actress. Erica makes up stories about herself to impress the other sixth graders and to hide the fact that she finds her family embarrassing. When a beautiful, rich, and intelligent new girl, Alison Ashley, shows up in her class, Erica instantly hates her and classifies her as a snob. Alison does appear to be perfect; she's even a skilled actress, getting cast as the lead role in a play at sixth grade camp. The two girls become incredibly competitive, but will one of them come out on top? Is Alison's life really as perfect as Erica believes? *Hating Alison Ashley* is a "fair dinkum beauty" (that's Australian for "true beauty") of a story. Go on, and give it a whirl!

What to read next?

- *Alice-Miranda at School* by Jacqueline Harvey
- *Playing Beatie Bow* by Ruth Park
- *Harriet the Spy* by Louise Fitzhugh
- *From the Mixed-Up Files of Mrs. Basil E. Frankweiler* by E. L. Konigsburg

Did you know?

Robin Klein is one of Australia's most popular authors. Her first short story was published when Robin was 16, and she has now written more than 40 novels.

Read it! ☐   Rating: ☆☆☆☆☆

Favorite Character: _____

Notes: _____

_____

Esperanza Rising
Written by Pam Muñoz Ryan

Tragedy, danger, great change, and a strong girl are what you will find in *Esperanza Rising*.

In 1930, during the Great Depression, Esperanza's father is murdered, and she and her mama have no choice but to flee from Mexico to California. Used to living a lush and privileged life on a Mexican ranch, Esperanza's life changes drastically. She goes from riches to rags and must adjust to her new life in a camp for Mexican farm workers. Fancy dresses and servants are replaced with hard work in order to make ends meet. The love of Esperanza's family is her only true treasure in the world. Esperanza's experiences help her become kinder and more appreciative, which makes her such an inspirational heroine. Even after living through murder, fire, illness, and financial troubles, she reminds us to not ever be afraid to start over. This story is as beautiful as any of your favorite childhood fairy tales. The happiness that shines through even the saddest parts will carry you through to the very last page.

Did you know?

Pam Muñoz Ryan's inspiration for *Esperanza Rising* came from her own family's struggles. In Spanish, the word *esperanza* means "hope."

What to read next?

- *A Little Princess* by Frances Hodgson Burnett
- *Inside Out and Back Again* by Thanhha Lai
- *The Dreamer* by Pam Muñoz Ryan
- *Walk Two Moons* by Sharon Creech

AGES:
10+

GENRE:
HISTORICAL FICTION

PUBLISHER:
SCHOLASTIC PRESS

PUBLICATION DATE:
2000

PAGE COUNT:
262

Read it! ☐   Rating: ☆☆☆☆☆

Favorite Character: _____

Notes: _____

_____

81 My Side of the Mountain

Written and Illustrated by Jean Craighead George

AGES:
10+

GENRE:
ADVENTURE

PUBLISHER:
PUFFIN BOOKS

1959

PUBLICATION DATE:
1959

PAGE COUNT:
192

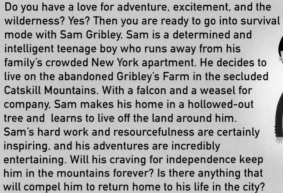

Do you have a love for adventure, excitement, and the wilderness? Yes? Then you are ready to go into survival mode with Sam Gribley. Sam is a determined and intelligent teenage boy who runs away from his family's crowded New York apartment. He decides to live on the abandoned Gribley's Farm in the secluded Catskill Mountains. With a falcon and a weasel for company, Sam makes his home in a hollowed-out tree and learns to live off the land around him. Sam's hard work and resourcefulness are certainly inspiring, and his adventures are incredibly entertaining. Will his craving for independence keep him in the mountains forever? Is there anything that will compel him to return home to his life in the city?

This is a novel that's easy to get lost in; no literary survival skills are necessary. The author has provided everything needed to keep you turning the page all the way to the end. Try reading this in your favorite outdoor spot, and you'll feel at one with nature, just like Sam Gribley!

What to read next?
- *On the Far Side of the Mountain* by Jean Craighead George
- *Frightful's Mountain* by Jean Craighead George
- *Hatchet* by Gary Paulsen
- *Where the Red Fern Grows* by Wilson Rawls

Did you know?

It took Jean Craighead George 30 years to write the sequel, On the *Far Side of the Mountain*. It took another 10 years after that to complete the trilogy, with *Frightful's Mountain*.

People who visit the area written about in the book often ask to see the abandoned Gribley's farm. However, the farm does not exist...it is a completely made up location.

Read it! ☐   Rating: ☆☆☆☆☆

Favorite Character: _____

Notes: _____

82 Blubber

Written by Judy Blume

AGES:

10+

GENRE:
REALISTIC

People can be cruel! After presenting a school report on whales, the other students in class pass around a note giving Linda, an overweight fifth grader, the nickname "Blubber." The teasing doesn't stop there. A group of mean girls torment Linda, physically and emotionally. They force her to say things like, "I am Blubber, the Smelly Whale of Class 206." Jill, one of the mean girls, narrates the story. While Jill may not be the main offender, she definitely participates, doing some really terrible things to Linda—things that will make your jaw drop! Nobody likes to be teased, and we all know that we shouldn't bully, so why is Jill so unkind to Linda? When things turn upside down and Jill finds herself on the other end of the bullying, the classroom dynamics really begin to change.

There is so much to think about after reading a book about bullying and how we treat one another. But the most important question is what will you take away from reading *Blubber*?

PUBLISHER:
ANTHEUM BOOKS
FOR YOUNG
READERS

Did you know?

The inspiration for *Blubber* came from a real experience that took place in Judy Blume's daughter's fifth grade class. A tormentor, who singled out one girl, led the entire class to bully her. Blume wrote *Blubber* to help readers see bullying for what it is and to encourage kids to speak up about it.

What to read next?

- *Are You There God? It's Me, Margaret* by Judy Blume
- *Slob* by Ellen Potter
- *Confessions of a Former Bully* by Trudy Ludwig
- *Wonder* by R.J. Palacio

PUBLICATION DATE:
1974

PAGE COUNT:
208

Read it! ☐   Rating: ☆☆☆☆☆

Favorite Character: _____

Notes: _____

Mary Poppins

Written by P.L. Travers • Illustrated by Mary Shepard

AGES:
10+

GENRE:
FANTASY

PUBLISHER:
HMH BOOKS
FOR YOUNG
READERS

**PUBLICATION
DATE:**
1934

PAGE COUNT:
208

There is no need for a spoonful of sugar to help this story go down!

Blown in by the blustery east wind, Mary Poppins arrives at Number Seventeen Cherry-Tree Lane, and "spit-spot," the Banks family is changed forever. Arriving with her umbrella and magical carpetbag, she is to be the new nanny to Jane, Michael, and twins John and Barbara. Having Mary Poppins around, even with her no-nonsense approach to maintaining order, ensures that every day is filled with mystery and magic. Mary Poppins may be a bit stiff and a tad bossy, but she has the kids enjoying tea on the ceiling, riding peppermint horses, and visiting polar bears as they fly around the world by way of a magic compass.

Adventures with Mary Poppins can have you feeling both happy to keep turning the page and sad for the end, as the line between real life and fantasy begins to blur. With Mary Poppins' help, you can find wonder, if you know where to look for it. And this book is surely one place to find wonder!

Did you know?

P.L. Travers was Helen Lyndon Goff's pen name. It was an abbreviation for Pamela, the name she used as an actress, Lynden, her middle name, and Travers, her father's first name.

What to read next?

- *Mary Poppins Comes Back* by P.L. Travers
- *Peter Pan* by J. M. Barrie
- *Bed-Knob and Broomstick* by Mary Norton
- *Chitty Chitty Bang Bang* by Ian Fleming

Did you know?

Travers has written many books but is best known for *Mary Poppins*, which has been translated into 17 different languages and adapted into a very popular Disney film.

"THERE WAS SOMETHING STRANGE AND EXTRAORDINARY ABOUT HER—SOMETHING THAT WAS FRIGHTENING AND AT THE SAME TIME MOST EXCITING."

Read it! ☐   Rating: ☆☆☆☆☆

Favorite Character: _____

Notes: _____

_____

84 Holes

Written by Louis Sachar

AGES:
10+

GENRE:
MYSTERY

PUBLISHER:
YEARLING

PUBLICATION DATE:
1998

PAGE COUNT:
233

Get ready to dig into this adventurous, often funny, and twisted mystery that flits between the past and the present. And did I mention the buried treasure?

Stanley Yelnats' family has a history of bad luck, and it seems Stanley has been afflicted with the same infamous curse that began with his "no-good-dirty-rotten-pig-stealing-great-great-grandfather." After being caught in the wrong place at the wrong time, the overweight 14-year-old has been unfairly sent to a boys' detention center, Camp Green Lake, where there is no lake...just a lot of holes dug by boys to help build their character. The holes are all exactly 5 feet wide and 5 feet deep, and it turns out that the warden, who paints her fingernails with rattlesnake venom, has an agenda much bigger than building character. The warden is looking for something that may be buried underneath the dried-up lake, but what could that be? Will Stanley's luck turn around, and can the curse be lifted from the Yelnats family? Thanks to the book's exciting twists and turns, you'll find it hard to put down!

What to read next?
- *Small Steps* by Louis Sachar
- *Fuzzy Mud* by Louis Sachar
- *Maniac Magee* by Jerry Spinelli
- *Hatchet* by Gary Paulsen

"NOTHING IN LIFE IS EASY. BUT THAT'S NO REASON TO GIVE UP."

Did you know?
Stanley Yelnats' name is a palindrome. It reads the same whether read backward or forward.

Read it! ☐   Rating: ☆☆☆☆☆

Favorite Character: _____

Notes: _____

_____

85 Smile

Written by Raina Telgemeier

AGES:
10+

GENRE:
GRAPHIC NOVEL

PUBLISHER:
GRAPHIX

PUBLICATION DATE:
2010

PAGE COUNT:
224

This is a graphic novel you'll want to sink your teeth into! The night that 12-year-old Raina trips, falls, and loses her two front teeth not only causes her physical pain, it leads to a traumatic four years filled with plenty of emotions. Raina spends a lot of time in dental appointments—she gets braces, surgery, headgear, and even a retainer with fake teeth. If that isn't enough, she has to deal with some troubling friendship issues, body changes, some boy stuff, and an earthquake too. *Whoa!*

Smile definitely doesn't cover Raina's finest years, but her ability to see the good in the bad sure makes for an excellent story. It's refreshing to know that things do get easier for Raina as she learns to stand up for herself and accept herself as she is. The full-color, cartoon-style illustrations are incredibly cheerful and humorous. And this might seem a tad obvious, but I'll let you in on a secret: Smile will make you smile. "Weird…Something happens when you smile at people. They smile back!"

What to read next?

- *Sisters* by Raina Telgemeir
- *Sunny Side Up* by Jennifer L. Holm
- *Roller Girl* by Victoria Jamieson
- *El Deafo* by Cece Bell

Did you know?

Smile is a true story. Raina Telgemeier really knocked out her teeth when she was in sixth grade. She wrote *Smile* to get the entire experience down on paper.

Read it! ☐   Rating: ☆☆☆☆☆

Favorite Character: _____

Notes: _____

_____

86 Inside Out and Back Again

Written by Thanhha Lai

In this story, readers experience the main character's joy, pain, anger, frustration, losses, and determination. It's a powerful novel inspired by Thanhha Lai's own memories as a Vietnamese refugee. *Inside Out and Back Again* is the story of 10-year-old Hà during 1975—a year known in history as the "Fall of Saigon." Along with her mother and three brothers (her father has been missing in action for nine years), Hà travels by boat to a tent city in Guam before moving to the United States, where she finds herself living in Alabama, sponsored by an "American cowboy" and his wife. Hà's family is treated like outcasts. If they are to be accepted as part of the community, they must learn to speak a new language, eat different food, and follow a different religion.

AGES:
10+

GENRE:
HISTORICAL FICTION

PUBLISHER:
HARPERCOLLINS

Did you know?

Thanhha Lai started a nonprofit organization called "Viet Kids Inc." The organization buys bicycles for poor students who would otherwise have to walk two hours to and from school. With a bike, the trip takes only 30 minutes, leaving the students with energy to spend in the classrooms.

From the delectable description of her most cherished fruit, the papaya, to the bitter differences between the home she's left behind and the challenges of her new home, Hà's life is told through amazing descriptions of smells, tastes, and touch. The story is divided into four bite-size parts with a series of deeply honest poems. *Inside Out and Back Again* is beautiful!

PUBLICATION DATE:
2011

What to read next?

- *Brown Girl Dreaming* by Jacqueline Woodson
- *Listen, Slowly* by Thanhha Lai
- *Full Cicada Moon* by Marilyn Hilton
- *The Crossover* by Kwame Alexander

PAGE COUNT:
272

Read it! ☐   Rating: ☆☆☆☆☆

Favorite Character: _____

Notes: _____

_____

The Golden Compass
Written by Philip Pullman

AGES:
10+

GENRE:
FANTASY

PUBLISHER:
YEARLING

PUBLICATION DATE:
1995

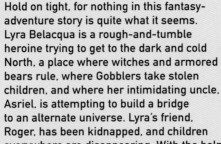

Hold on tight, for nothing in this fantasy-adventure story is quite what it seems. Lyra Belacqua is a rough-and-tumble heroine trying to get to the dark and cold North, a place where witches and armored bears rule, where Gobblers take stolen children, and where her intimidating uncle, Asriel, is attempting to build a bridge to an alternate universe. Lyra's friend, Roger, has been kidnapped, and children everywhere are disappearing. With the help of a magical instrument that tells the future, Lyra is determined to rescue Roger and save the children who are being experimented on.

Filled with gripping action, darkness, betrayal, grand battles, and dramatic escapes, readers will be kept on the edge of their seat as Lyra does her best to outwit the evildoers. Grab your compass, navigate your way to the most comfortable reading spot you can find, and get ready to stay a while because *The Golden Compass* is a real page-turner.

PAGE COUNT:
432

What to read next?
- *The Subtle Knife* by Philip Pullman
- *The Amber Spyglass* by Philip Pullman
- *The Hobbit* by J. R. R. Tolkien
- *The Girl Who Circumnavigated Fairyland in a Ship of Her Own Making* by Catherynne M. Valente

Did you know?
In most countries outside of the United States, *The Golden Compass* is actually titled *Northern Lights*.

"YOU CANNOT CHANGE WHAT YOU ARE, ONLY WHAT YOU DO."

Read it! ☐   Rating: ☆☆☆☆☆

Favorite Character: _____

Notes: _____

_____

88 Black Beauty

Written by Anna Sewell

AGES:
10+

GENRE:
ANIMALS

PUBLISHER:
PENGUIN
CLASSICS

PUBLICATION DATE:
1877

PAGE COUNT:
245

Attention animal lovers: This is a pedigree story told through the eyes of a horse. Thanks to a stable fire, a dangerous bridge, and a slew of memorable characters, *Black Beauty* is filled with plenty of page-turning suspense. Black Beauty is a lovely black horse that begins his career as a carriage horse, but after he's injured, his wealthy owner decides he's no longer good enough for the job. From this moment, Black Beauty is passed from owner to owner and used for hard manual labor. Even though many inhumane things happen to Black Beauty at the hands of unkind humans, he lives up to his name both on the outside and the inside by remaining a kind and respectful horse.

This story of Black Beauty's life, from birth to old age, is so beautifully descriptive that everything from his sprightly days as a colt in a farm pasture to a hard life pulling taxicabs on cobblestone paths in London can be easily envisioned. Each chapter has an excellent message to take away, usually about animal welfare, kindness, sympathy, and respect. It's time to find a nice sunny pasture, grassy field, or comfortable chair, and settle into *Black Beauty*, a well-bred story sure to reach your heart and stay there forever.

What to read next?
- *The Black Stallion* by Walter Farley
- *Misty of Chincoteague* by Marguerite Henry
- *My Friend Flicka* by Mary O'Hara
- *The Georges and the Jewels* by Jane Smiley

Did you know?

After an illness, Anna Sewell eventually became unable to walk. She depended on horse-drawn transportation, and this nurtured her great respect for horses.

"IT IS GOOD PEOPLE WHO MAKE GOOD PLACES."

Read it! ☐   Rating: ☆☆☆☆☆☆

Favorite Character: _____

Notes: _____

_____

89

The Little Prince

Written and Illustrated by Antoine de Saint-Exupéry

AGES:
10+

GENRE:
FANTASY

PUBLISHER:
HARCOURT

PUBLICATION
DATE:
1943

PAGE COUNT:
96

This is an honest and beautiful story about loneliness, friendship, sadness, and love. The Little Prince is a small boy from a tiny planet—an asteroid to be precise—who travels the universe, from planet to planet, seeking wisdom. On his journey, he discovers the unpredictable nature of adults. As Saint-Exupéry writes, "All grown-ups were once children...but only few of them remember it."

The story begins on Earth, with the narrator, a pilot who has crashed in the Sahara Desert. One day, while repairing his wrecked plane, a small and oddly dressed boy shows up, insisting the pilot draw him a sheep. The pilot obeys the boy's odd request, which leads to him discovering more about the Little Prince and where he came from.

What unfolds is a marvelous story that some will find happy and others will find sad. Either way, all readers will have their minds opened wide and will (hopefully) grow up to be adults who always remember they were once children too. *The Little Prince* is a thin book, but don't be fooled by its small size, it is an intelligent story meant to be thought about deeply and encourage you to build castles in the air.

What to read next?
- *Peter Pan* by J. M. Barrie
- *The Phantom Tollbooth* by Norton Juster
- *The Complete Tales of Winnie the Pooh* by A. A. Milne
- *A Wrinkle in Time* by Madeleine L'Engle

Did you know?

The Little Prince was translated into English from the original French. Antoine de Saint-Exupéry was a French pilot. Similar to the pilot in his story, while flying a mission during World War II, his plane was shot down, disappearing somewhere over the Mediterranean.

"THE MOST BEAUTIFUL THINGS IN THE WORLD CANNOT BE SEEN OR TOUCHED, THEY ARE FELT WITH THE HEART."

Read it! ☐   Rating: ☆☆☆☆☆

Favorite Character: _____

Notes: _____

_____

90 The Evolution of Calpurnia Tate

Written by Jacqueline Kelly

AGES:
10+

GENRE:
HISTORICAL FICTION

PUBLISHER:
SQUARE FISH

PUBLICATION DATE:
2009

PAGE COUNT:
352

It's 1899, and it's time to spend a year growing up with 11-year-old Calpurnia Virginia Tate, the only girl in a family of six brothers. Callie has more ambition than the average young girl of her time. Although she is expected to behave like a "lady," cooking and such with her mother, she is much happier exploring and studying the natural world, collecting specimens. One day in her backyard, she wonders why the yellow grasshoppers are bigger than the green grasshoppers. When she asks her prickly grandfather, who typically shows no interest, he replies that she will figure it out on her own. As she investigates the grasshopper situation, her connection with her grandfather grows, and together they discover the answer. Much to her mother's disappointment, her grandfather does a great job teaching Callie about the natural world and evolution—not typical teachings for a girl in 1899. It's even possible that the pair discovers an unknown plant species!

Although there are plenty of great things to chew on throughout this story, one main question arises: Can Callie enjoy her life as a budding naturalist while meeting her mother's expectations? Fitting in and finding a place in the world can be difficult, but Callie is an excellent problem solver, and her curiosity and bravery will have you cheering for her all the way to the last page.

What to read next?
- *The Curious World of Calpurnia Tate* by Jacqueline Kelly
- *The Green Glass Sea* by Ellen Klages
- *Chasing Secrets* by Gennifer Choldenko
- *The Penderwicks* by Jeanne Birdsall

Read it! ☐   Rating: ☆☆☆☆☆

Favorite Character: _____

Notes: _____

_____

91 Twenty Thousand Leagues Under the Sea

Written by Jules Verne

Are you fascinated by science and the unexplained? *Twenty Thousand Leagues Under the Sea* is the tale of an astonishing and mystical world beneath the sea that wide-eyed readers have been exploring for over 140 years. When Professor Aronnax boards a ship to investigate a series of attacks by a strange sea monster, the real monster turns out to be an amazing submarine, the *Nautilus*, piloted by the villainous Captain Nemo. A gigantic explosion leaves Professor Aronnax, his servant Conseil, and the harpoonist Ned Land captive on the submarine, and they are taken around the world on a perilous journey as Captain Nemo seeks revenge. They encounter shipwrecks and their ghostly passengers, a squad of monstrous squid, and treacherous icy waters.

Twenty Thousand Leagues Under the Sea flows with intriguing scientific and historical findings. This may be the most challenging story in our book, but if you dare to embark on this voyage with a crew of commanding characters, you'll never forget it!

What to read next?
- *The City of Ember* by Jeanne DuPrau
- *A Wrinkle in Time* by Madeleine L'Engle
- *The Little Prince* by Antoine de Saint-Exupéry
- *Treasure Island* by Robert Louis Stevenson

Did you know?

Jules Verne was a French writer, and his books are some of the most translated works in history. There are so many translations, in fact, that you might want to have a quick chat with your school or local librarian to help you decide which is best for you.

AGES:
10+

GENRE:
ADVENTURE

PUBLISHER:
STERLING

PUBLICATION DATE:
1870

PAGE COUNT:
336

Read it! ☐   Rating: ☆☆☆☆☆

Favorite Character: _____

Notes: _____

_____

92 Treasure Island

Written by Robert Louis Stevenson

AGES:
10+

GENRE:
ADVENTURE

PUBLISHER:
SIMON &
SCHUSTER

1883

**PUBLICATION
DATE:**
1883

PAGE COUNT:
304

Avast ye, me mateys and landlubbers! *Treasure Island* is the most famous, adventurous adventure ever written about pirates. Batten down the hatches because this tale begins with Jim Hawkins, a brave and honest young cabin boy who finds a treasure map in the sea chest of a strange sailor who dies at the Admiral Benbow Inn. Along with his friends, Captain Smollett, Squire Trelawney, and Dr. Livesey, Jim sets sail in the *Hispaniola* on a mission to find the treasure. The friends soon discover there are buccaneers who want the map and the buried loot it leads to for themselves, and Jim must use both his brains and his bravery to fight off the mutinous pirates, who are led by the one-legged Long John Silver.

Just as the ocean swells and moves quickly in a storm, so too does this tale with its crew of both treacherous and heroic characters. Who will get to the buried pirate booty first? Shiver me timbers, this is indeed a splendid choice for adventure-seeking scallywags.

Did you know?

Treasure Island began as a map that Robert Louis Stevenson created while drawing with his stepson on a rainy day. In the book, the island is described as looking like "a fat dragon standing up." Once he added harbors and bays, a brilliant story started coming to life.

What to read next?
- *Peter and the Starcatchers* by Dave Barry
- *Nick of Time* by Ted Bell
- *Robinson Crusoe* by Daniel Defoe
- *Peter Pan* by J. M. Barrie

Did you know?

There are five real-life pirates in *Treasure Island*: William Kidd, Blackbeard, Edward England, Howell Davis, and Bartholomew Roberts.

"SEAWARD HO! HANG THE TREASURE! IT'S THE GLORY OF THE SEA THAT HAS TURNED MY HEAD."

Read it! ☐ Rating: ☆☆☆☆☆

Favorite Character: _____

Notes: _____

_____

One Crazy Summer
Written by Rita Williams-Garcia

AGES:
11+

GENRE:
HISTORICAL
FICTION

PUBLISHER:
AMISTAD

**PUBLICATION
DATE:**
2010

PAGE COUNT:
240

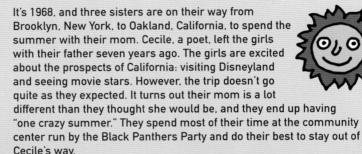

It's 1968, and three sisters are on their way from Brooklyn, New York, to Oakland, California, to spend the summer with their mom. Cecile, a poet, left the girls with their father seven years ago. The girls are excited about the prospects of California: visiting Disneyland and seeing movie stars. However, the trip doesn't go quite as they expected. It turns out their mom is a lot different than they thought she would be, and they end up having "one crazy summer." They spend most of their time at the community center run by the Black Panthers Party and do their best to stay out of Cecile's way.

In *One Crazy Summer*, the author does a magnificent job of telling the story of how the sisters work to regain the love of their mother during a revolutionary time in African-American history. The sisters are amazing characters that draw you deep into the story. You'll love all three of their individual, powerful voices, as together they discover much about themselves, their family, their culture, and the general unfairness that is part of their life. This is an unforgettable and moving book punctuated with humor in all of the right places. Come on now— it's time to go crazy over *One Crazy Summer*!

What to read next?
- *P.S. Be Eleven* by Rita Williams-Garcia
- *Gone Crazy in Alabama* by Rita Williams-Garcia
- *The Watsons Go to Birmingham—1963* by Christopher Paul Curtis
- *The Penderwicks* by Jeanne Birdsall

Did you know?
Rita Williams-Garcia won three huge awards for this book: the Newbery Honor, the Coretta Scott King Award, and the Scott O'Dell award for Historical Fiction.

"WE ALL HAVE OUR LA-LA-LA SONG. THE THING WE DO WHEN THE WORLD ISN'T SINGING A NICE TUNE TO US. WE SING OUR OWN NICE TUNE TO DROWN OUT THE UGLY."

Read it! ☐   Rating: ☆☆☆☆☆

Favorite Character: _____

Notes: _____

_____

94 Roll of Thunder, Hear My Cry

Written by Mildred D. Taylor

AGES:
11+

GENRE:
HISTORICAL
FICTION

PUBLISHER:
PUFFIN BOOKS

1976

**PUBLICATION
DATE:**
1976

PAGE COUNT:
288

It's southern Mississippi in the 1930s, a time of depression and segregation. Money is hard to come by for most, and black people are treated poorly because of the color of their skin. The Logans, an African American family, are struggling. Through the eyes of 9-year-old Cassie Logan, we learn what it was like to grow up during this time. Until now, Cassie's family has protected her from racism. She has no idea just how important it is that her family has their own piece of land. She learns about discrimination and intolerance quickly the year the Night Riders come to town and many dangerous and scary things begin to happen. Ultimately, Cassie learns that she and her family have something that nobody can take away from them.

Thanks to Cassie's ability to speak her mind, readers experience the heavy truth of the brutal ways African Americans were treated. "There are things you can't back down on, things you gotta take a stand on. But it's up to you to decide what them things are," she says. "You have to demand respect in this world, ain't nobody just gonna hand it to you. How you carry yourself, what you stand for—that's how you gain respect. But, little one, ain't nobody's respect worth more than your own." What will you decide? Will you read this book? Please do!

What to read next?
- *Song of the Trees* by Mildred D. Taylor
- *Let the Circle Be Unbroken* by Mildred D. Taylor
- *The Road to Memphis* by Mildred D. Taylor
- *The Land* by Mildred D. Taylor

Read it! ☐   Rating: ☆☆☆☆☆

Favorite Character: _____

Notes: _____

_____

95 The Arrival

Written and Illustrated by Shaun Tan

Most people feel a need to belong somewhere, and everyone experiences new beginnings. Because of that, everyone can get something from reading *The Arrival*, told in a format that's a cross between a wordless picture book and a graphic novel. Fantastic illustrations reveal a story about a man who sets off across the ocean, tearfully leaving his wife and child behind in order to build a brighter future for his family in a new and unknown country. Now a stranger in a land filled with strange-looking animals and floating objects, the man must find a place to live, food to eat, and secure a job to earn money. Even though he doesn't speak the same language, many strangers greet him with kindness, and he begins to find his way in the new city. Will the man find a better future and a new home?

Because there are no words in this book, readers are able to sink deeply into a new world that balances itself carefully between the familiar and fantastical. You get to be the main character and experience everything he does. Reading it feels more like watching a silent movie than reading a book. The illustrator wants you to pause, think, and let your imagination take over. And because you'll be dying to discuss the meaning of the book when you've finished, have your bestie read it at the same time!

What to read next?

- *Tales from Outer Suburbia* by Shaun Tan
- *The Rabbits* by John Marsden
- *The Invention of Hugo Cabret* by Brian Selznick
- *The Encyclopedia of Early Earth* by Isabel Greenberg

AGES:
11+

GENRE:
GRAPHIC NOVEL

PUBLISHER:
ARTHUR A. LEVINE BOOKS

2007

PUBLICATION DATE:
2007

PAGE COUNT:
128

Did you know?

Shaun Tan won an Academy Award for the animated film version of his picture book, *The Lost Thing*.

Read it! ☐   Rating: ☆☆☆☆☆

Favorite Character: _____

Notes: _____

_____

Anne Frank: The Diary of a Young Girl
Written by Anne Frank

AGES:
11+

GENRE:
AUTOBIOGRAPHY

PUBLISHER:
BANTAM

PUBLICATION DATE:
1947

PAGE COUNT:
304

This is the very real diary written by a Jewish teenager, Anne Frank. It was found in an attic in Amsterdam after World War II. The diary tells Anne's story of how her family was forced to leave their home during World War II and hide from the Nazis in an attic in Amsterdam. Her family lived in tight quarters with others, and Anne writes of the hunger and boredom they experienced. She also writes about the brave people who tried to keep them safe—to be discovered meant certain death. At times, Anne makes readers laugh with her descriptions and unique teen voice, but it's important to know that readers will almost certainly feel a deep sadness when they finish this book. *The Diary of a Young Girl* is a powerful and emotional read that reminds us that war is horrific, and we should always strive for peace.

What to read next?
- *Anne Frank: Her life in words and pictures from the archives of The Anne Frank House* by Menno Metselaar and Ruud van der Rol
- *Number the Stars* by Lois Lowry
- *Inside Out and Back Again* by Thanhha Lai
- *A Long Walk to Water* by Linda Sue Park

Did you know?
Anne Frank was born in Germany in 1929. In 1933, her family moved to Amsterdam, which is where the Gestapo, the official secret police of Nazi Germany and German-occupied Europe, eventually captured them. Anne died in the Bergen-Belsen concentration camp in 1945.

Read it! ☐   Rating: ☆☆☆☆☆

Favorite Character: _____

Notes: _____

_____

The Dreamer

Written by Pam Muñoz Ryan • Illustrated by Peter Sís

Calling artists, nature lovers, and all other readers, this enchanting and thoughtful book will make your heart grow and your imagination blossom. Shy Neftali is a very gifted boy who has a way with words. He is a natural-born poet, but this is a talent that does not sit well with his father, who wants him to be a doctor. When the beauty of Neftali's surroundings in Chile provoke him to daydream and write, his inner strength helps him continue pursuing his true calling, and at 18, Neftali creates a new identity, calling himself Pablo Neruda.

Despite living beneath the shadow of a daunting father and being bullied at school, Pablo Neruda grew up to be a Nobel Prize-winning poet. *The Dreamer* is his inspiring true story mixed beautifully with fictional elements, as told by the talented author Pam Muñoz Ryan. The illustrations by Peter Sís provide extra insights into each new chapter. We should all be able to share our creative gifts with the world, and thanks to Pablo Neruda, we can be empowered to do so.

What to read next?

- *A River of Words: The Story of William Carlos Williams* by Jen Bryant
- *Echo* by Pam Muñoz Ryan
- *The Color of My Words* by Lynn Joseph
- *Love that Dog* by Sharon Creech

AGES:
11+

GENRE:
HISTORICAL
FICTION

PUBLISHER:
SCHOLASTIC
PRESS

**PUBLICATION
DATE:**
2010

Did you know?

Pablo Neruda wrote a book called *The Book of Questions*, which inspired the questions asked in Peter Sís' illustrations throughout *The Dreamer*.

PAGE COUNT:
400

Read it! ☐   Rating: ☆☆☆☆☆

Favorite Character: _____

Notes: _____

_____

Hatchet

Written by Gary Paulsen

AGES:
11+

GENRE:
ADVENTURE

PUBLISHER:
SIMON & SCHUSTER
BOOKS

PUBLICATION DATE:
1987

Are you in need of an exciting, gritty, and action-packed adventure book? *Hatchet* is the ultimate survival story and the first in a series of five books. Traveling in a single-engine airplane, 13-year-old Brian Robeson is on his way to spend the summer with his father in Northern Canada. When the pilot suffers a heart attack and dies, Brian does his best to land the plane, but it crashes into a lake in the middle of the wilderness. Brian, now stranded, must go into survival mode. The only things he has on him are the clothes he is wearing, a tattered windbreaker, and the hatchet his mom gave him before boarding the plane.

Brian's instincts to survive and his can-do attitude help him gain many survival skills. He makes a fire with his hatchet as well as hunting tools. He even makes himself a shelter. Alone in the wilderness, Brian also has plenty of time to think about the family secret that led to his parents' divorce, but self-pity has no use in the wilderness. Faced with life-threatening situations, Brian must stay alive long enough to be rescued, and you'll be gripping your copy of *Hatchet*, dying to find out if he makes it.

Did you know?

Gary Paulsen has written more than 200 books, for grown-ups and kids, and he receives hundreds of fan letters each day.

What to read next?

- *Brian's Winter* by Gary Paulsen
- *Robinson Crusoe* by Daniel Defoe
- *Holes* by Louis Sachar
- *Where the Red Fern Grows* by Wilson Rawls

PAGE COUNT:
192

Did you know?

Brian's time spent in the Canadian wilderness is based on nature-loving Paulsen's own experiences of two forced landings and his time spent living in the woods where he hunted with a bow.

"PATIENCE, HE THOUGHT. SO MUCH OF THIS WAS PATIENCE—WAITING, AND THINKING AND DOING THINGS RIGHT. SO MUCH OF ALL THIS, SO MUCH OF ALL LIVING WAS PATIENCE AND THINKING."

Did you know?

Hatchet should be the first book you read in the Brian Saga. After that, it doesn't matter which order you read the books in.

Read it! ☐   Rating: ☆☆☆☆☆

Favorite Character: _____

Notes: _____

_____

99 A Long Walk to Water

Written by Linda Sue Park

AGES:
11+

GENRE:
HISTORICAL
FICTION

PUBLISHER:
HMH BOOKS
FOR YOUNG
READERS

**PUBLICATION
DATE:**
2010

PAGE COUNT:
128

This is Linda Sue Park's incredible story about the Lost Boys of Sudan, a real part of history involving more than 20,000 boys who were separated from their families during the Second Sudanese Civil War in Africa. One story follows a boy, Salva, and one story follows a girl, Nya. They're both 11 years old and live in Sudan, but their stories take place during different decades. Nya, whose story takes place in 2008, walks twice a day to fetch water from a pond two hours from her home—that makes eight hours of walking each day! Salva, whose story takes place in 1985, is a refugee walking through Africa, often alone, looking for his family and searching for safety. After fleeing an explosion at his school caused by attacking rebels, crossing a crocodile-infested river, and withstanding many other difficulties, Salva's story joins beautifully with Nya's and shows readers that no matter how difficult it is to walk a path, keep going. There is always hope.

What to read next?

- *A Single Shard*
  by Linda Sue Park
- *When My Name Was Keoko*
  by Linda Sue Park
- *Parched* by Melanie Crowder
- *The Red Pencil*
  by Andrea Davis Pinkney

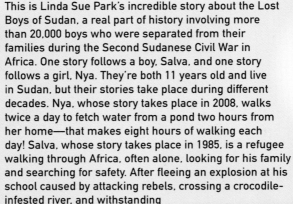

Did you know?

Salva Dut is a real person who led the Lost Boys of Sudan to a refugee camp. He is a friend of Linda Sue Park and her inspiration for this story. When Salva came to America, he started a volunteer group that drills for wells in Sudan so that families don't have to walk for hours for clean water. His group is called Water for South Sudan. Now some kids, like the fictional Nya, have time to go to school and read books just like you!

Read it! ☐   Rating: ☆☆☆☆☆

Favorite Character: _____

Notes: _____

_____

The Secret Garden

Written by Frances Hodgson Burnett

Just as a brown and drab winter blossoms into an alluring and colorful spring, *The Secret Garden* is a story filled with characters who bloom. Sour-faced and spoiled orphan Mary Lennox has come to live with her uncle at Misselthwaite Manor, a cheerless mansion with nearly 100 rooms, most of them locked. Her uncle keeps to himself, and her tantrum-throwing and sickly cousin, Colin, is confined to his room. To amuse herself, Mary explores the surrounding gardens, except for the secret garden that has been locked for many years. If only Mary could find the key! Could she bring this magical oasis back to life? Maybe, like the flowers, she'd grow and change her ways. And, perhaps, life at Misselthwaite Manor could return to more places than the garden alone.

AGES:
11+

GENRE:
FRIENDSHIP

PUBLISHER:
HARPERCOLLINS

Did you know?

The original title for *The Secret Garden* was *Mistress Mary*, inspired by a well-known English nursery rhyme that captures the essence of both the main character and the story itself. The rhyme goes as follows:

Mary, Mary, quite contrary,
How does your garden grow?
With silver bells, and
* cockle shells,*
And pretty maids all in a row.

Here's a little secret: Mary does find the key, and what unravels is a captivating story of friendship and the healing powers of nature. For full effect, the perfect time to read *The Secret Garden* is when winter transitions into spring.

What to read next?
- *A Little Princess* by Frances Hodgson Burnett
- *Ballet Shoes* by Noel Streatfeild
- *Heidi* by Johanna Spyri
- *Anne of Green Gables* by L. M. Montgomery

PUBLICATION DATE:
1911

PAGE COUNT:
331

Read it! ☐   Rating: ☆☆☆☆☆

Favorite Character: _____

Notes: _____

101 Wonder

Written by R.J. Palacio

AGES:
11+

GENRE:
REALISTIC

PUBLISHER:
KNOPF BOOKS
FOR YOUNG
READERS

PUBLICATION DATE:
2012

PAGE COUNT:
320

Have you ever wondered what it is like to be someone else? Ten-year-old August (Auggie) Pullman, a kind of medical mystery who was born with rare facial deformities, wants nothing more than to be treated like an ordinary kid. He loves *Star Wars* and his Xbox as much as the next person, yet people always act differently around him. Auggie has had 27 surgeries, both big and small, and a lot of illness in his life. Up until now, he's been homeschooled. Now he's entering 5th grade at Beecher Prep. The other kids stare at Auggie, and they whisper to each other to stay away from him. Some kids are utterly unkind—in fact, they are bullies.

Readers will hear the story of Auggie's challenging first year of school from Auggie himself, but they'll also get to hear the story from the point of view of his classmates and sister, among others. It's so awesome to hear different sides of the same story: what it feels like to be Auggie, what it feels like to get to know him, what it feels like to be his sister, and all the while learning that there's more than one way to hurt someone's feelings. It's not easy being different, but Auggie is definitely someone we could all hope to be like. He is brave and has a big heart. He reminds us to be our best selves, and he can even make us laugh. Everyone should read this book! Everyone who is ready to choose kindness, that is. And everyone who is ready to *wonder* what it would be like to be in Auggie's shoes!

What to read next?
- *Auggie & Me: Three Wonder Stories* by R.J. Palacio
- *365 Days of Wonder: Mr. Browne's Book of Precepts* by R.J. Palacio
- *Out of My Mind* by Sharon M. Draper

Did you know?

R.J. Palacio was inspired to write *Wonder* after her 3-year-old son cried at an ice cream store when he sat next to a little girl with a severe facial deformity. To protect the girl's feelings, Palacio grabbed her kids and left the store. Looking back, she wished she had used the moment to teach her kids there was nothing to fear.

"THE THINGS WE DO OUTLAST OUR MORTALITY. THE THINGS WE DO ARE LIKE MONUMENTS THAT PEOPLE BUILD TO HONOR HEROES AFTER THEY'VE DIED. THEY'RE LIKE THE PYRAMIDS THAT THE EGYPTIANS BUILT TO HONOR THE PHARAOHS. ONLY INSTEAD OF BEING MADE OUT OF STONE, THEY'RE MADE OUT OF THE MEMORIES PEOPLE HAVE OF YOU."

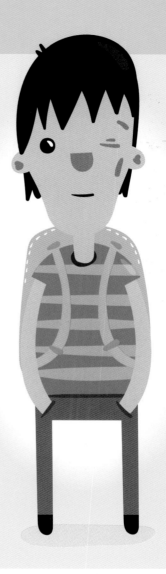

Read it! ☐   Rating: ☆☆☆☆☆

Favorite Character: _____

Notes: _____

_____

141

Titles by Genre

About the Author

Bianca Schulze is the founder of *The Children's Book Review*, a resource devoted to children's literature and recognized by the American Library Association as a "Great Website for Kids." She is a reader, reviewer, mother, and children's book lover. Combining her love of books and experience as a children's bookseller, Bianca's goal is to share her passion in order to help create a new generation of readers.

Born and raised in Sydney, Australia, she now lives with her husband and three children in Boulder, Colorado.

You can visit her at www.thechildrensbookreview.com.